Cognitive Behavioral Therapy for Psychosis as a Syndrome

Edo S. Jaya

Cognitive Behavioral Therapy for Psychosis as a Syndrome

A Symptom-Based Management Approach

Springer

Edo S. Jaya
Faculty of Psychology
Universitas Indonesia
Depok, Indonesia

Indonesian Psychological Healthcare Center
Jakarta, Indonesia

ISBN 978-981-95-9202-9 ISBN 978-981-95-9203-6 (eBook)
https://doi.org/10.1007/978-981-95-9203-6

This Springer imprint is published by the registered company Springer Nature Singapore Pte Ltd.
The registered company address is: 152 Beach Road, #21-01/04 Gateway East, Singapore 189721, Singapore

The original version of this book was published without the Acknowledgements section. This has now been added.

Preface

Psychosis remains one of the most challenging mental health conditions to treat effectively, often requiring a carefully orchestrated combination of pharmacological and psychological interventions. While antipsychotic medications play a crucial role in managing symptoms, psychological treatments—particularly Cognitive Behavioral Therapy (CBT)—have emerged as vital components in helping individuals achieve lasting recovery and improved quality of life.

This treatment manual presents a novel, symptom-based approach to CBT for psychosis that draws inspiration from internal medicine's management of complex syndromes. Just as physicians don't treat "sepsis" as a single entity but rather address its various manifestations through targeted interventions, this manual advocates for treating psychosis as a syndrome requiring individualized, symptom-specific strategies.

The manual is written primarily for clinical psychologists, psychiatrists, and mental health practitioners who work with individuals experiencing psychosis. It offers a structured yet flexible framework that can be adapted to meet the unique needs of each patient. Rather than providing a one-size-fits-all approach, it emphasizes the importance of understanding each individual's specific symptom profile and selecting appropriate therapeutic techniques accordingly.

What sets this manual apart is its systematic integration of various evidence-based CBT techniques targeted at specific symptoms and comorbidities commonly seen in psychosis. From addressing insomnia and depression to managing social anxiety and improving emotional regulation, each chapter provides practical, step-by-step guidance while maintaining sight of the broader goal: helping individuals with psychosis lead more fulfilling lives.

The manual also recognizes the reality of practicing in resource-limited settings. While comprehensive assessment and treatment are ideal, we provide guidance on prioritizing interventions when time or resources are constrained. This pragmatic approach ensures the manual's utility across diverse clinical settings, from well-resourced specialty clinics to community mental health centers.

This work reflects not only years of clinical experience and research but also countless hours of learning from patients themselves. Their experiences, challenges, and triumphs have shaped this approach and continue to inform our understanding of how best to help individuals managing psychosis.

Jawa Barat, Indonesia Jaya S. Edo

Acknowledgements The development of this manual would not have been possible without the support and contributions of many individuals. I am particularly indebted to HS, one of my first patients with psychosis who was open to CBT. His willingness to engage in therapy helped shape my early thinking about this approach to treating psychosis. Though he is no longer with us, his influence on this work remains profound.

I am deeply grateful to my colleagues at the Indonesian Psychological Healthcare Center, particularly Bianca Sutjiono and Shafira Fawzia Ahmad, with whom I collaborated on a pivotal case study published in Behavior Change that helped crystallize many of the ideas presented here. The countless patients who have trusted us with their care at the Center have also been instrumental in refining this approach.

My understanding of syndrome-based treatment has been significantly enriched through conversations with Jason Amidjoyo, an internist in Germany, whose insights into internal medicine's approach to complex diseases shaped the theoretical framework of this manual. I am also profoundly grateful to Professor Tania Lincoln, whose mentorship and expertise in psychosis research provided me with the methodological foundation necessary to develop this innovative treatment strategy.

I owe a deep debt of gratitude to my parents, who shaped my fundamental approach to problem-solving and research. My mother, Dr. Sri Lily Djajakesukma, instilled in me the importance of methodological rigor, diligence, and precision—qualities essential to developing this manual. My father, Dr. Jap Tji Beng, taught me the value of deep, solution-focused thinking. Cognitive Behavioral Therapy for Psychosis as a Syndrome 6 and the courage to explore unconventional approaches while maintaining an engineer's pragmatism.

At the Faculty of Psychology, Universitas Indonesia, I am especially grateful to Professor Corinna Debora Silalahi for her steadfast mentorship and guidance throughout my academic journey. I am equally grateful to Professor Bagus Takwin, whose emphasis on philosophy—from its classical roots to Stoicism—has provided an intellectual foundation that continues to shape my understanding of CBT to this day.

On a personal note, I want to thank my wife, Julia Dharmawan, for her unwavering support throughout the development of this work.

It is my hope that this manual will serve as a practical guide for clinicians while also advancing our collective understanding of how to better serve individuals experiencing psychosis. The journey toward recovery from psychosis is rarely straightforward, but with the right tools and approach, meaningful progress is possible.

Faculty of Psychology, Universitas Indonesia Edo S. Jaya
Indonesian Psychological Healthcare Center, Jakarta
January 2026

Competing Interests The author has no competing interests to declare that are relevant to the content of this manuscript.

Praise for *Cognitive Behavioral Therapy for Psychosis as a Syndrome*

"This book brings CBTp back into the realm of *medicine*: not as a protocol for a diagnostic label, but as a relational craft embedded in dimensional, symptom-based formulation. Edo Jaya shows—with pragmatism and clinical tact—how psychosis care becomes more humane and more effective when we stop reifying 'schizophrenia' and instead treat what is *there*, in the person, now".

—Jim van Os, *Professor of Psychiatric Epidemiology and Public Mental Health, UMC Utrecht, the Netherlands*

"Edo S. Jaya offers a sophisticated and practical reframing of cognitive behavioral therapy (CBT) for psychosis, viewing it as a constellation of symptoms requiring tailored interventions. He integrates evidence-based techniques that target specific symptoms and common comorbidities with clarity and clinical precision. Adaptable across a variety of practice contexts, this manual equips practitioners with actionable and compassionate strategies—an essential guide for clinicians committed to improving outcomes for individuals living with psychosis".

—Bagus Takwin, *Professor of Social Psychology, Faculty of Psychology, Universitas Indonesia*

"This book is strongly recommended to anyone working with psychosis. Taking a personalized and comprehensive approach, it will guide practitioners in selecting the interventions that best fit the symptom profile and needs of their patient. It includes numerous validated tools for assessment, helpful guidance on treatment planning, and multiple options for intervention. An invaluable resource".

—Tania Lincoln, *Professor of Clinical Psychology and Psychotherapy, Universität Hamburg, Hamburg, Germany*

"Using physical-illness analogies, Edo Jaya conceptualizes schizophrenia as a dynamic systemic syndrome. Although the precipitating factors are highly diverse and often difficult to identify, intervention can already take place by identifying the presenting symptoms and selecting an appropriate cluster of techniques to address them. This approach offers renewed hope and optimism in the treatment of schizophrenia".

—Kristi Poerwandari, *Professor of Clinical Psychology, Universitas Indonesia*

"As someone who has long advocated for psychology that is scientifically grounded and resistant to speculative or mystical approaches, I appreciate the clarity and seriousness of Edo S. Jaya's work. This book offers a genuinely novel contribution, showing how careful scholarship, the synthesis of evidence, and original research can translate into real innovation in clinical care. It provides a thoughtful and disciplined advancement of CBT for psychosis".

—Hamdi Muluk, *Vice Rector for Research and Innovation, Universitas Indonesia*

Contents

About the Author

Dr. phil. Edo S. Jaya, M.Psi., Psikolog is a clinical psychologist and tenured lecturer in the Faculty of Psychology, Universitas Indonesia. He is the founder and director of Indonesian Psychological Healthcare Center, a psychotherapy clinic in Jakarta dedicated to promoting evidence-based practices and supporting research projects in psychopathology.In service to his profession, he is a board member of the Indonesian Clinical Psychology Association and National Board of Clinical Psychologists (Indonesia). In service to academia, he is the Editor-in-Chief of Makara Human Behavior Studies in Asia, an open-access journal published by Universitas Indonesia, and a reviewer at journals such as Schizophrenia Bulletin and Psychological Medicine.With a doctorate in clinical psychology from Universität Hamburg in Germany, Dr. Jaya has published peer-reviewed research in leading journals including Schizophrenia Research and Journal of Psychiatric Research, and has collaborated with international authors from Germany, the Netherlands, the United Kingdom, and the United States in the field of psychosis and cognitive behavioral therapy.

Part I
An Introduction to Cognitive Behavioral Therapy for Psychosis: Symptom-Based Approach

Chapter 1
Introduction to Psychosis

Abstract This chapter defines psychosis as a condition involving impaired reality testing and introduces its core symptom domains: positive symptoms, negative symptoms, disorganization, and neurological soft signs. Hallucinations, delusions, and thought disorder are described with clear phenomenological distinctions and clinical examples. Negative symptoms—including avolition, anhedonia, alogia, and affective flattening—are elaborated as deficits that substantially impair functioning. This chapter also contextualizes "rational cognition" (in contrast to psychoticism) as a historically recent human development emphasizing that psychotic experience must be understood against the broader backdrop of cultural shifts. A historical overview traces the conceptual evolution from *dementia praecox* (premature or early dementia) to schizophrenia, the emergence of the psychosis continuum, and the modern reframing of schizophrenia as a syndrome rather than a discrete disease. Finally, this chapter summarizes major treatment modalities—pharmacotherapy, psychotherapy, rTMS, ECT, and psychosurgery—highlighting their roles and limitations in contemporary practice.

Keywords Psychotic symptoms · Positive symptoms · Negative symptoms · Psychosis continuum · Schizophrenia syndrome

1.1 What Are Psychotic Symptoms? What Do they Look like?

Psychosis is a psychological condition where a person has difficulty distinguishing between what is real and what is not real. There are many symptoms and signs of psychosis. Symptoms of psychosis are generally divided into positive and negative symptoms. Positive symptoms are termed "positive" because they do not exist in non-psychotic conditions. This includes hallucinations, delusions, and disorganized thinking. For example, people without psychosis don't experience hallucinations or false beliefs. On the other hand, negative symptoms are called "negative" because they involve the absence or reduction of normal functions. These include things like

E. S. Jaya, *Cognitive Behavioral Therapy for Psychosis as a Syndrome*, https://doi.org/10.1007/978-981-95-9203-6_1

flat affect (feeling/showing little to no emotion), lack of motivation (amotivation/avolition), reduced speech (alogia), lack of pleasure (anhedonia), and sometimes catatonia (reduced movement). For instance, people without psychosis usually have the motivation to socialize, but those with negative symptoms may withdraw from interactions. In addition to these symptoms, psychosis can also be identified through signs like problems with gait (how a person walks) and memory.

While we describe these phenomena as *symptoms*—clinical indicators of dysfunction—it is crucial to remember that what we now idealize as "rational," bias-free, and empirically grounded thinking is a relatively recent cultural development, not a universal human default.

This cognitive style began to crystallize in Western Europe during the seventeenth and eighteenth centuries, particularly through Enlightenment thinkers such as René Descartes (*Discourse on Method*, 1637) and Immanuel Kant (*Critique of Pure Reason*, 1781), who sought to separate reason from faith, imagination, and superstition. As Michel Foucault (1961/1965) observed in *Madness and Civilization*, this period marked a profound historical rupture: "unreason" was segregated and pathologized as the counterpart of "reason."

Even within the West, this transformation was not universal nor immediate. The rational-scientific worldview did not become culturally dominant in the United States and Western Europe until the late nineteenth to early twentieth century, when industrialization, compulsory education, and scientific institutions consolidated secular norms of knowledge. In other words, the widespread internalization of "rational" cognition in everyday life is only about 100–150 years old—roughly the temporal distance between the invention of the telegraph (1844) and the rise of the Internet (1990s).

To put this in perspective, the Enlightenment's emergence roughly 250–300 years ago is astonishingly recent. It's the same span that separates Aristotle's Greece (300 BC) from the birth of Christ (0 AD), or the early medieval world (700 AD) from the first great cathedrals of Europe (1000 AD). In the scale of human history—tens of thousands of years of mythic and spiritual cognition—that is effectively *yesterday*.

From the standpoint of human evolution, rational cognition is an exceptionally new adaptation. For most of our species' history, people organized thought through mythic, relational, and spiritual logics that would now be considered "irrational." Clinicians should help patients and families appreciate that the modern demarcation between "psychotic" and "non-psychotic" experience is both culturally contingent and historically novel, not a timeless feature of the human mind.

1.1.1 Positive Symptoms of Psychosis: Hallucinations

A hallucination is a perception that occurs in the absence of an external stimulus but has the qualities of a real perception. It differs from several related experiences. For example, hallucinations are distinct from dreaming (which happens during REM sleep and does not involve wakefulness), pseudohallucinations (which do not mimic real perception and are recognized as unreal), and illusions (which are distorted or misinterpreted perceptions of actual stimuli). They are also different from mental imagery, which is under voluntary control and does not resemble real perception. Additionally, hallucinations are not the same as "delusional perceptions", where a real stimulus is accurately sensed and interpreted (i.e., a real perception) but is given extra significance. Hallucinations can affect any of the senses, including visual, auditory, olfactory, gustatory, tactile, and less common senses like proprioception (awareness of body position), equilibrioception (balance), nociception (pain), thermoception (temperature), and chronoception (sense of time).

Auditory hallucinations, where sounds are heard without an external source, are especially common and can be divided into simple and complex types. They can also be either verbal or non-verbal, with auditory verbal hallucinations being more common. Simple auditory hallucinations may include hearing sounds like your name being called when in a crowd or the sound of someone knocking on your door. Similarly, tinnitus is the perception of sounds like ringing, buzzing, or hissing in the ears without an external source. While typically caused by factors like loud noise or hearing loss, tinnitus is sometimes regarded as a form of simple auditory hallucination. On the other hand, complex hallucinations involve hearing voices, music, or other sounds. These voices or sounds may be clear or unclear, familiar or unfamiliar, and they can range from being friendly to hostile.

A visual hallucination is the experience of seeing something that appears real but is not present in the external environment. This phenomenon is distinct from a visual illusion, which involves a distortion of an actual external stimulus. Visual hallucinations are further categorized into simple or complex types. Simple visual hallucinations are often described as non-specific visual sensations, including lights, colors, geometric shapes, or vague objects. Within this category, there are phosphenes, which are simple visual hallucinations lacking distinct structure, and photopsias, which are simple visual hallucinations featuring geometric patterns. On the other hand, complex visual hallucinations entail vivid, detailed images or scenes, such as people, animals, objects, or places.

Olfactory hallucinations occur when a person perceives a smell that does not really exist. In contrast, olfactory illusions happen when an actual odor is detected but perceived differently from how it's remembered. These experiences involve distortions in the sense of smell (olfactory system) and are often not indicative of a serious underlying condition. Typically, they resolve on their own over time. Potential causes include nasal infections, nasal polyps, dental issues, migraines, head injuries, seizures, strokes, or brain tumors. Environmental factors, such as smoking, exposure to specific chemicals (e.g., insecticides or solvents), or radiation therapy for head or neck cancer, can also trigger these olfactory disturbances.

Tactile hallucinations involve the sensation of being touched or feeling pressure on the skin or other body parts, even though no physical contact is occurring. One example of this is mistakenly thinking that your phone vibrates in your pocket even though there is no activity in the phone. These false sensations can range from light touches or tingling to more intense feelings of pressure or pain. Individuals may perceive crawling, pinching, or temperature changes on their skin.

1.1.2 Positive Symptoms of Psychosis: Delusions

A delusion is a fixed false belief that is not amenable to change even in the face of conflicting evidence. Delusions can be categorized as bizarre or non-bizarre. Bizarre delusions are those that are clearly implausible and incomprehensible to others from the same cultural background; they do not arise from everyday experiences. In contrast, non-bizarre delusions involve beliefs that could theoretically happen in real life. For example, a person might mistakenly believe they are being constantly monitored by the police. Delusions can manifest in various themes. Here are a few examples, along with case illustrations.

Persecutory delusions are marked by the false belief that one is being targeted or persecuted by others. These beliefs can lead to significant paranoia and distress, often affecting an individual's behavior and relationships. For example, Patient John firmly believed that he was under constant surveillance by a shadowy organization intent on harming him. This belief was unfounded and caused extreme distress. He felt as though every move he made was being monitored and suspected that strangers on the street were spies reporting on his activities. As a result of these persecutory delusions, John experienced social withdrawal, avoiding what he believed were spies. He lived in constant fear, unsure why the organization was watching him or what harm they intended. His behavior became erratic, responding to perceived threats from the organization. This paranoia led him to change his living arrangements out of suspicion that the head spy had moved close to him, and ultimately resulted in job loss, as he struggled to concentrate at work due to the overwhelming need to evade the imagined spies.

Delusion of control involves the false belief that external entities—such as individuals, groups, or even external forces—exert control over an individual's thoughts, emotions, impulses, or actions. This delusion can create a sense of helplessness and a perceived lack of agency in one's life. For example, Patient Michael was convinced that a government agency had specifically targeted him, believing they possessed the ability to influence people's thoughts. He thought a microchip had been implanted in his brain, enabling this agency to manipulate his thoughts, emotions, and behaviors at will. Michael felt that he was constantly under surveillance, convinced that his thoughts were being redirected to serve a mysterious and malevolent agenda.

Thought broadcasting is a delusion in which individuals falsely believe that their thoughts are accessible to others. For example, Patient John, who experienced thought broadcasting delusion, expressed a deep conviction that his thoughts were no longer private and that anyone around him could listen in on his inner dialogue. He worried that people would judge him harshly because he sometimes thought negatively about others. This belief was particularly distressing for him, leading to significant social withdrawal as he sought to prevent anyone from overhearing his thoughts and to regain a sense of privacy.

Thought insertion involves the belief that external forces are implanting thoughts into one's mind. For instance, David's experience of thought insertion was a central feature of his clinical presentation. He firmly believed that intrusive thoughts, which he did not originate, were being forced into his mind. These thoughts were often disturbing and unwelcome, featuring derogatory or distressing content. David's distress arose from his inability to control or silence these intrusive thoughts, which he felt were imposed on him.

Delusion of reference involves attributing personal meaning or significance to seemingly insignificant remarks, events, or objects in one's surroundings. The meanings assigned are typically negative, though they can occasionally take on a grandiose quality. This delusion demonstrates how the human mind can misconstrue everyday occurrences. For example, Michael's delusion of reference was characterized by a profound belief that the world around him was filled with hidden messages specifically meant for him. He thought that strangers' casual conversations contained concealed references to his life and personal experiences. Michael became especially fixated on uncovering hidden meanings in news headlines, advertisements, and everyday objects, believing they were tailored to convey messages related to his existence. This delusion led him to engage in excessive note-taking and decoding activities.

Delusional jealousy revolves around the unwarranted conviction that a spouse or romantic partner is having an affair, despite a complete absence of evidence supporting such a claim. Those affected by delusional jealousy experience intense emotional turmoil and relational challenges. For example, Sarah's delusional jealousy was characterized by the firm conviction that her spouse was having an affair. She believed that her spouse was being unfaithful to her and engaging in a secret relationship. Sarah was convinced that she could see subtle signs of this infidelity in her spouse's behavior, expressions, and interactions with others, even when others perceived these behaviors as completely innocent.

Erotomania is a delusion in which individuals falsely believe that someone else is deeply in love with them. For example, Daniel's erotomania was marked by a fervent belief that an older female celebrity was secretly in love with him. He interpreted her public appearances, social media posts, and interviews as hidden declarations of love directed at him. Daniel even believed they had communicated through coded messages and secret signs.

Religious delusions revolve around the belief that one possesses divine qualities or has been chosen to act as a god. For instance, Rachel's religious delusion centered around the belief that she had been divinely chosen to act as a prophet and messenger of God. She believed that she was the sole recipient of divine revelations and that her life was guided by divine intervention. Rachel felt that she had a unique and sacred role to fulfill and considered herself to be endowed with extraordinary spiritual powers.

1.1.3 Positive Symptoms of Psychosis: Disorganization

Disorganized speech and behavior are core features of schizophrenia, but it is important to note that they are NOT required for a diagnosis of schizophrenia.

Disorganized speech is a symptom of psychosis characterized by incoherent, tangential, or loosely connected thoughts and speech that lacks logical structure or coherence. It often includes the use of neologisms (made-up words) and clang associations (where words are chosen for their sound rather than their meaning). Here is an example of disorganized speech:

> **Interviewer**: John, can you tell me about your day today and how you've been feeling?
> **John**: Oh, you know, the day, it's like, just spinning, like a top, but not a toy top, more like, um, a top of the world, if you know what I mean. I was walking down the street, saw a cat, and you know, cats, they're like those furry whisker things, but they don't know where they're going. And the sun, it was shining, really bright, like my mom's kitchen, but that's a different kind of shine. And I was going to get coffee, or maybe tea, because the birds told me that tea is like a hug, but without the arms. And then, you see, it's like this, my mind is like a puzzle, but all the pieces are in the wrong box, and I can't find the picture on the lid, you know?

In this example, John's speech is disorganized and tangential, as he jumps between unrelated ideas and metaphors without clear connections or a coherent narrative. His responses lack logical structure and consistency, making it challenging for the interviewer to understand his thoughts and feelings.

Disorganized behavior refers to erratic and unpredictable actions or routines, often marked by difficulties in maintaining personal hygiene, completing tasks, adhering to schedules, and organizing living spaces, resulting in impaired daily functioning. Here is an example of disorganized behavior. Michael struggled to maintain personal hygiene, often going for days without showering or changing clothes. He sometimes wore mismatched outfits without realizing it, like pairing a formal shirt with worn-out jeans, creating an unintentional fashion statement. His daily routine lacked structure and his sleep schedule was an unpredictable rollercoaster, with waking times shifting from day to day. Meals were often skipped, and his eating habits appeared to follow no regular pattern. This lack of routine spilled into his professional life as well, causing him to arrive late for job interviews, miss appointments, and even neglect job responsibilities. Michael's living space painted a clear picture of his disorganized life. His room was a maze of unfinished projects and cluttered spaces. Partially painted canvases leaned against the wall, forgotten puzzles lay incomplete, and books were marked with bookmarks, but the pages remained untouched. The kitchen was no different; Michael would start cooking a meal and then leave the stove unattended, with food still simmering. Time management remained a constant challenge. Appointments became a puzzle of uncertainty, as Michael would either underestimate or overestimate how much time he had for various activities. This inconsistency led to countless missed opportunities and social gatherings that he never attended. It also extended to his financial management, where bill payments became a jumbled mess of missed deadlines, and budgeting felt like an elusive concept.

1.1.4 *Negative Symptoms of Psychosis*

The negative symptoms of psychosis include affective flattening, alogia, anhedonia, avolition, asociality, apathy, cognitive impairment, and poor self-expectations. Here are some examples of these negative symptoms:

1. **Affective Flattening**: Reduced emotional expression, which may manifest as a lack of facial expressions, voice modulation, or gestures.
   Here is an example:

   Clinician: Good morning, how are you feeling today?
   Patient: (Monotonous tone) Morning. I'm... fine, I guess.
   Clinician: Can you tell me more about how you've been feeling recently?
   Patient: (With a lack of emotion) Not much to say, really. Just... here.
   Clinician: I understand. Have you noticed any changes in your mood or emotions lately?
   Patient: (Blank expression) No, not really. Everything's just... flat.
   Clinician: Can you explain what you mean by "flat"?
   Patient: (Showing little emotion) It's like there's not much happening inside. I used to feel happy sometimes, or even sad, but now... it's just all the same. I don't feel much of anything anymore.

2. **Alogia**: Impoverished thinking and reduced speech output, characterized by brief or monosyllabic responses and difficulty conveying meaningful information.
   Here is an example:

   Clinician: Good afternoon, how have you been today?
   Patient: (Pauses for a moment) Uh, yeah, okay, I guess.
   Clinician: Can you tell me more about how you've been feeling recently?
   Patient: (Briefly) Well, not much happening, you know.
   Clinician: (Encouraging) It's alright. I'm here to listen. Can you share a bit more about what's been on your mind lately?
   Patient: (Pauses again) Uh, not really. Just regular stuff.
   Clinician: (Exploring further) Regular stuff like daily routines, work, or hobbies?
   Patient: (With some difficulty) Yeah, those things. Just... usual stuff.

3. **Anhedonia**: Decreased ability to experience pleasure or interest in previously enjoyable activities, resulting in reduced participation in social and recreational pursuits.
   Here is an example:

   Clinician: Good afternoon. How has your day been so far?
   Patient: (With a lack of enthusiasm) It's been alright, I suppose.
   Clinician: Can you tell me if you've enjoyed or found pleasure in any activities recently?
   Patient: (With a lack of enthusiasm) Not really. I used to like reading, but it's just not the same anymore.
   Clinician: (Showing concern) I see. What about spending time with friends or family? Has that brought you any joy?
   Patient: (With a hint of sadness) Not really. I've been with them, but it's like I'm just going through the motions.
   Clinician: (Exploring further) Is there anything in particular that you used to find enjoyable, but no longer do?
   Patient: (With a sense of loss) Yeah, I used to love playing games, but now it's just collecting dust in the corner.

4. **Avolition**: Diminished motivation to initiate and complete purposeful activities, leading to reduced self-care, work, and social engagement.
   Here is an example:

   Clinician: Good morning. How are you feeling today?
   Patient: (Displays minimal enthusiasm) Morning. I'm… alright, I guess.
   Clinician: Can you tell me if there's anything specific you'd like to accomplish or do today?
   Patient: (With reluctance) Not really. I don't feel like doing much.
   Clinician: (Observing the patient's appearance) I noticed that your hair appears greasy and unkempt, and there's a faint, lingering odor. Have you been taking care of yourself, making sure to eat well and maintain your personal hygiene?
   Patient: (Admits) Not really. I've been skipping meals, and, well, I don't remember the last time I showered. It's been like a month. I haven't been brushing my teeth much either.

5. **Asociality**: Impaired social functioning and difficulty forming or maintaining relationships due to decreased interest in social interactions.
   Here is an example:

   Clinician: Good afternoon. How have you been today?
   Patient: (Displays disinterest) Afternoon. I'm… here, I guess.
   Clinician: Can you tell me if you've spent time with friends or family recently, or engaged in social activities?
   Patient: (With a lack of enthusiasm) Not really. I've just been keeping to myself.
   Clinician: (Observing the patient's demeanor) I've noticed that you haven't mentioned any recent social interactions or gatherings. It seems like you've been withdrawing from social activities. Can you tell me more about that?
   Patient: (Admits) Yeah, I haven't really felt like being around people. It's just easier to be alone.

6. **Apathy**: A lack of interest, enthusiasm, or initiative in engaging in goal-directed activities or interacting with others.
   Here is an example:

   Clinician: Good morning. How have you been feeling today?
   Patient: (With a sense of indifference) Morning. I'm here, I guess.
   Clinician: Can you tell me if there's anything you're looking forward to or any goals you have in mind?
   Patient: (With disinterest) Not really. There's nothing I'm particularly excited about.
   Clinician: (Exploring further) Is there something that used to motivate you or give you a sense of purpose, even in small ways?
   Patient: (With apathy) I used to enjoy reading books, but now, it's like I don't care anymore. I just don't see the point.

7. **Cognitive Impairment**: Deficits in cognitive functioning, including difficulties with attention, memory, problem-solving, and executive functions, leading to impaired decision-making and functioning.
   Here is an example:

   Clinician: Good afternoon. How have you been today?
   Patient: (With noticeable difficulty) Afternoon. I've been… um… well, you know, just… trying to… my head is all over the place.

Clinician: (Observing the patient's struggles) I can see that you might be finding it a bit hard to express yourself today. Is that correct?
Patient: (Nods) Yeah, it's... (pauses) words are like... playing hide-and-seek in my mind. I can't find them when I need them.

8. **Poor Self-Expectations**: Reduced sense of self-efficacy and low expectations for future success and personal achievements.
   Here is an example:

Clinician: Good morning. How are you feeling today?
Patient: (With lowered self-expectation) Morning. I'm just... not expecting much from today.
Clinician: Can you tell me if you have any goals or things you hope to achieve in the near future?
Patient: (With a sense of resignation) Not really. I've learned not to set my expectations too high.
Clinician: (Curious) It's important to have some aspirations and goals. Is there a particular reason why you don't set high expectations for yourself?
Patient: (Expressing low self-expectation) Well, every time I did, I ended up disappointed. So, now I just go with the flow and see where it takes me.

1.1.5 Neurological Signs of Psychosis

Neurological soft signs are often observed in individuals with schizophrenia and can assist in distinguishing schizophrenia from other diagnoses. These signs are minor neurological abnormalities related to sensory and motor performance, detected during clinical examinations. They are termed "soft" rather than "hard" because they do not indicate obvious localized pathological lesions. Generally, neurological soft signs are categorized into three domains: deficits in integrative sensory function, motor coordination, and motor sequencing. Deficits in integrative sensory function are evident in impaired audio-visual integration, agraphaesthesia (inability to recognize symbols written on the skin), and astereognosis (inability to identify objects by touch alone). Problems in motor coordination can be observed in general coordination tests, intention tremor, finger-thumb opposition, balance, and gait. Issues in motor sequencing are evident in tests that require repetitive alternating hand positions, such as fist-edge-palm, fist-ring, and the Ozeretski test.

Abnormalities in gait and overall walking style are frequently observed in individuals with schizophrenia. Their movements often appear slowed and effortful, marked by reduced walking speed, shorter stride length, decreased arm swing, and subtle postural instability—sometimes giving the impression of cautious or hesitant movement. These changes are thought to reflect disruptions in motor planning, basal ganglia function, and psychomotor coordination. In my experience, studying the gait patterns of individuals with Parkinson's disease can provide valuable parallels: both groups may show reduced stride amplitude, diminished automaticity, and a "shuffling" quality in their steps, although the underlying mechanisms differ. For a clear illustration of these motor patterns, refer to this video from *The Lancet*, which demonstrates the progression of Parkinsonian gait from mild to severe stages: https://youtu.be/pFLC9C-xH8E?si=fjrOt9gYGR1kaN6h

1.1.6 Signs of Schizophrenia

While the previous sections described symptoms of psychosis, here are some signs of schizophrenia. These signs are useful to differentiate schizophrenia from other diagnoses, such as severe obsessive-compulsive disorder.

Bizarre delusions are typically unique to schizophrenia and rarely seen in other conditions. For example, a bizarre paranoid delusion might involve the belief that one is being stalked by a spirit named John, who resides between heaven and hell. In contrast, non-bizarre paranoid delusions could involve an unfounded belief that someone harbors ill intentions, even though there is no evidence to support this. This is often colloquially referred to as paranoia, overthinking, or jumping to conclusions. Certain delusional symptoms are particularly indicative of schizophrenia. If a patient experiences thought insertion (believing external forces are inserting thoughts into their mind), thought blocking (sudden interruptions in thinking), or thought broadcasting (believing their thoughts are being transmitted for others to hear), it is highly likely that their psychosis is related to schizophrenia.

Auditory hallucinations are another common feature of schizophrenia. In individuals without a diagnosis, auditory hallucinations might be relatively benign, such as thinking someone is calling them in a crowded place but realizing no one is there. In non-schizophrenia cases, auditory hallucinations might manifest as whispers or imagined voices, similar to how one might mentally assign voices to different characters when reading a novel. However, in schizophrenia, commanding voices and commenting voices are more characteristic. Commanding voices may be loud, authoritative, or even whispering, urging the individual to perform specific actions. For example, a voice might command someone to jump or harm a friend, under the false promise that the voice will disappear afterward. These voices can be forceful and deceptive. Commenting voices, on the other hand, provide a running commentary on the individual's thoughts and actions, similar to a sports commentator. These voices often make critical or demeaning remarks, which can be distressing. Such auditory hallucinations are rarely experienced by those without schizophrenia, but it's important to note that not all individuals with schizophrenia will experience these specific types of voices.

Disorganized symptoms are also a hallmark of schizophrenia, though they can occur due to other factors like substance use or neurodegenerative conditions such as Alzheimer's. Disorganized behavior in schizophrenia may sometimes be a result of other symptoms. For instance, if someone is experiencing commanding voices that demand they jump repeatedly, they might engage in sudden, erratic behaviors, like randomly jumping, which might appear unusual to others.

1.2 A Brief History of Psychosis: From Dementia Praecox to Schizophrenia, the Psychosis Continuum, and Reinventing Schizophrenia

In this section, we'll explore the origins of the term *dementia praecox*, its evolution into *schizophrenia*, the development of the *psychosis continuum*, and the ongoing debate about whether schizophrenia as a distinct entity truly exists. Finally, we will establish the position of this book, presenting schizophrenia as a syndrome.

The history of schizophrenia is a complex and evolving narrative, spanning over a century. From the initial diagnosis of "dementia praecox" to the modern-day recognition of a "psychosis continuum," the understanding of this intricate mental disorder has been shaped by significant milestones and paradigm shifts, deeply rooted in the historical, social, and scientific context of each era.

1.2.1 The Emergence of Dementia Praecox in the Industrial Age

The foundation of our understanding of schizophrenia was laid during the late nineteenth century, a period of rapid societal change brought on by the Industrial Revolution. In this context, German psychiatrist Emil Kraepelin introduced the term "dementia praecox" (1905/1913). The industrial age had brought about unprecedented changes in society, with urbanization, mechanization, and the rapid expansion of cities. These changes, along with the stressors of modernization, were accompanied by the emergence of new forms of mental distress. Kraepelin sought to categorize and make sense of these conditions, distinguishing "dementia praecox" from other mental illnesses.

In this tumultuous environment, Kraepelin's work marked a pivotal moment in the understanding of severe mental illnesses. He introduced "dementia praecox" as a diagnostic category to distinguish it from other mental illnesses. Kraepelin emphasized that this condition typically had an early onset, often in young adulthood, and was characterized by a progressive course leading to severe cognitive decline. The Latin phrase "dementia praecox" literally translates to "premature dementia," reflecting the prevailing belief that the disorder resulted in cognitive deterioration similar to dementia. The term itself captured the essence of the era—the fear of cognitive decline amid the rapid changes of the Industrial Revolution.

Kraepelin's groundbreaking work was instrumental in drawing a distinction between this class of disorders and other forms of mental illness that were more common in a society undergoing rapid transformation.

1.2.2 Eugen Bleuler and the Birth of Schizophrenia

The next significant chapter in the history of schizophrenia unfolded in the early twentieth century. In 1911, Swiss psychiatrist Eugen Bleuler introduced the term "schizophrenia" (Bleuler, 1950). His work was influenced not only by medical and scientific developments but also by the cultural and social milieu of the time. As Europe grappled with the aftermath of World War I and the looming uncertainties of a changing world, Bleuler's conceptualization of "schizophrenia" reflected the era's prevailing sense of instability and fragmentation.

Bleuler observed that not all individuals with the disorder experienced the progressive cognitive decline implied by "dementia praecox." Instead, he focused on the fragmentation of thought processes, emotional withdrawal, and the concept of a "split mind" as central characteristics of the condition. The term "schizophrenia," derived from the Greek words, combined "schizein" (to split) and "phrēn," (mind). It underscored the division in the patients' mental functions, capturing the zeitgeist of a world grappling with a sense of internal division and disintegration.

Bleuler's conceptualization expanded the understanding of schizophrenia, highlighting that cognitive deficits were only one part of the disorder. The shift from "dementia praecox" to "schizophrenia" was pivotal in acknowledging the complexity and diversity of the illness, setting the stage for a more comprehensive approach to its study and treatment.

1.2.3 The Psychosis Continuum

As the world moved into the modern age, the understanding of schizophrenia continued to evolve. It became increasingly evident that psychotic disorders were not neatly compartmentalized but existed on a spectrum. This recognition led to the development of the concept of a "psychosis continuum", particularly from Strauss (Strauss, 1969) to the work of Professor Jim van Os and Professor Richard Linscott (e.g., Linscott & van Os, 2010, 2013).

In this framework, psychotic disorders such as schizophrenia, schizoaffective disorder, and bipolar disorder with psychotic features were seen as sharing common elements, suggesting shared underlying mechanisms. For example, auditory hallucinations are argued to not be qualitatively different across schizophrenia, other mental disorders, or even normal experiences. The distinction lies in quantitative factors such as frequency, intensity of distress, location, and degree of control. In schizophrenia, auditory hallucinations—such as commanding voices—may occur daily for a few minutes and are highly distressing. They are also likely perceived as coming from outside the person and are uncontrollable or difficult to dismiss. In contrast, in normal experiences, similar hallucinations might occur once in a lifetime for a second or two, cause no distress, are perceived as coming from within the person's own mind, and are more easily controlled or dismissed.

The psychosis continuum concept highlights the overlap of symptoms across diagnoses, emphasizing the need for more individualized and nuanced approaches to diagnosis and treatment. It challenges traditional boundaries between psychotic disorders and underscores the interconnected nature of these conditions.

1.2.4 Reinventing Schizophrenia: The Schizophrenia Research Journal

In contemporary times, the landscape of schizophrenia research continues to evolve, driven by multidisciplinary collaboration and technological advancements. The "Reinventing Schizophrenia" special issue, published by the *Schizophrenia Research* journal, represents a modern-day call to action (Tandon et al., 2022).

This initiative brings together cutting-edge research and insights from diverse fields, including psychiatry, psychology, genetics, neuroscience, and more. It challenges conventional notions of schizophrenia and explores innovative approaches to its diagnosis, treatment, and support. The issue reflects a recognition that traditional frameworks need to be reevaluated and reimagined in a rapidly changing world, offering hope for continued progress in the field of schizophrenia research.

In this special issue, the majority of the authors agree to retain the term "schizophrenia" due to its clinical utility. However, some authors argue for its abolition, acknowledging that the term is no longer scientifically valid. The debate over the validity of the schizophrenia construct has even led the journal *Schizophrenia Bulletin* to change its name to *Journal of Psychotic Disorders*. Many authors advocate for redefining schizophrenia as a syndrome rather than a disorder, particularly Professor William Carpenter (Carpenter, 2016, 2022). Many authors also underline the need to recognize its multidimensional nature, and its treatment requirement should also be multidimensional.

In conclusion, the history of schizophrenia spans over a century and is deeply intertwined with the historical, social, and scientific context of each era. From Kraepelin's "dementia praecox" in the Industrial Age to Bleuler's "schizophrenia" in the aftermath of World War I, our evolving understanding of this disorder has transformed how we perceive and approach it. The emergence of the "psychosis continuum" paradigm challenges traditional classifications, emphasizing the interconnected nature of psychotic disorders in a globalized world. The "Reinventing Schizophrenia" initiative in the *Schizophrenia Research* journal represents a modern response to the dynamic and rapidly changing landscape of schizophrenia research, offering hope for a future with enhanced understanding and support for those affected by this complex condition.

1.3 Overview of Treatment for Psychosis: Pharmacotherapy, Psychotherapy, and ECT

There are various treatment modalities for psychosis. The most common are pharmacotherapy and psychotherapy; however, other options include electroconvulsive therapy, transcranial magnetic stimulation, and psychosurgery.

1.3.1 Pharmacotherapy

Pharmacotherapy, or medication-based treatment, is a cornerstone of managing psychosis. Antipsychotic medications, which include both typical and atypical antipsychotics, are prescribed to alleviate symptoms by modulating neurotransmitter activity in the brain, particularly dopamine.

Typical antipsychotics, such as haloperidol, effectively address positive symptoms like hallucinations and delusions, but they may cause movement-related side effects. Atypical antipsychotics, like olanzapine and risperidone, are often preferred for their broader efficacy, including the treatment of negative symptoms like social withdrawal and lack of motivation. However, they may lead to metabolic side effects.

The choice of medication depends on the specific symptoms, their severity, and the individual's response to treatment. Finding the right medication and dosage often involves a trial-and-error process under the supervision of a healthcare provider.

1.3.2 Psychotherapy

Psychotherapy, or talk therapy, plays a crucial role in managing psychosis. Cognitive behavioral therapy for psychosis (CBTp) is the most widely used approach. It helps individuals recognize and manage symptoms, identify triggers for psychosis, and develop coping strategies.

CBTp focuses on changing thought patterns and behaviors related to delusions and hallucinations. It empowers individuals to challenge irrational beliefs, reduce distress, and improve their overall quality of life. Therapy is typically conducted on an individual or group basis, depending on the preferences and needs of the individual.

Recovery-oriented approaches, such as the Recovery Model and the Open Dialogue Approach, emphasize collaboration between the individual, their support network, and healthcare professionals. These models prioritize holistic well-being, social connections, and personalized care.

1.3.3 Electroconvulsive Therapy (ECT)

ECT is a medical procedure primarily used when psychosis is severe and other treatments have been ineffective or when there's an urgent need for intervention. During ECT, a controlled electric current is applied to the brain, inducing a brief seizure. This process is believed to reset abnormal brain activity associated with severe symptoms of psychosis.

ECT is particularly useful for individuals with conditions like catatonia, severe depression with psychotic features, or treatment-resistant schizophrenia. While it can be highly effective, it is typically considered only after other options have been exhausted due to its invasiveness and potential side effects.

1.3.4 Repetitive Transcranial Magnetic Stimulation (rTMS)

rTMS is a non-invasive neurostimulation technique that uses magnetic fields to stimulate specific areas of the brain. It has shown promise in treating psychosis, particularly in cases of treatment-resistant schizophrenia. By modulating neural activity, rTMS aims to alleviate symptoms and improve cognitive functioning.

1.3.5 Psychosurgery

Psychosurgery, also known as neurosurgery for mental disorder (NMD), is a highly specialized and invasive treatment option considered only in extreme cases of severe, treatment-resistant psychosis. Psychosurgery involves the surgical alteration of brain tissue to alleviate symptoms. Procedures like prefrontal lobotomy have largely been replaced by more precise techniques, such as deep brain stimulation (DBS), which target specific brain regions to modulate neural activity.

The choice of treatment depends on the specific diagnosis, the individual's preferences, and the severity of symptoms. Regular assessment and collaboration between healthcare providers and the individual are essential for tailoring the treatment plan to achieve the best possible outcomes. In summary, the treatment of psychosis encompasses a range of interventions. The choice of treatment should be individualized and regularly reviewed to ensure the most effective and personalized approach to managing psychosis.

References

Bleuler, E. (1950). *Dementia praecox or the group of schizophrenias*. International Universities Press.

Carpenter, W. T. (2016). Shifting paradigms and the term schizophrenia. *Schizophrenia Bulletin, 42*(4), 863–864. https://doi.org/10.1093/schbul/sbw050

Carpenter, W. T. (2022). Schizophrenia: A view of immediate future. *Schizophrenia Research, 242*, 15–16. https://doi.org/10.1016/j.schres.2021.12.004

Linscott, R. J., & van Os, J. (2010). Systematic reviews of categorical versus continuum models in psychosis: Evidence for discontinuous subpopulations underlying a psychometric continuum. Implications for DSM-V, DSM-VI, and DSM-VII. *Annual Review of Clinical Psychology, 6*(1), 391–419. https://doi.org/10.1146/annurev.clinpsy.032408.153506

Linscott, R. J., & van Os, J. (2013). An updated and conservative systematic review and meta-analysis of epidemiological evidence on psychotic experiences in children and adults: On the pathway from proneness to persistence to dimensional expression across mental disorders. *Psychological Medicine, 43*(6), 1133–1149. https://doi.org/10.1017/S0033291712001626

Strauss, J. S. (1969). Hallucinations and delusions as points on continua function: Rating scale evidence. *Archives of General Psychiatry, 21*(5), 581–586. https://doi.org/10.1001/archpsyc.1969.01740230069010

Kraepelin, E. (1913). *Lectures on clinical psychiatry* (T. Johnstone, trans.). William Wood & Company. (Original work published 1905).

Tandon, R., Keshavan, M., & Nasrallah, H. (2022). Reinventing schizophrenia: Updating the construct. *Schizophrenia Research, 242*, 1–3. https://doi.org/10.1016/j.schres.2022.02.024

Chapter 2
Overview of Cognitive Behavioral Therapy

Abstract This chapter provides a concise overview of Cognitive Behavioral Therapy (CBT), presenting it as an empirically supported, skills-based psychotherapy that links thoughts, emotions, and behaviors. It outlines core components of CBT—cognitive restructuring, guided discovery, exposure, behavioral activation, journaling, relaxation training, and successive approximation—demonstrating their relevance across clinical presentations. The chapter also describes CBT's historical origins from Beck, Ellis, and later European developments, clarifying the theoretical foundations that inform its structured, collaborative practice. Mechanisms of change are reviewed from both specific-technique and common-factor perspectives. Evidence is examined showing that targeted interventions (e.g., metacognitive training, insomnia treatment) can reduce specific symptoms, while therapeutic alliance often drives broader clinical improvement. The chapter concludes by framing CBT as a synergy of technique and relationship, setting the conceptual foundation for applying CBT within a symptom-based framework for psychosis.

Keywords Cognitive restructuring · Behavioral activation · Exposure therapy · Therapeutic alliance · Mechanisms of change

2.1 What Is Cognitive Behavioral Therapy?

Cognitive Behavioral Therapy (CBT) is a leading, empirically supported psychotherapy approach grounded in the principle that thoughts, emotions, and behaviors are intimately inter-connected; altering maladaptive cognitions and behavioral patterns can reduce distress and improve functioning. In structured, collaborative sessions, clinicians help clients identify automatic thoughts, core beliefs, and maintaining behaviors, then use techniques such as cognitive restructuring, behavioral activation, exposure, and skills training. CBT's strong evidence base, adaptability across disorders and emphasis on skill-building have made it a mainstay in contemporary clinical practice.

E. S. Jaya, *Cognitive Behavioral Therapy for Psychosis as a Syndrome*,
https://doi.org/10.1007/978-981-95-9203-6_2

Historically, CBT draws on the cognitive tradition pioneered by Aaron T. Beck (whose landmark work *Cognitive Therapy of Depression* was published in 1979) together with earlier behavioral traditions influenced by Albert Ellis's rational-emotive work, and subsequent European/UK adaptations (for example, by David M. Clark and Paul Salkovskis). This blend of cognitive and behavioral methods gives CBT both theoretical coherence and practical flexibility.

This section offers only a concise overview of CBT's concept and foundation. Readers seeking a more detailed theoretical and historical treatment are encouraged to consult Beck's original works and major comprehensive texts in the field.

2.2 Components of Cognitive Behavioral Therapy

Cognitive Behavioral Therapy (CBT) is a multifaceted therapeutic approach that clinical psychologists employ to address a range of emotional and psychological issues. It comprises several core components, each serving a distinct purpose within the therapy process. Firstly, the cognitive component involves identifying and challenging irrational or negative thought patterns that contribute to distress. It encourages clients to reevaluate their beliefs and adopt more constructive thinking. Secondly, the behavioral component focuses on changing maladaptive behaviors through techniques like exposure therapy and behavioral experiments, promoting healthier responses to triggers. Additionally, the emotional component involves understanding and managing emotional reactions more effectively, thereby enhancing emotional regulation. Communication and interpersonal skills are honed through the interpersonal component, fostering healthier relationships. Overall, CBT's adaptability and comprehensive nature empower clinical psychologists to tailor treatment strategies to the unique needs of their clients, making it an indispensable tool in the field of clinical psychology. Here are some techniques in CBT:

1. **Cognitive restructuring or reframing**
   This process involves thoroughly examining negative thought patterns, which may include tendencies to over-generalize, anticipate the worst outcomes, or excessively focus on minor details. Such thinking patterns can significantly impact actions and potentially become self-fulfilling prophecies. The therapist will inquire about the thought process in specific situations to help the patient recognize negative patterns. Once identified, the therapist, together with the patient, will try to find ways to reframe those thoughts in a more objective manner. For instance, the thought, "I failed the report because I'm utterly incompetent" can transform into, "While the report was a failure, it is incorrect to assume that I am utterly incompetent, as I received a promotion this year and last year."
2. **Guided discovery**
   Guided discovery entails the therapist familiarizing themselves with your perspective and then posing questions designed to challenge your beliefs and

broaden your perspectives. You might be prompted to provide evidence supporting your assumptions as well as contrasting evidence that contradicts them. This process helps you explore alternative viewpoints, especially those you might not have considered previously, aiding you in choosing more beneficial paths.

3. **Exposure therapy**
   Exposure therapy is a method used to confront fears and phobias gradually. The therapist gradually exposes you to anxiety-provoking stimuli while guiding you in developing coping mechanisms. This exposure occurs in small, manageable steps. Ultimately, it aims to reduce vulnerability and enhance your confidence in managing such situations.
4. **Journaling and thought records**
   Writing serves as an effective way to connect with your thoughts. Your therapist may encourage you to document negative thoughts that arise between sessions and explore positive alternatives. Another writing exercise involves tracking new thoughts and behaviors practiced since the last session. This written record helps you recognize your personal progress.
5. **Activity scheduling and behavior activation**
   Integrating avoided or procrastinated activities into your schedule can alleviate decision-making burdens, potentially increasing follow-through. By scheduling activities, you establish constructive routines and create ample opportunities to apply the strategies you've learned.
6. **Behavioral experiments**
   Behavioral experiments involve predicting outcomes before engaging in anxiety-inducing tasks. By discussing whether these predictions come true, you can gradually reveal the discrepancy between anticipated and actual outcomes, which helps reduce the anxiety associated with these tasks.
7. **Relaxation and stress reduction techniques**
   CBT often includes teaching progressive relaxation techniques such as deep breathing exercises, muscle relaxation, and guided imagery. These practical skills help reduce stress and empower individuals to effectively manage phobias, social anxieties, and other stressors.
8. **Role playing**
   Engaging in role-playing scenarios allows individuals to navigate potential challenging situations, reducing fear and anxiety. This technique facilitates improvement in problem-solving abilities, builds confidence in specific contexts, practices social skills, provides assertiveness training, and enhances communication skills.
9. **Successive approximation**
   This strategy involves breaking daunting tasks into smaller, manageable steps. By progressively building on these steps, individuals gain confidence incrementally, overcoming overwhelming tasks bit by bit.

2.3 Mechanisms of Cognitive Behavioral Therapy

The mechanisms underlying Cognitive Behavioral Therapy (CBT) remain a subject of ongoing debate. While CBT's clinical efficacy is well established, its precise mechanisms of change are less clearly delineated. Critics have argued that despite numerous randomized controlled trials (RCTs) demonstrating its effectiveness, few studies have directly tested *how* CBT achieves symptom reduction. Most RCTs emphasize outcomes over process, making it difficult to determine which therapeutic components are responsible for change. For example, Morrison et al. (2014) conducted an RCT of CBT for psychosis in which a range of manualized techniques were available, yet not all participants received every technique—raising the question of which specific interventions accounted for improvement.

Two main research traditions have emerged in response to this mechanistic gap. The first emphasizes specific mechanisms, examining whether particular CBT components produce targeted effects. For instance, Freeman et al. (2017) demonstrated that CBT interventions for insomnia and anxiety in psychosis led to measurable symptom improvements, while Moritz and Lysaker (2014) found that metacognitive training targeting reasoning biases reduced paranoid ideation. This line of inquiry supports the view that symptom change in CBT arises, at least in part, from the successful application of specific cognitive and behavioral techniques.

The second tradition highlights common factors in psychotherapy—particularly the therapeutic alliance—as a general mechanism of change. Proponents of this perspective argue that the quality of the therapist–client relationship may account for much of the observed improvement across modalities. Meta-analyses (e.g., Cuijpers et al., 2021, 2023) have shown that distinct therapies, such as CBT and psychoanalysis, can yield comparable outcomes in depression, suggesting that shared relational processes contribute substantially to therapeutic success.

In this manual, we recognize that both perspectives are valid. Specific techniques can lead to specific changes—for example, relaxation can reduce tension and anxiety, which in turn may lead to broader improvements such as reduced irritability and better interpersonal relationships. Conversely, general processes such as the therapeutic alliance can also drive specific changes: when a therapist demonstrates trustworthiness to a paranoid patient, this relationship itself becomes a behavioral experiment that challenges persecutory beliefs and fosters corrective learning. At the same time, that same alliance may bring about general improvements, as the patient—therapist relationship becomes a living model of trust and psychological safety.

Ultimately, this book holds that meaningful therapeutic change in CBT arises from the synergy between targeted techniques and the relational context that allows those techniques to work.

References

Cuijpers, P., Quero, S., Noma, H., Ciharova, M., Miguel, C., Karyotaki, E., Cipriani, A., Cristea, I. A., & Furukawa, T. A. (2021). Psychotherapies for depression: a network meta-analysis covering efficacy, acceptability and longterm outcomes of all main treatment types. *World Psychiatry, 20*, 283–293. https://doi.org/10.1002/wps.20860.

Cuijpers, P., Miguel, C., Harrer, M., Plessen, C. Y., Ciharova, M., Ebert, D., & Karyotaki, E. (2023). Cognitive behavior therapy vs. control conditions, other psychotherapies, pharmacotherapies and combined treatment for depression: A comprehensive meta-analysis including 409 trials with 52,702 patients. *World Psychiatry, 22*(1), 105–115. https://doi.org/10.1002/wps.21069

Freeman, D., Sheaves, B., Goodwin, G. M., Yu, L. M., Nickless, A., Harrison, P. J., Waite, F., et al. (2017). The effects of improving sleep on mental health (OASIS): A randomized controlled trial with mediation analysis. *The Lancet Psychiatry, 4*(10), 749–758. https://doi.org/10.1016/S2215-0366(17)30328-0

Moritz, S., & Lysaker, P. H. (2014). Metacognitive training for schizophrenia spectrum patients: A review and synthesis of neurocognitive, social cognitive, and metacognitive perspectives. *Psychological Medicine, 44*(3), 647–658.

Morrison, A. P., Turkington, D., Pyle, M., Spencer, H., Brabban, A., Dunn, G., Christodoulides, T., Dudley, R., Chapman, N., Callcott, P., Grace, T., Lumley, V., Drage, L., Tully, S., Irving, K., Cummings, A., Byrne, R., Davies, L. M., & Hutton, P. (2014). Cognitive therapy for people with schizophrenia spectrum disorders not taking antipsychotic drugs: A single-blind randomised controlled trial. *The Lancet, 383*(9926), 1395–1403. https://doi.org/10.1016/S0140-6736(13)62246-1

Chapter 3
Rationale for Symptom-Based Management Approach

Abstract This chapter argues for conceptualizing psychosis as a syndrome rather than a discrete disorder, drawing analogies from internal medicine. Using sepsis, diabetes, and irritable bowel syndrome (IBS) as models, it explains how syndromes rely on targeted management of multiple contributing dysfunctions rather than pursuit of a single etiological cure. Psychosis similarly exhibits heterogeneous pathways, variable severity, and fluctuating presentations, making symptom-level intervention more pragmatic than disorder-level treatment. The chapter proposes a "syndromic logic" for CBT: clinicians should select treatment modules based on presenting symptoms—e.g., insomnia treatment for patients with insomnia, social anxiety modules for those with social fear—mirroring how medical management individualizes treatment combinations. This approach accommodates the vast heterogeneity of psychosis ("no two patients with schizophrenia are alike") and provides a systematic rationale for integrating diverse CBT techniques within a unified, symptom-based clinical framework.

Keywords Syndromic model · Symptom-level intervention · Individualized treatment · Transdiagnostic approach · Clinical heterogeneity

3.1 How Does Internal Medicine Treat Syndrome?

In clinical psychology, psychopathology is often approached with an "infectious disease" or "disorder" mindset. The infectious disease model treats mental illness as something foreign that needs to be eradicated. For example, antibiotics are used to treat bacterial infections, such as an E. coli-induced stomachache, while antivirals are prescribed for viral infections like the flu. Similarly, Cognitive Behavioral Therapy (CBT) for depression is used to treat depression but would not typically be applied to panic disorder.

In contrast, the "disorder" mindset views mental illness as a dysregulation of normal processes, with treatment aimed at restoring balance. For example, hypertension is characterized by elevated blood pressure, and medication is used to lower

E. S. Jaya, *Cognitive Behavioral Therapy for Psychosis as a Syndrome*,
https://doi.org/10.1007/978-981-95-9203-6_3

it to normal levels. Phobias, similarly, represent an exaggerated fear response that can be normalized through exposure therapy. Despite these perspectives, psychopathology is rarely framed in a "syndrome" mindset.

In internal medicine, syndromes like sepsis, irritable bowel syndrome (IBS), and diabetes are often managed rather than cured. Treatments do not directly target the syndrome itself but aim to control the symptoms and various conditions contributing to it. For instance, sepsis—a condition where the body's immune response to infection causes tissue and organ damage—cannot be "cured" but can be managed. Sepsis management protocols, such as the "Sepsis Six" (resuscitation, oxygen titration, blood cultures, intravenous antibiotics, lactate measurement, and urine output monitoring), along with early-goal-directed therapy, have been shown to reduce mortality (Levy et al., 2018). Schizophrenia, in many ways, resembles sepsis in that it involves multiple pathways, crisis management is crucial, and the ultimate treatment often targets underlying causes (e.g., treating the cause of an infection in sepsis or addressing life stressors in schizophrenia).

Similarly, diabetes is a group of metabolic disorders characterized by prolonged high blood sugar levels due to insufficient insulin production or insulin resistance. While there is no "cure" for diabetes, its management is essential to prevent complications. Type 1 diabetes is often genetic, while Type 2 diabetes is commonly linked to lifestyle factors like obesity. Management programs, such as the Saxon Diabetes Management Program, emphasize integrated guidelines, care structures, quality management, and patient education. The UK Prospective Diabetes Study demonstrated that complications from Type 2 diabetes could be reduced through improved glucose and blood pressure control (Holman et al., 2008). However, diabetes management rarely aims for remission; instead, the focus is on avoiding complications. This stands in contrast to psychosis, where patients often prioritize functional outcomes over symptom management alone. Like diabetes, the management of psychosis should involve multidisciplinary teams, which may include dentists, psychologists, and other healthcare professionals.

Irritable Bowel Syndrome (IBS), another example of a syndrome that lacks a definitive cure, is characterized by abdominal pain, bloating, and altered bowel movements. IBS is now recognized as a disease of gut-brain interaction, and its diagnosis is typically one of exclusion (Ford et al., 2014). Although its etiology remains unknown, IBS is managed by addressing symptoms through diet modifications, increased fiber intake, and medications like antidepressants. Research on IBS management is still relatively new, and while there have been RCTs on individual therapies targeting individual symptoms within IBS, there is currently no comprehensive RCT on overall IBS management.

3.2 Applying Lessons from Internal Medicine to Psychosis

Metaphors and analogies are often used to clarify complex phenomena. Here, I draw on concepts from internal medicine to illuminate psychosis as a syndrome. Building on earlier examples, I discuss sepsis, irritable bowel syndrome (IBS), and diabetes as medical analogies that highlight different dimensions of psychosis.

Sepsis resembles schizophrenia in several ways. Both are syndromes arising from diverse precipitating factors and showing highly variable outcomes. Some patients with sepsis do not survive; others recover fully and resume normal lives. Likewise, while many individuals with schizophrenia struggle with functional independence, others—such as John Nash (Nobel prize winner)—achieve remarkable accomplishments, illustrating the wide outcome spectrum. Sepsis typically presents with four key features: fever, tachycardia, tachypnea, and confusion, though numerous other signs may occur. Schizophrenia, too, has defining symptom clusters—positive symptoms (e.g., hallucinations, delusions) and negative symptoms (e.g., amotivation, social withdrawal)—within a broader spectrum of manifestations.

The analogy, however, lies in *syndromic heterogeneity*, not in biological mechanism. In sepsis, the infectious trigger and biomarkers are usually identifiable; in schizophrenia, causal pathways remain elusive. Yet both conditions challenge the clinician to recognize and stabilize a dysregulated system rather than search for a single cause. It is often possible to identify who is at risk of sepsis (for example, critically ill inpatients), but predicting who will develop schizophrenia remains far more uncertain. It is easy to say who will not develop sepsis imminently; the same confidence cannot be applied to psychosis.

Irritable bowel syndrome (IBS) illustrates a different but complementary parallel. Both IBS and psychosis have unclear etiologies, fluctuating courses, and widely varying prognoses. In both cases, the primary treatment goal is to manage symptoms sufficiently so that they do not disrupt daily life.

This approach reflects a broader medical principle: in many internal medicine conditions, clinicians do not wait to resolve etiology before intervening. They focus instead on alleviating identifiable dysfunctions—reducing inflammation, relieving pain, normalizing rhythm—trusting that systemic balance will gradually re-establish itself once acute stressors are removed. Psychosis management should follow the same logic: we target distress, sleep, and functioning directly rather than chase an unseen "root cause" or focus on difficult, often unmodifiable targets such as delusions. Stabilization, rather than cure, becomes the path through which recovery unfolds.

Taken together, these analogies show that psychosis, like many internal medicine syndromes, should not be understood through a single-deficit lens. It is best approached as a dynamic system of interacting biological, psychological, and environmental processes—sometimes acute and catastrophic, sometimes chronic and functional, but always multifactorial. As in internal medicine, clinical progress depends less on identifying one etiological agent than on restoring equilibrium through careful symptom management and support for the system's own self-regulation.

3.3 Applying Lessons from Internal Medicine to CBT

Various techniques in CBT can be employed similarly to how various medications and approaches are used in the treatment of sepsis in internal medicine. For example, in the management of diabetes, a diabetic patient with hypertension will receive blood pressure medications and a diabetic patient with normal tension will not receive blood pressure medications. Likewise, a psychotic patient with insomnia should receive CBT for insomnia and those without insomnia should not receive CBT for insomnia.

Specificity of technique for CBT for various disorders is ubiquitous. For instance, in Clark and Wells' CBT for social anxiety, specific techniques tailored to this condition are rarely found in CBT for other disorders. This approach emphasizes behavioral experiments, with sessions typically lasting 90 min, compared to the usual 60-min duration of a typical CBT session. Additionally, confederates are sometimes used to simulate feared social situations, such as conversing with the opposite sex for romantic purposes. In contrast, CBT for insomnia does not incorporate behavioral experiments or confederates. Instead, it emphasizes sleep monitoring, which involves using a diary to record pre-sleep activities and assess sleep quality—a technique that is clearly not applicable to social anxiety. These two examples demonstrate that the techniques utilized in CBT are specifically tailored to the condition being treated.

Unlike social anxiety and insomnia, psychosis is formulated here as a syndrome. Thus, in applying CBT for psychosis, we adopt the same principle of selecting appropriate techniques tailored to the specific problems at hand, similar to how sleep monitoring is used in insomnia treatment and behavioral experiments are applied in social anxiety. However, this application occurs at a higher level. Rather than focusing solely on individual techniques for specific problems (e.g., journaling before bedtime to address ruminations that contribute to insomnia), we consider a collective group of techniques (e.g., those used in CBT for insomnia) aimed at addressing a range of related issues (e.g., insomnia). This approach is essential given the heterogeneous nature of psychosis, as many authors have noted that "no two patients with schizophrenia are alike." Consequently, while one patient may benefit from techniques used in CBT for insomnia, another may require those from CBT for social anxiety.

References

Ford, A. C., Talley, N. J., Schoenfeld, P. S., Quigley, E. M. M., & Moayyedi, P. (2014). Efficacy of antidepressants and psychological therapies in irritable bowel syndrome: Systematic review and meta-analysis. *Gut, 63*(6), 997–1007.

Holman, R. R., Paul, S. K., Bethel, M. A., Matthews, D. R., & Neil, H. A. W. (2008). 10-year follow-up of intensive glucose control in type 2 diabetes. *The New England Journal of Medicine, 359*(15), 1577–1589. https://doi.org/10.1056/NEJMoa0806470

Levy, M. M., Evans, L. E., & Rhodes, A. (2018). The surviving sepsis campaign bundle: 2018 update. *Intensive Care Medicine, 44*(6), 925–928. https://doi.org/10.1007/s00134-018-5085-0

Part II
Assessment and Formulation

Chapter 4
Assessment of Psychosis

Abstract This chapter outlines core assessment tools used in evaluating psychosis within a symptom-based CBT framework. It reviews standardized measures—including PSYRATS, BPRS, CAINS, CAPE-42, the Neurological Evaluation Scale, and the Bush-Francis Catatonia Scale—highlighting their structure, utility, and relevance for diagnostic clarification, baseline mapping, and treatment planning. The chapter emphasizes the need for multidimensional assessment that incorporates positive symptoms, negative symptoms, neurological soft signs, comorbidities, and risk factors. By grounding assessment in validated instruments, clinicians can generate a precise clinical profile that enables targeted intervention and objective monitoring of therapeutic progress.

Here, we outline common measures for psychosis, categorized based on principle of open-access and evidence-based approaches.

Keywords Psychosis assessment · Symptom severity scales · Negative symptoms · Clinical rating scales · Neurological soft signs

4.1 The Psychotic Symptom Rating Scales (PSYRATS)

The Psychotic Symptom Rating Scales (PSYRATS) is a semi-structured interview designed to assess the dimension and severity of auditory hallucinations and delusions (Haddock et al., 1999). This interview consists of two subscales: the auditory hallucinations subscale (AH) and the delusions subscale (DS). The AH comprises 11 items that evaluate general symptoms, including frequency, duration, severity, intensity of distress, and specific dimensions of auditory hallucinations such as controllability, loudness, location, negative content, degree of negative content, beliefs about the origin of voices, and disruption. The DS consists of six items assessing the dimensions of delusions, including preoccupation, duration, conviction, distress, intensity of distress, and disruption. Both subscales are rated on a five-point ordinal scale (0–4). Good reliability and validity have been reported in patients with chronic

E. S. Jaya, *Cognitive Behavioral Therapy for Psychosis as a Syndrome*,
https://doi.org/10.1007/978-981-95-9203-6_4

schizophrenia and those experiencing their first episodes of schizophrenia or related disorders (Drake et al., 2007).

4.2 The Brief Psychiatric Rating Scale (BPRS)

The Brief Psychiatric Rating Scale (BPRS) has been widely used as an assessment tool to monitor treatment change across several symptoms characteristics. Initially, the scale consisted of 16 items (Dazzi et al., 2016; Overall & Gorham, 1962), but later, two additional items were added to create the standard 18-item version (Dazzi et al., 2016; Overall, 1974). To capture more aspects of schizophrenia, a comprehensive 24-item version known as the Brief Psychiatric Rating Scale Expanded (BPRS-E) was developed. This expanded version includes items related to bizarre behavior, self-neglect, suicidality, elevated mood, motor hyperactivity, and distractibility. The latest version, BPRS-E 4.0, incorporated two new items: conceptual disorganization and bizarre behavior (Dazzi et al., 2016; Ventura et al., 1993). The scoring for the BPRS-E is measured using a 7-point Likert Scale, ranging from 0 (not assessed) and 7 (extremely severe) for each dimension, including bizarre behavior, conceptual disorganization, impoverished thinking, poor attention, and inappropriate affect.

4.3 The Clinical Assessment Interview for Negative Symptoms (CAINS)

The Clinical Assessment Interview for Negative Symptoms (CAINS) is a standardized interview composed of 13 items, divided into two scales: expression and motivation/pleasure (Kring et al., 2013). The expression scale consists of four items that assess vocal prosody, facial expressions, gestures, and speech. In contrast, the other scale contains nine items measuring motivation and pleasure across various life domains, including social, vocational, and recreational activities. Each item is rated on a five-point scale from 0 (not present) to 4 (severe). A notable feature of this interview is its clear treatment objectives that have a strong basis in neuroscience, specifically targeting emotional expression and motivation/pleasure. Furthermore, the motivation/pleasure scale has shown associations with all aspects of functioning, while the expression scale is associated with living independently and family functioning. The CAINS demonstrates good reliability and strong convergent validity in patients with schizophrenia or schizoaffective disorder (Kring et al., 2013).

4.4 The Community Assessment of Psychic Experiences (CAPE-42)

The Community Assessment of Psychic Experiences (CAPE) is a 42-item self-report questionnaire that evaluates lifetime psychotic experiences, focusing on both the frequency and levels of distress associated with these experiences. It assesses three dimensions: positive symptoms, such as bizarre experiences, hallucinations, paranoia, magical thinking, and grandiosity; negative symptoms, including affective flattening, social withdrawal, and avolition; and additional depressive symptoms (Jaya, 2017; Stefanis et al., 2002). The questionnaire is structured with four columns corresponding to each subscale (frequency and distress), with scores ranging from 0 (never) to 3 (nearly always).

4.5 The Neurological Evaluation Scale (NES)

The Neurological Evaluation Scale (NES) is a standardized instrument designed to assess neurological signs associated with schizophrenia, which can be easily administered by clinicians (Buchanan & Heinrichs, 1989). It consists of 26 items that represent three functional areas of interest: sensory integration, motor coordination, and sequencing of complex motor acts. It also assesses cerebral dominance, short-term memory, frontal release signs, and eye movement abnormality. Each item includes specific instructions to measure the relevant areas (e.g., demonstrating how the patient walks, kicks a ball, matches a set of tapping sounds with one of three sets of dots presented). In total, 14 items are tested and scored separately for the right and left sides of the body. Each item is scored on a 3-point scale (0 = no abnormality, 1 = mild but definite impairment, 2 = marked impairment). A total score (the sum of all items) can also be obtained. Preliminary data indicate that the NES demonstrates good reliability and can effectively discriminate between patients with schizophrenia and nonpsychiatric controls (Buchanan & Heinrichs, 1989).

4.6 The Bush-Francis Catatonia Scale

The Bush-Francis Catatonia Scale is a structured and measurable assessment for catatonia, aimed at detecting and diagnosing its presence (Bush et al., 1996). The instrument is composed of a 23-item scale, where the first 14 items comprise the Bush-Francis Catatonia Screening Instrument (BFCSI). For screening purposes, these initial 14 items are rated on a scale from 0 (absent) to 3 (present). If two or more of the screening items persist for 24 h or longer, this aligns with the diagnostic criteria for catatonia as proposed by Bush et al. (1996). Regarding the severity assessment, all 23 items are rated on a scale from 0 to 3. The total BFCRS score is determined by summing the responses to all 23 items. Additionally, the rating scale is accompanied by a standardized examination procedure consisting of nine steps.

References

Buchanan, R. W., & Heinrichs, D. W. (1989). The neurological evaluation scale (NES): A structured instrument for the assessment of neurological signs in schizophrenia. *Psychiatry Research, 27*(3), 335–350.

Bush, G., Fink, M., Petrides, G., Dowling, F., & Francis, A. (1996). Catatonia. 1. Rating scale and standardized examination. *Acta Psychiatrica Scandinavica, 93*(2), 129–136. https://doi.org/10.1111/j.1600-0447.1996.tb09814.x

Dazzi, F., Shafer, A., & Lauriola, M. (2016). Meta-analysis of the brief psychiatric rating scale–expanded (BPRS-E) structure and arguments for a new version. *Journal of Psychiatric Research, 81*, 140–151. https://doi.org/10.1016/j.jpsychires.2016.07.001

Drake, R., Haddock, G., Tarrier, N., Bentall, R., & Lewis, S. (2007). The psychotic symptom rating scales (PSYRATS): Their usefulness and properties in first episode psychosis. *Schizophrenia Research, 89*(1–3), 119–122.

Haddock, G., McCarron, J., Tarrier, N., & Faragher, E. B. (1999). Scales to measure dimensions of hallucinations and delusions: The psychotic symptom rating scales (PSYRATS). *Psychological Medicine, 29*(4), 879–889.

Jaya, E. S. (2017). Confirmatory factor analysis of the Indonesian version of community assessment of psychic experiences. *Makara Human Behavior Studies in Asia, 9*(1), 1–12. https://doi.org/10.7454/mssh.v21i1.3495

Kring, A. M., Gur, R. E., Blanchard, J. J., Horan, W. P., & Reise, S. P. (2013). The clinical assessment interview for negative symptoms (CAINS): Final development and validation. *American Journal of Psychiatry, 170*(2), 165–172. https://doi.org/10.1176/appi.ajp.2012.12010109

Overall, J. E. (1974). The brief psychiatric rating scale in psychopharmacology research. In P. Pichot & E. Olivier-Martin (Eds.), *Psychological measurements in psychopharmacology: Modern problems in psychopharmacology* (pp. 67–78). Karger.

Overall, J. E., & Gorham, D. R. (1962). The brief psychiatric rating scale. *Psychological Reports, 10*, 799–812. https://doi.org/10.2466/pr0.1962.10.3.799

Stefanis, N. C., Hanssen, M., Smirnis, N. K., Avramopoulos, D. A., Evdokimidis, I. K., Stefanis, C. N., Verdoux, H., & Van Os, J. (2002). Evidence that three dimensions of psychosis have a distribution in the general population. *Psychological Medicine, 32*(2), 347–358. https://doi.org/10.1017/s0033291701005141

Ventura, J., Lukoff, D., Nuechterlein, K. H., Liberman, R. P., Green, M. F., & Shaner, A. (1993). Brief psychiatric rating scale (BPRS) expanded version: Scales, anchor points, and administration manual. *International Journal of Methods in Psychiatric, 3*, 227–243.

Chapter 5
Common Comorbidities, Risk Factors, and Protective Factors in People with Psychosis

Abstract This chapter details the psychiatric comorbidities and psychosocial factors that shape the course and treatment response of psychosis. It reviews common co-occurring disorders—including depression, anxiety disorders, substance use, OCD-spectrum symptoms, and personality pathology—and explains how these conditions influence symptom severity, functioning, and relapse risk. Risk factors such as trauma history, discrimination, social undermining, and adverse life events are contrasted with protective factors including supportive relationships, coping skills, and environmental stability. The chapter highlights the importance of identifying these contextual contributors during assessment to guide treatment prioritization and optimize outcomes within a symptom-based CBT approach.

Keywords Psychiatric comorbidity • Psychosocial risk • Protective factors • Functional impairment • Recovery predictors

The undeniable clinical diversity within schizophrenia manifests uniquely in each patient, with hardly any presenting an identical array of symptoms. Furthermore, within the same individual, symptoms exhibit remarkable variability over time, showcasing significant interactions among different symptom clusters. For instance, the alleviation of "secondary" negative symptoms often accompanies the resolution of positive symptoms, such as patient who no longer refuses to take a shower because he no longer thinks that the FBI is watching his shower box, contrasting with a possible enduring nature of core "deficit" negative symptoms, such as the patient's refusal to routinely engage with family and friends, that tend to exacerbate throughout the illness's longitudinal course.

Schizophrenia commonly coexists with various psychiatric conditions, while a multitude of identified risk and protective factors contribute significantly to the onset and progression of psychosis. This intricate web of factors significantly contributes to the individualized clinical heterogeneity observed in patients diagnosed with schizophrenia.

E. S. Jaya, *Cognitive Behavioral Therapy for Psychosis as a Syndrome*,
https://doi.org/10.1007/978-981-95-9203-6_5

5.1 Psychiatric Comorbidities

Schizophrenia is almost always accompanied by prevalent coexisting conditions such as depression, anxiety, and substance abuse, which can significantly influence its clinical presentation. These secondary conditions intricately interplay with the primary symptoms of schizophrenia. For instance, depression may trigger additional negative symptoms, panic attacks can fuel paranoia, and cannabis abuse can exacerbate both positive and disorganization symptoms. Treating the positive symptoms often alleviates depressive symptoms during an acute psychotic episode, but these may resurface in the "postpsychotic" phase, potentially worsening the long-term trajectory of the illness.

Anxiety and depression are pervasive throughout the illness, with estimated rates of 15% for panic disorder, 29% for posttraumatic stress disorder (PTSD), and 23% for obsessive—compulsive disorder (OCD) (Buckley et al., 2009). Furthermore, they also found that approximately half of all patients experience comorbid depression, while a conservative estimate suggests that 47% also have a lifetime diagnosis of substance abuse disorder.

The lifetime prevalence rates for any anxiety disorder range from 30% to 85%, notably higher than the general population (Pokos & Castle, 2006). In over half of patients, the onset of anxiety disorders precedes the manifestation of psychosis. Studies report a wide variability in the prevalence of panic attacks (7.1%–63%) and panic disorder (3.3%–29.5%) among individuals with schizophrenia, with an estimated average prevalence of 25% for panic attacks and 15% for panic disorder. Comparatively, the lifetime prevalence of panic disorder in the general US population ranges from 2.0% to 5.1%. Regarding PTSD, research indicates a prevalence ranging from 0% to 67% among individuals with schizophrenia, suggesting an approximate 29% prevalence of PTSD in this population compared to a 7.8% estimated lifetime prevalence in the general population. Obsessive-compulsive symptoms (OCS) and OCD are frequently observed in schizophrenia, with studies suggesting a higher prevalence of both conditions in this population. Estimates indicate a rough average of 25% prevalence for OCS and 23% prevalence for OCD among individuals with schizophrenia.

The correlation between psychotic and affective symptoms remains central to psychiatric classification debates. Evidence suggests that schizophrenia and bipolar disorder might exist along a dimensional spectrum, leading to ongoing discussions about the nosological status of "schizoaffective" disorder (Buckley et al., 2009).

5.2 Risk and Protective Factors

Many risk and protective factors of psychosis have been identified. Major life events, characterized by substantial positive or negative changes coupled with a sense of threat, often coincide with the onset or recurrence of psychosis. A meta-analysis revealed a significant association between major life events and both psychotic disorder and subclinical psychotic experiences (Beards et al., 2013).

Moreover, various social risk factors significantly contribute to the development of psychotic symptoms. These encompass childhood trauma, experiences of bullying during childhood or adulthood, feelings of social exclusion, instances of social undermining, low socioeconomic status, limited social support and network, minority status, and perceived discrimination (Hennig et al., 2017; Hermanto et al., 2020; Jaya, 2017; Jaya et al., 2022; Jaya & Lincoln, 2016; Lincoln et al., 2017; Octavia et al., 2019). Additionally, high levels of negative schemas, both of oneself and others, have demonstrated a correlation with the manifestation of psychotic symptoms (Beck et al., 2017; Gollwitzer et al., 2018; Jaya et al., 2018; Jorovat et al., 2025).

Conversely, certain protective factors have been identified. These include good emotional regulation skills, having a partner, substantial social and emotional support, active participation in community activities, and a stable economic and financial status (Crush et al., 2018; Kuranova et al., 2020; Lim et al., 2014; Lincoln et al., 2017). Furthermore, possessing positive schema, both of oneself and others, appears to act as a protective factor against the emergence of psychotic symptoms (Beck et al., 2017).

References

Beards, S., Gayer-Anderson, C., Borges, S., Dewey, M. E., Fisher, H. L., & Morgan, C. (2013). Life events and psychosis: A review and meta-analysis. *Schizophrenia Bulletin, 39*(4), 740–747. https://doi.org/10.1093/schbul/sbt065

Beck, A. T., Himelstein, R., & Grant, P. M. (2017). In and out of schizophrenia: Activation and deactivation of the negative and positive schemas. *Schizophrenia Research, 203*, 55. https://doi.org/10.1016/j.schres.2017.10.046

Buckley, P. F., Miller, B. J., Lehrer, D. S., & Castle, D. J. (2009). Psychiatric comorbidities and schizophrenia. *Schizophrenia Bulletin, 35*(2), 383–402. https://doi.org/10.1093/schbul/sbn135

Crush, E., Arseneault, L., Moffitt, T. E., Danese, A., Caspi, A., Jaffee, S. R., Matthews, T., & Fisher, H. L. (2018). Protective factors for psychotic experiences amongst adolescents exposed to multiple forms of victimization. *Journal of Psychiatric Research, 104*, 32–38. https://doi.org/10.1016/j.jpsychires.2018.06.011

Gollwitzer, A., Wilczynska, M., & Jaya, E. S. (2018). Targeting the link between loneliness and paranoia via an interventionist-causal model framework. *Psychiatry Research, 263*, 101–107. https://doi.org/10.1016/j.psychres.2018.02.050

Hennig, T., Jaya, E. S., & Lincoln, T. M. (2017). Bullying mediates between attention-deficit/hyperactivity disorder in childhood and psychotic experiences in early adolescence. *Schizophrenia Bulletin, 43*(5), 1036–1104. https://doi.org/10.1093/schbul/sbw139

Hermanto, E., Asih, S. R., & Jaya, E. S. (2020). The role of perceived discrimination in mediating the relationship between minority status and psychotic symptoms in a community sample. *Konselor, 8*(4), 104. https://doi.org/10.24036/0201983105924-0-00

Jaya, E. S. (2017). Confirmatory factor analysis of the Indonesian version of community assessment of psychic experiences. *Makara Human Behavior Studies in Asia, 9*(1), 1–12. https://doi.org/10.7454/mssh.v21i1.3495

Jaya, E. S., & Lincoln, T. M. (2016). Social adversities and psychotic symptoms: A test of predictions derived from the social defeat hypothesis. *Psychiatry Research, 245*, 466–472. https://doi.org/10.1016/j.psychres.2016.09.002

Jaya, E. S., Ascone, L., & Lincoln, T. M. (2018). A longitudinal mediation analysis of the effect of negative-self-schemas on positive symptoms via negative affect. *Psychological Medicine, 48*(8), 1299–1307. https://doi.org/10.1017/S003329171700277X

Jaya, E. S., Pillny, M., Lincoln, T. M., & Riehle, M. (2022). Does social defeat cause negative symptoms? A prospective study in a multi-national community sample. *Comprehensive Psychiatry, 113*, 152289. https://doi.org/10.1016/j.comppsych.2021.152289

Jorovat, A., Twumasi, R., Mechelli, A., & Georgiades, A. (2025). Core beliefs in psychosis: A systematic review and meta-analysis. *Schizophrenia, 11*(1), 38. https://doi.org/10.1038/s41537-025-00577-2

Kuranova, A., Booij, S. H., de Jonge, P., Jeronimus, B., Lin, A., Wardenaar, K. J., Wichers, M., & Wigman, J. T. W. (2020). Don't worry, be happy: Protective factors to buffer against distress associated with psychotic experiences. *Schizophrenia Research, 223*, 79. https://doi.org/10.1016/j.schres.2020.05.019

Lim, M. H., Gleeson, J. F., Jackson, H. J., & Fernandez, K. C. (2014). Social relationships and quality of life moderate distress associated with delusional ideation. *Social Psychiatry and Psychiatric Epidemiology, 49*(1), 97–107. https://doi.org/10.1007/s00127-013-0738-3

Lincoln, T. M., Marin, N., & Jaya, E. S. (2017). Childhood trauma and psychotic experiences in a general population sample: A prospective study on the mediating role of emotion regulation. *European Psychiatry, 42*, 111–119. https://doi.org/10.1016/j.eurpsy.2016.12.010

Octavia, S., Jaya, E. S., & Asih, S. R. (2019). Does negative-self-schema link the relationship between childhood trauma and psychotic symptoms in a community sample of Indonesians? *Konselor, 8*(3), 85. https://doi.org/10.24036/0201983105885-0-00

Pokos, V., & Castle, D. J. (2006). Prevalence of comorbid anxiety disorders in schizophrenia spectrum disorders: A literature review. *Current Psychiatry Reviews, 2*(3), 285–307. https://doi.org/10.2174/157340006778018193

Chapter 6
Planning and Applying Symptom-Based Approach for Psychosis in Psychotic Disorders

Abstract This chapter provides the overarching framework for implementing a symptom-based CBT strategy in psychotic disorders. It begins with comprehensive assessment, then introduces three pillars for treatment planning: functional levels, psychotherapy requirements, and the combinability of therapeutic modules. The chapter outlines psychotherapy milestones, emphasizing stabilization of acute symptoms before higher-order cognitive work. It conceptualizes CBT for psychosis as a syndromic intervention, selecting modules such as insomnia treatment, anxiety management, or schema work based on the individual's presenting problems. The chapter stresses that heterogeneity in psychosis necessitates flexible sequencing and prioritization, ensuring that each patient receives only the interventions that match their symptom profile and functional stage.

Keywords Treatment formulation · Functional outcomes · Multimodal intervention · CBTp planning · Psychotherapy readiness

6.1 Comprehensive Assessment

A comprehensive assessment is key to formulating an effective treatment plan and is one of the most important factors in ensuring effective and efficient treatment. However, a comprehensive assessment may not always be possible in a low-resource context, in which many people with schizophrenia unfortunately are found. Here are some principles that can be used if one must choose assessments.

The first priority is to quantify the patient's psychotic symptoms. This is important for two reasons: 1) to track the patient's improvement, and 2) to determine whether the treatment plan is effective. Self-report measures are preferred for documenting the patient's initial condition and subsequent progress, as they minimize clinician subjectivity and mitigate the risk of perceived scoring bias—a relevant concern when working with populations prone to suspiciousness or paranoia. For a general assessment of psychotic symptoms, the Community Assessment of Psychic Experiences (CAPE) may be suitable, while the Paranoia Checklist (PCL) might be

E. S. Jaya, *Cognitive Behavioral Therapy for Psychosis as a Syndrome*,
https://doi.org/10.1007/978-981-95-9203-6_6

more appropriate if the primary symptom is paranoid delusion. Structured interviews like the Positive and Negative Syndrome Scale (PANSS) or the Psychotic Symptoms Rating Scale (PSYRATS) can also be instrumental. In low-resource settings, therapists may opt to focus on one or two key symptoms, selecting one or two specific questions from these scales.

The second priority is the comorbidity assessment. This can be conducted comprehensively using structured interviews, such as using the Structured Clinical Interview for Diagnosis (SCID), or through general screening questionnaires like the Patient Health Questionnaire (PHQ), which measures six of the most common mental disorders. Alternatively, targeted interviews or questionnaires can be used to focus on disorders that the clinician suspects are present and most relevant to the patient's functioning.

The third priority is the functioning assessment. The goal is to assess the patient's current level of functioning, identify target areas for improvement, and plan how to achieve these goals within the available number of sessions or time frame. The WHO Disability Assessment Schedule 2.0 (WHO DAS) can be used, either the 12-item version, which takes about 5 min, or the 36-item version, which takes around 20 min. It can be administered via self-report or interview. Ideally, the WHO DAS should be administered before treatment, during, and after treatment to assess progress and psychotherapy milestones. As an alternative, a brief anamnesis and observation based on WHO DAS domains—such as understanding and communicating, mobility, self-care, getting along with people, life activities, and participation in society—can be used to gage functioning.

At a minimum, in a low-resource setting, the clinician should aspire to at least take one general self-report measure of psychotic symptoms such as the CAPE, one quick measure of general comorbidity such as the PHQ, and one short measure of functioning such as the WHO DAS 12-item version. These three self-report questionnaires combined should take less than 30 min to administer.

6.2 Treatment Mechanism: Levels of Functioning, Psychotherapy Requirement, and Combinability of Treatment

The choice of CBT techniques or group of techniques to be delivered, as well as the order in which they are delivered, can be determined based on functioning, the putative psychopathology network, and the combinability of treatments.

6.2.1 *The Intersection with Levels of Functioning*

For assessing functioning, we can use the WHO Disability Assessment Schedule (WHO DAS), a standardized and widely used tool developed by the World Health Organization (WHO) to measure health and disability across different cultures and populations. It is designed to evaluate an individual's functioning across various domains of life.

The WHO DAS assesses disability and functioning in six main domains:

1. **Cognition**: This domain evaluates understanding and communication, such as concentration, memory, and learning.
2. **Mobility**: It assesses an individual's ability to move and get around, including standing, walking, and using transportation.
3. **Self-care**: This domain examines an individual's ability to manage personal hygiene, dressing, eating, and staying alone.
4. **Getting along**: It focuses on an individual's interactions with others, including friends, family, and the community, measuring their ability to maintain relationships.
5. **Life activities**: This area evaluates participation in work, school, and other everyday activities, assessing productivity and involvement.
6. **Participation**: This domain assesses involvement in community, social, and civic life, including engagement in leisure activities and responsibilities.

The WHO DAS uses a structured questionnaire with multiple items in each domain to evaluate an individual's level of difficulty in performing various activities. Responses are typically rated on a scale that indicates the severity or extent of difficulties experienced, ranging from 'none' to 'extreme/cannot do'.

The WHO DAS has been adapted into various languages and cultural contexts to ensure its applicability and reliability across diverse populations, making it a valuable tool for assessing disability and functioning worldwide.

The scoring system of WHO DAS provides a numerical representation of an individual's functioning in each domain. It uses Likert-type scales where respondents indicate the level of difficulty they experience in performing specific activities. Scoring can vary based on the version or specific adaptation being used. In general, the scoring ranges from 0 to 100, with higher scores indicating higher levels of disability or difficulty. The scoring may be further interpreted as follows:

- 0 to 4: No or none to mild difficulties
- 5 to 24: Moderate difficulties
- 25 to 49: Severe difficulties
- 50 to 100: Extreme difficulties or inability to perform activities

Here are case vignettes illustrating different levels of functioning based on the WHO Disability Assessment Schedule (WHO DAS) scoring, focusing on individuals diagnosed with schizophrenia:

1. **No or Mild Difficulties (0–4):**

   Emily, a 32-year-old diagnosed with schizophrenia, has been managing her condition effectively with medication and therapy. She experiences occasional mild hallucinations but can distinguish them from reality. Emily works part-time in an administrative role, manages her household tasks independently, and maintains social connections. She rates her functioning as 3 on the WHO DAS scale due to occasional mild difficulties in concentration and minimal impact on her daily life.

2. **Moderate Difficulties (5–24):**

   Alex, a 40-year-old with schizophrenia, experiences moderate symptoms, including auditory hallucinations and occasional disorganized thinking. He works part-time but struggles to maintain focus and concentration, leading to reduced productivity. Alex requires some assistance in managing his finances and occasionally forgets to take his medication. His functioning is rated as 15 on the WHO DAS scale due to moderate difficulties in work performance and self-care.

3. **Severe Difficulties (25–49):**

   Rachel, a 28-year-old diagnosed with schizophrenia, experiences severe symptoms, including persistent delusions and disorganized thoughts. She requires constant supervision and support from family members to perform daily activities. Rachel is unable to work due to the severity of her symptoms and needs assistance in managing personal hygiene and medication adherence. Her functioning is rated as 35 on the WHO DAS scale due to severe impairment in self-care and social functioning.

4. **Extreme Difficulties or Inability to Perform Activities (50–100):**

   James, a 50-year-old with schizophrenia, experiences extreme symptoms, including severe auditory and visual hallucinations, paranoid delusions, and complete withdrawal from reality. He is unable to maintain personal hygiene, communicate effectively, or perform any meaningful activities. James requires full-time care in a specialized facility due to the severity of his symptoms, and his functioning is rated as 70 on the WHO DAS scale due to the extreme impairment in all aspects of daily life.

These vignettes illustrate hypothetical scenarios depicting varying levels of functioning among individuals diagnosed with schizophrenia, based on the WHO DAS scoring system.

Once we assess the patient's functioning level, we then identify the specific psychopathologies or comorbidities that impede the desired functional milestones. For instance, upon evaluating grooming habits, we might find that depressive symptoms, such as amotivation and reduced energy, hinder basic self-care. In response, we apply a range of Cognitive Behavioral Therapy (CBT) techniques for depression until grooming becomes less challenging. Similarly, individuals experiencing psychosis may encounter obstacles in social interactions. This could stem from social withdrawal due to psychosis symptoms, lack of energy caused by depression, or disrupted sleep patterns from insomnia. In such cases, we pivot our approach, transitioning from addressing depressive symptoms with CBT techniques to tackling insomnia using CBT for insomnia methods. The goal is to enhance the patient's sleep quality, potentially elevating their energy levels and thereby facilitating improved social engagement.

Moreover, the psychotherapist can ingeniously combine similar techniques, often rooted in related psychopathologies, either to enhance effectiveness or due to the interplay between these psychopathologies. Consider this example of technique amalgamation for improved efficiency: when treating a patient with schizophrenia alongside comorbid panic and depressive disorders, the therapy plan prioritizes addressing panic disorder before tackling other comorbidities. The therapist might focus on addressing the panic-inducing symptom of heart palpitations through interoceptive exposure, such as jointly ascending stairs during sessions. Concurrently, they introduce behavioral activation by encouraging the patient to consistently opt for stairs instead of using the elevator. Following 2 weeks of this practice, a reduction in both panic and depressive symptoms may be observed.

Another scenario necessitating the fusion of multiple CBT techniques arises when psychopathologies interact. For instance, consider a patient with schizophrenia, comorbid social anxiety disorder and depression. The therapeutic strategy outlines addressing depression first, followed by targeting social anxiety and other comorbidities. Initially employing behavioral activation to address fundamental activities like grooming, meals, and sleep, the therapist successfully encourages the patient to occasionally leave their room. However, efforts to engage the patient in social interactions remain unsuccessful despite the alleviation of depressive symptoms. At this juncture, the therapist shifts focus to employing CBT techniques tailored for social anxiety. This may involve behavioral experiments designed to gradually reintroduce social interactions into the patient's life. After improvement of social anxiety symptoms, the psychotherapist may shift back to behavioral activation or CBT for depression to improve the patient's depressive symptoms until recovery or remission and then perhaps return to targeting the social anxiety symptoms if needed. The decision to merge techniques should be guided by the therapist's judgment based on the specific needs and progress of the patient.

6.2.2 *The Requirement for Psychotherapy*

The requirement for psychotherapy is rarely discussed in contemporary CBT treatment manuals. However, because psychosis encompasses a wide range of patient presentations, it may be relevant to outline the requirement for this psychotherapy. The requirements are as follows: 1) The patient can communicate and follow instructions, 2) The patient can reach an agreement concerning the milestones and stages, and 3) The patient has the necessary resources to complete the agreed-upon psychotherapy sessions.

6.2.3 *The End Goal: Psychotherapy Milestones and Stages*

In this psychotherapy there are specific milestones and stages. The psychotherapy milestones are patient-centered end goals of the treatment, while the psychotherapy stages are the stages that psychotherapists and patients need to go through to reach the desired milestones.

There are four psychotherapy milestones in this treatment: 1) Basic functioning (e.g., can eat independently, drink independently, shower, brush teeth; overall quite competent to live independently when provided with the necessary resources), 2) Non-psychotic symptoms alleviation, 3) Basic living (e.g., having one friend, having independent income, living independently, and avoiding perpetual poor decisions such as drug abuse or fighting with people, which add stress and inhibit potential), and 4) Ordinary happiness (e.g., having good self-esteem, positive self and other-schemas, low negative self and other-schemas, meaningful relationships, meaningful life goals). Psychotherapists are instructed to discuss these milestones in relation to the patient's current resources so that they can work together to achieve the desired and agreed-upon milestones.

There are seven stages in this psychotherapy. These stages include: 1) thoroughly examining psychotic disorders, 2) psychoeducating the patient and their family about psychotic symptoms, 3) examining comorbidities and identifying risk and protective factors, 4) treating and managing comorbidities, 5) reducing risk factors and improving protective factors, 6) re-examining psychotic disorders, comorbidities, and both internal and external environments, and 7) preventing relapse and nurturing protective factors. All patients should be informed about the seven stages, and an agreement should be reached between the psychotherapist and patients regarding the depth of each stage.

6.2.4 CBT for Psychosis as a Syndrome: Mechanisms and Principles

The main principle of therapy mechanisms involves psychoeducation about the patient's mental condition so that they understand what occurs in their mind and brain. Addressing comorbidities aims to disrupt the vicious cycle, promoting natural recovery through homeostasis. Creating a safe internal and external environment is crucial, including avoiding obvious triggers such as poverty. There are steps outlined in a flowchart based on symptom mapping and weighting for intervention delivery (see Fig. 6.1).

The first set of principles to keep in mind when delivering CBT for psychosis as a syndrome is the priority principles of care. Here are the priority principles in care: 1) physical before psychological, 2) address potential life-threatening issues first (such as addressing depression with suicidality first until suicidality diminishes instead of panic attack complaints), 3) combinability principle (e.g., behavioral activation for depression can be combined with sleep hygiene for insomnia), 4) brevity principle (e.g., behavioral activation is faster than cognitive restructuring, so try behavioral activation first before altering thinking patterns), 5) psychopathological dynamics principle (e.g., if depression persists due to a patient having social anxiety disorder, treat depression until no suicidality with behavioral activation, then shift to social anxiety treatment with CBT Clark and Wells until socialization is possible,

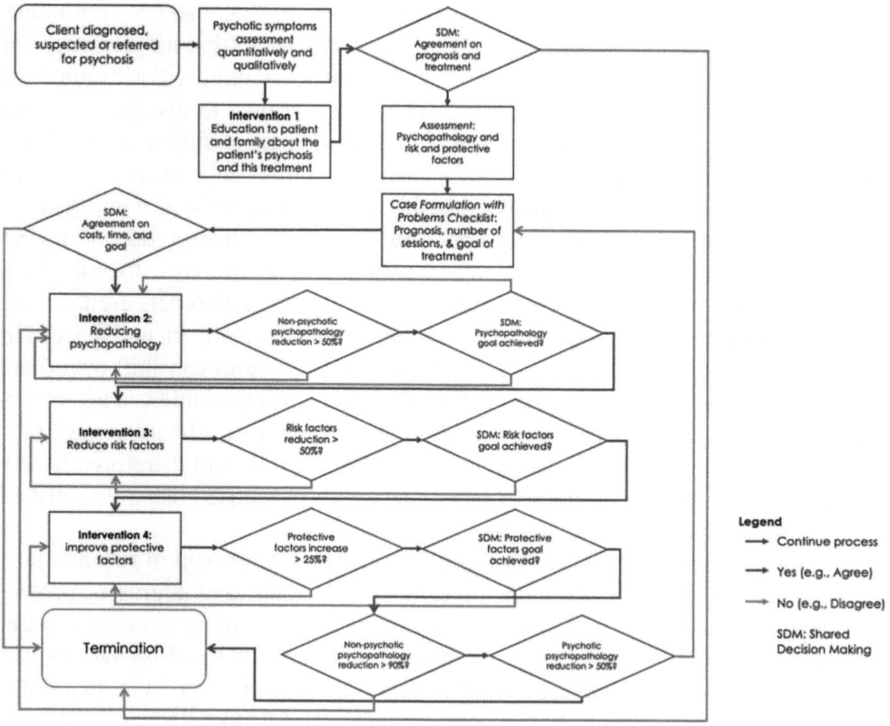

Fig. 6.1 Treatment algorithm flowchart

before returning to behavioral activation), 6) Reformulation and assessment upon completion of a treatment target (for instance, behavioral activation is delivered for depressive symptoms until no suicidal behavior as a treatment target and once suicidal behavior disappears, the patient is given a PHQ-9 questionnaire to reassess depressive symptoms).

One of the main driving mechanisms for this CBTp is psychoeducation. At this stage of psychotherapy, the goal is to help patients understand their condition so they can regain a sense of control over their symptoms. The process can be compared to managing chronic medical conditions such as diabetes or hypertension: patients who understand their illness can live stable, fulfilling lives because they learn to manage it—rather than be controlled by it. Just as the manifestations of diabetes or hypertension differ from one person to another, psychotic symptoms also vary widely between individuals. For instance, one person with diabetes may find that daily morning walks keep their blood sugar stable, while another may discover that eliminating sugar from their diet works best. Likewise, each person with psychosis must learn to distinguish which of their symptom patterns and triggers are identifiable and consistent, and which occur unpredictably or without clear cause. A key task of the psychotherapist is to help patients observe, recognize, and remember these distinctions as part of building self-awareness and mastery over their condition.

The second driving mechanism of this CBTp is the management of comorbidities. The main principle at this stage of therapy is to ensure that no permanent or semi-permanent factors continue to sustain psychotic symptoms. For example, if psychosis is driven by daily methamphetamine use—known to disrupt dopamine regulation—the most direct intervention is to help the patient stop using methamphetamine. A less straightforward case involves comorbid depression, which has been shown in multiple studies to influence the severity and persistence of psychotic symptoms. Moreover, psychotic features observed during therapy do not always indicate schizophrenia; they may instead suggest schizoaffective disorder or a depressive episode with psychotic features. Because mental disorders are theoretical and pragmatic constructs—*utilitarian* rather than *realistic* in the sense that infectious diseases like COVID-19 are—diagnostic boundaries can shift over time. Following the same logic as in the methamphetamine example, addressing comorbid depression often reduces psychotic symptoms indirectly, as the depressive process itself may be a hidden maintaining factor. Clinicians should therefore identify and treat common comorbidities in individuals with psychosis, using established clinical guidelines to ensure comprehensive management.

The third driving mechanism for this CBTp is the management of risk and protective factors. The primary principle in reducing risk factors and improving protective factors at stage five is similar to the principle of managing comorbidities at stage four: ensuring that no factors sustain psychotic symptoms. Risk factors like bullying, loneliness, low self-esteem, and unhealthy social circles require psychologist attention and individualized management. Protective factors such as good emotional regulation, effective anger management, supportive family or friendships, occupation or meaningful activities, and a healthy lifestyle need to be nurtured and maintained.

Furthermore, when delivering this CBTp, psychotherapists are faced with possibly nearly one hundred techniques to choose from. The guiding principles for choosing techniques include: 1) ease of implementation, 2) has not been tried previously, and 3) combinable with other techniques that will be provided. Another important principle is sidestepping psychotic symptoms. It is important that the technique being delivered does not directly provoke or exacerbate these symptoms.

In summary, the psychotherapy should be conducted in the following steps: 1) Comprehensive assessment of symptoms, risk, and/or protective factors, 2) Compilation of a list of symptoms, risk, and/or protective factors, and 3) Formulation of a treatment plan using the priority principles of care and shared decision-making with the patient.

Chapter 7
Planning and Applying Symptom-Based Approach for Psychosis in Personality Disorders

Abstract This chapter addresses the unique clinical challenges of psychosis occurring within personality disorders, highlighting how maladaptive interpersonal patterns, emotional dysregulation, and chronic schema disturbances influence psychotic symptoms. It emphasizes the need to differentiate trait-based vulnerabilities from state-related psychotic features to avoid misattribution and mistreatment. Treatment planning must account for issues such as mistrust, affective instability, impulsivity, and relational conflict, which may complicate alliance-building and technique delivery. The chapter provides a framework for adapting CBT modules—prioritizing stabilization, emotional regulation, and schema-focused strategies—before applying standard CBT techniques for psychosis. This ensures therapeutic safety and improves engagement in complex personality-psychosis presentations.

Keywords Personality pathology · Psychotic features · Symptom formulation · Differential diagnosis · Integrated psychotherapy

Personality disorder diagnoses have evolved across different classification systems over time, notably within the International Classification of Diseases (ICD) and Diagnostic and Statistical Manual of Mental Disorders (DSM). The ICD-10 delineates ten distinct personality disorders, encompassing paranoid, schizoid, schizotypal, dissocial, emotionally unstable (borderline type and impulsive type), histrionic, narcissistic, anankastic, anxious (avoidant), dependent, and additional categories that are diagnosable in its own. In contrast, the ICD-11 classifies personality disorder as a single diagnosis on a spectrum of mild, moderate, or severe, and then there are six specific traits that can be added as diagnosis modifiers: negative affectivity, detachment, dissociality, disinhibition, anankastia, and borderline pattern. Meanwhile, the DSM has transitioned in its approach from DSM-II, III, and IV, where personality disorders were placed on a separate axis, to DSM-5, which allows personality disorder to be diagnosed as a primary condition. DSM-III to DSM-5 retains the same types of personality disorders: paranoid, schizoid, and schizotypal for Cluster A; antisocial, borderline, histrionic, and narcissistic for Cluster B; and avoidant, dependent, and obsessive-compulsive for Cluster C.

E. S. Jaya, *Cognitive Behavioral Therapy for Psychosis as a Syndrome*,
https://doi.org/10.1007/978-981-95-9203-6_7

The application of CBT for psychosis symptom-based approach is contingent upon the specific diagnoses and available treatments. At present, borderline personality disorder is the only personality disorder diagnosis that has garnered substantial attention in treatment literature. Longitudinal studies, like those conducted by Gunderson et al. (2011), have shown satisfactory remission rates, and numerous randomized controlled trials have demonstrated the efficacy of psychotherapies such as Dialectical Behavioral Therapy (Linehan et al., 2006; McMain et al., 2022) and Mentalization Based Therapy (Carlyle et al., 2020) in alleviating its symptoms. Consequently, for individuals presenting both borderline personality disorder and significant psychosis, a CBT for psychosis symptom-based approach may be suitable. However, it is advisable for the patient, if feasible, to prioritize seeking treatment specifically for their borderline personality disorder, viewing the CBT for psychosis symptom-based approach as a complementary treatment. In instances where evidence-based treatments for other personality disorders are lacking, employing a CBT approach targeting psychosis symptoms might serve as a suitable intervention for psychotic manifestations.

References

Carlyle, D., Green, R., Inder, M., Porter, R., Crowe, M., Mulder, R., & Frampton, C. (2020). A randomized-controlled trial of mentalization-based treatment compared with structured case management for borderline personality disorder in a mainstream public health service. *Frontiers in Psychiatry, 11*, 561916. https://doi.org/10.3389/fpsyt.2020.561916

Gunderson, J. G., Stout, R. L., McGlashan, T. H., Shea, M. T., Morey, L. C., Grilo, C. M., Zanarini, M. C., Yen, S., Markowitz, J. C., Sanislow, C., Ansell, E., Pinto, A., & Skodol, A. E. (2011). Ten-year course of borderline personality disorder: Psychopathology and function from the collaborative longitudinal personality disorders study. *Archives of General Psychiatry, 68*(8), 827–837. https://doi.org/10.1001/archgenpsychiatry.2011.37

Linehan, M. M., Comtois, K. A., Murray, A. M., Brown, M. Z., Gallop, R. J., Heard, H. L., Korslund, K. E., Tutek, D. A., Reynolds, S. K., & Lindenboim, N. (2006). Two-year randomized controlled trial and follow-up of dialectical behavior therapy vs therapy by experts for suicidal behaviors and borderline personality disorder. *Archives of General Psychiatry, 63*(7), 757–766. https://doi.org/10.1001/archpsyc.63.7.757

McMain, S. F., Chapman, A. L., Kuo, J. R., Dixon-Gordon, K. L., Guimond, T. H., Labrish, C., Isaranuwatchai, W., & Streiner, D. L. (2022). The effectiveness of 6 versus 12 months of dialectical behavior therapy for borderline personality disorder: A noninferiority randomized clinical trial. *Psychotherapy and Psychosomatics, 91*(6), 382–397. https://doi.org/10.1159/000525102

Chapter 8
Planning and Applying Symptom-Based Approach for Psychosis in Mood Disorders

Abstract This chapter explains how psychosis manifests within mood disorders and outlines principles for integrating symptom-based CBT within these presentations. It distinguishes psychotic symptoms emerging from depressive, manic, or mixed states, emphasizing their fluctuating intensity and state dependence. Treatment planning requires coordination with pharmacotherapy, careful monitoring of mood episodes, and prioritization of foundational interventions such as sleep normalization, anxiety reduction, and behavioral activation. CBT techniques targeting hallucinations or delusions are applied only after mood stabilization, ensuring that interventions align with the patient's functional stage and emotional capacity. The chapter highlights the importance of dynamic treatment steering, adjusting module selection as mood states shift.

Keywords Affective psychosis · Mood-congruent symptoms · Bipolar psychosis · Psychotic depression · Transdiagnostic treatment

In managing mood disorders with psychotic features, the recommended approach for psychotherapists is to prioritize addressing mood symptoms. Subsequently, attention can be directed toward managing anxiety symptoms, sleep disturbances, and then focusing on assessing and managing risk and protective factors. Due to the generally more optimistic prognosis associated with mood disorders with psychotic features in contrast to schizophrenia, the therapeutic goals should differ regarding targeted functioning, number of sessions required, and psychotherapy milestones compared to patients diagnosed with schizophrenia. Patients with mood disorders with psychotic features can be targeted to attain a functioning level with either no or mild difficulties, undergo approximately half the recommended number of sessions, and should strive to achieve all psychotherapy milestones.

In instances where a mood disorder patient's significant psychotic features warrant this treatment, therapists may use this treatment manual. However, it is

E. S. Jaya, *Cognitive Behavioral Therapy for Psychosis as a Syndrome*,
https://doi.org/10.1007/978-981-95-9203-6_8

essential not to overlook the crucial phase of psychoeducation about psychosis. Therapists using this treatment manual should note that the psychoeducation stage pertaining to psychotic symptoms, as outlined in the subsequent chapter, remains a pivotal and mandatory component of this therapeutic approach.

Part III
Treatment Modules: Orientation of CBT for Psychosis

Chapter 9
Psychoeducation

Abstract This chapter outlines the foundational role of psychoeducation in CBT for psychosis as a syndrome approach of this book. Psychoeducation is emphasized as the first-stage intervention before any symptom-specific module is implemented. This chapter covers psychoeducation for hallucinations, delusions, and disorganized symptoms and provides explanations, instructions, and vignettes that can be useful to psychotherapists in helping patients understand these experiences without judgment or mystification. The chapter also reviews psychoeducation regarding the etiology of psychotic symptoms, integrating biological, psychological, and environmental explanations to reduce stigma and enhance treatment engagement. Finally, it presents a systematic approach for communicating the overall CBT-for-psychosis treatment plan, helping patients understand how comorbidities, risk factors, and protective factors will be managed within a structured, symptom-based framework.

Keywords Illness insight · Symptom awareness · Treatment adherence · Patient engagement · CBTp orientation

9.1 Psychoeducation of Psychotic Symptoms

In essence, the primary objectives of psychoeducating patients about psychotic symptoms are centered on fostering their comprehension and sense of empowerment over their lives, rather than allowing these symptoms to dictate their existence. Toward this goal, key psychoeducation techniques can be broadly classified into three categories: 1) normalizing the patient's experience of psychosis, 2) elucidating the continuum of psychosis relevant to the patient's symptoms, and 3) outlining the ramifications of these symptoms—how they can cause annoyance, hinder concentration, and impede the patient's functional capabilities. The implementation of these techniques revolves around two primary methods: 1) educational sessions coupled with counseling, and 2) role-playing exercises. During role-playing, therapists take on the role of the patient, immersing themselves in a certain environment that mirrors the patient's experiences and symptoms (e.g., experiencing auditory

E. S. Jaya, *Cognitive Behavioral Therapy for Psychosis as a Syndrome*,
https://doi.org/10.1007/978-981-95-9203-6_9

hallucinations while doing household chores with dad). This serves a dual purpose: firstly, to confirm the psychotherapist's grasp of the patient's symptoms and, secondly, to illustrate to the patient that their experiences are being comprehended and acknowledged.

The following are further tips and examples for delivering psychoeducation on specific symptoms of psychosis.

9.1.1 Psychoeducation About Hallucinations

Patients require a comprehensive understanding of the scientific definition of hallucinations and their contextual relevance within their specific disorder. The primary goal is to empower patients with a heightened sense of control over their symptomatic experiences. Hallucinations, emerging from diverse scenarios, encompass substance use, sensory deafferentation (an absence of sensory experiences compelling the brain to generate sensory perceptions against the natural degenerative processes), environmental circumstances such as mistaking wartime sounds during peacetime or sensing a vibrating phone in one's pocket when none exists, physiological contexts such as upon awakening, spontaneous occurrences such as sudden auditory sensations in public places, or manifestations attributed to psychological conditions such as depression or psychotic disorders. Fundamentally, hallucinations denote irregularities in perception, where perceptions arise without corresponding stimuli.

An illustrative neutral example involves the concept of phantom limb, particularly phantom limb pain, wherein an individual who has undergone amputation perceives sensations in the absent limb. This information serves to validate the patient's understanding that hallucinations do not signify insanity or unreality but are mere phenomena associated with brain function. The analogy of phantom limb can effectively elucidate the patient's experience of hallucinations. For instance, one could inquire of a non-amputee patient: "Have you ever encountered an experience akin to phantom limb, such as hearing sounds, experiencing visual perceptions, or sensing unusual sensations?" Educating patients on managing hallucinations necessitates adopting a rational, non-interpretative, and emotionally detached approach. To instill this mindset, employing the analogy of phantom limb proves useful. For example: "If you were to experience phantom limb sensations, such as an itch in a nonexistent limb, how would you respond? Consider repetitively contemplating and analyzing the cause of the itch. Imagine attempting to scratch the absent limb (gesture as if demonstrating this action to accentuate its peculiarity). How might observers perceive us if they witnessed such an action? Apply this same methodology uniformly to other hallucinatory experiences. Now, discern what distinguishes hallucination from reality? This intricate distinction remains a focal point throughout psychotherapy." By employing educational strategies using such analogies, patients grasp that their encountered hallucinations, despite differing in form and intensity, are shared by others. This approach cultivates a heightened sense of control and self-assurance by showcasing instances where patients adeptly handled diverse hallucinatory encounters, such as correctly discerning perceived calls without over-interpreting, thereby leading to their eventual cessation.

9.1.2 Psychoeducation About Delusion

Patients need comprehensive education regarding the various scientifically defined types of delusions and an understanding of the continuum of psychosis within delusions. This continuum encompasses normal, subclinical, and clinical delusions. It is essential for patients to visualize how others might experience delusions and consider what actions they might take to assist these individuals (this serves as a technique for self-assessment). To impart knowledge on delusions, adopt an approach similar to a game or quiz, akin to learning the Latin names of human muscles for anatomy studies. Different types of delusions should be presented in their normal, subclinical/non-bizarre, and clinical/bizarre forms. It is vital to cover specific delusion types that the patient is likely to experience, such as paranoid/persecutory delusions, grandiose delusions, erotomanic delusions, delusions of being controlled, delusional jealousy, delusions of guilt or sin, delusions of mind being read, delusions of thought insertion, delusions of reference, religious delusions, somatic delusions, and delusions of poverty. If the psychotherapist or patient wants to save time in this process, the psychotherapist can simply provide a one-sentence example of each delusion and confirm to the patient whether he or she has never experienced it.

1. When educating on paranoid/persecutory delusions, explain normal types, such as the reluctance to walk alone in front of the house at night due to feeling unsafe, despite no concrete evidence of danger (e.g., no recent criminal incidents in the area). Discuss subclinical/non-bizarre types, such as avoiding the use of WhatsApp out of concern that personal data might be owned by Facebook/Meta and then passed on to the United States government, complicating daily life. Also, cover clinical/bizarre types, such as believing there is an invisible surveillance device in the practice room that remains continuously active without a clear power source, transmitting information actively monitored by the military, directly relayed to the President, and purposefully disrupting his life by consuming his favorite meatball order from the nearest vendor.
2. When educating on grandiose delusions, illustrate normal types, such as being confidently certain of graduating from a bachelor's program despite attending university for the first time. Describe subclinical/non-bizarre types, like being confident of securing a promotion and eventually becoming a director within a company, despite ten available director positions. Also, discuss clinical/bizarre types, such as believing oneself to be an incarnation of a deity responsible for ending human suffering.

3. For educating on erotomanic delusions, cover normal types, such as feeling that a friend has a secret crush without any clear or concrete evidence, like a written declaration of affection. Explain subclinical/non-bizarre types, such as firmly believing that a friend has a crush, leading to behaviors like online or offline stalking and altered behavior toward that individual. Also, discuss clinical/bizarre types, such as firmly believing that a celebrity (whom the individual does not know personally) harbors affection for them, conveyed through hidden codes in mass media (delusions of reference).
4. When educating on delusions of being controlled (the belief that another entity controls one's thoughts or behavior), explain normal types, such as feeling compelled to behave rudely toward someone because of their irritating behavior. Discuss subclinical/non-bizarre types, like feeling unable to leave an abusive partner because they have total control over one's thoughts and life situations. Also, define clinical/bizarre types, such as believing that a school teacher who despises them is controlling their thoughts to hinder them from studying.
5. In educating on delusional jealousy, portray normal types, such as feeling jealous when seeing a partner interact with someone of the opposite sex for work purposes. Describe subclinical/non-bizarre types, such as experiencing jealousy every time the partner interacts with someone of the opposite sex. Also, discuss clinical/bizarre types, such as feeling jealous when the partner uses a mobile phone, suspecting potential infidelity with an American celebrity, whom they objectively cannot possibly know.
6. For delusions of guilt or sin, delineate normal types, such as feeling guilty for not tipping, even though there is no norm mandating it. Describe subclinical/non-bizarre types, such as feeling guilty toward a colleague who has to work extra due to their maternity leave, despite it being their right to take leave. Also, explain clinical/bizarre types, such as feeling responsible for causing global warming, thus accelerating the extinction of humanity.
7. When educating on delusions of mind being read, discuss normal types, such as when having a conversation with a close friend, they finish your sentences, making you feel like your friend can read your mind. Explain subclinical/non-bizarre types, such as fearing that if they lie to a teacher, their intention to deceive will be detectable. Also, define clinical/bizarre types, such as feeling that an unfamiliar motorcyclist can read their thoughts.
8. For educating on delusions of thought insertion, elaborate on normal types, such as being reminded to revise a thesis chapter while meeting a co-student in a mall and attributing the thought to them ("Ah, it is because of you that I am thinking about the thesis"). Describe subclinical/non-bizarre types, like when conversing with an ex-acquaintance who was once their partner, suddenly recalling their ex's work and attributing the recollection to the acquaintance. Also, discuss clinical/bizarre types, like walking in a mall, considering purchasing an unnecessary item, and feeling as if the thought was implanted by a passing stranger (which can be connected with paranoid delusion: perhaps that

person is a store employee who used to bully them, now coercing them to buy unnecessary items, leading to bankruptcy and humiliation).

9. A delusion of reference involves connecting everything together (often implicitly to them). This tendency to link various events or situations that are actually unrelated often involves believing that small events in life are signs or messages from the universe, even though there's no scientific or logical evidence supporting these connections. When teaching about delusions of reference, illustrate normal types, such as feeling successful in a job interview tomorrow due to the specific lunar phase. Discuss subclinical/non-bizarre types, like feeling confident about acing a job interview today because they saw a gray cat this morning, and the interviewer wore a red shirt (considered lucky omens). Also, describe clinical/bizarre types, such as interpreting specific letters in the news as indicative that the FBI and CIA control the world, attempting to convey messages to ensure personal safety from bullies at school. Note: It is challenging to construct subclinical examples, as this delusion type tends to lean toward normal or clinical/bizarre.
10. When educating on religious delusions, clarify normal types like feeling obliged to attend church on Sundays, fearing damnation otherwise. Explain subclinical/non-bizarre types, like occasionally believing one can perform miracles when praying for someone's recovery. Also, discuss clinical/bizarre types, such as believing oneself to be a prophet for various religions—including Christianity, Catholicism, Islam, and even Confucianism—despite the fact that Confucianism does not have prophets, as it focuses more on teachings.
11. In educating on somatic delusions, discuss normal types, such as fearing they have cancer after reading about their headache online. Describe subclinical/non-bizarre types like being convinced that there is a severe illness inside them, leading them to visit a doctor multiple times. Also, define clinical/bizarre types like a man believing that he is pregnant or sensing a tumor on the palm of his hand causing five protuberances (although it's just five fingers), or feeling the color of his penis head is abnormal, wishing it were black or brown instead of its actual color.
12. When explaining delusions of poverty, elaborate on normal types, like feeling extremely regretful for missing a discount due to fears of continuous loss leading to poverty. Discuss subclinical/non-bizarre types, like reacting with fear and/or intense anger upon realizing they lost a month's salary when purchasing a motor vehicle. Also, define clinical/bizarre types, such as feeling destitute and homeless despite living in a house (not on the streets) with provided meals. Special note: According to Western literature, this type of delusion is rarely encountered, but personal clinical practices with non-schizophrenic patients indicate its prevalence among patients in Jakarta, Indonesia. While these beliefs are often not clearly visible and may manifest as stinginess or unpleasantness, they actually conceal irrational fears related to poverty deep within their minds.

9.2 Psychoeducation of Etiology of Psychotic Symptoms

Psychotic symptoms appear probabilistically. It is difficult to predict when exactly psychotic symptoms will appear, but various risk factors increase the likelihood. These include genetic/hereditary predispositions, trauma, unsafe environments (e.g., war zones, abusive homes), substance use, pollution, head trauma, stroke, Alzheimer's disease, malnutrition, and other psychopathologies (McGrath et al., 2015).

Heritability studies indicate that approximately 79% of monozygotic twins show concordance for psychosis, suggesting a high genetic variance (Hilker et al., 2018). However, genome-wide association studies (GWAS) have only found small genetic effects, such as DRD2, contributing less than 1% to the overall risk (Schizophrenia Working Group of the Psychiatric Genomics Consortium, 2014).

Additionally, environmental factors contribute to the onset of psychosis. Cannabis-induced psychosis, for instance, is often transient, subsiding with cessation of use, but persists with continued consumption (Murray et al., 2017). This suggests that risk factors must be actively maintained for psychotic symptoms to persist.

9.3 Treatment Planning of CBT for Psychosis Syndrome: A Systematic Approach to Managing Comorbidity, Risk and Protective Factors

CBT for psychosis syndrome is founded on a central premise: psychotic symptoms persist because they are maintained by unhealthy conditions. Therefore, our aim is to systematically discover and improve both the risk factors and protective factors associated with psychotic symptoms.

Our treatment strategy addresses two fundamental goals. First, we work to remove secondary emotional reactions to psychotic symptoms. By the end of this initial phase, patients should be able to discuss their symptoms with their psychotherapist without experiencing overwhelming distress or shame. While it is natural and acceptable for patients to feel distressed by the content of their experiences (such as the content of voices), they should not be severely distressed by the mere presence or sudden appearance of these symptoms, as these would have been present for some time before beginning therapy.

The second goal involves systematically addressing risk factors while enhancing protective factors. To accomplish this, the patient and psychotherapist collaboratively complete a comprehensive checklist. This process requires careful attention to ensure no problems are overlooked due to negligence, shame, or fear. The checklist serves as both an assessment tool and a framework for treatment planning, with each factor assigned a specific number of required sessions based on empirical evidence.

Upon completing the checklist, we determine the total number of sessions required for treatment. This prognosis guides a treatment strategy that adheres to four fundamental principles: combinability (how interventions can work together), brevity (efficient use of session time), speed of efficacy in improving quality of life, and plausibility of order. The last principle is particularly important—for instance, attempting to improve self-esteem while a patient is severely depressed is unlikely to be effective.

To illustrate this systematic approach, let's examine a case involving John, a 21-year-old male patient with schizophrenia and several comorbid conditions: insomnia, depression, specific phobia, social anxiety, generalized anxiety disorder, OCD, and substance use (marijuana) that is shown in a checklist in Table 9.1.

Through the checklist process in Table 9.1, both John and his psychotherapist independently evaluated how each condition affected his quality of life. John's assessment revealed that insomnia and depression had the most severe impact on his daily functioning, particularly through suicidal thoughts and chronic fatigue. These conditions created a debilitating cycle: depression led to feelings of weakness, lack of motivation, and pessimism, which triggered suicidal thoughts that interfered with sleep. The resulting insomnia forced him to take daytime naps, further disrupting his functioning and narrowing his focus to mere survival.

While John rated his OCD symptoms as having moderate impact and viewed his GAD, phobia, and social anxiety as minimal concerns, he did not perceive his marijuana use as problematic. In contrast, his psychotherapist identified both the OCD and marijuana use as significant issues requiring attention. This divergence in perspective highlights the importance of gathering both patient and clinician viewpoints.

When considering protective factors, John recognized the potential value of improving his emotional regulation skills and addressing both positive and negative schemas. He also acknowledged the importance of strengthening relationships and developing stronger reasons for living, though he initially struggled to understand the concept of self-compassion.

The checklist system reconciles these different perspectives by averaging the ratings and considering the typical number of sessions needed for effective treatment of each condition. This calculation produces a "speed efficacy" score that helps guide treatment sequencing. Though the initial data suggested beginning with insomnia and depression, followed by OCD and substance use, collaborative discussion led to a modified sequence. The final plan prioritized insomnia and depression, followed by addressing anxiety disorders (beginning with specific phobia and GAD), before tackling the more complex issues of OCD and substance use.

This systematic approach ensures that treatment planning remains both evidence-based and patient-centered. The checklist provides objective data while allowing for flexible modification based on clinical judgment and patient readiness. Most importantly, it creates a transparent framework for monitoring progress and maintaining collaborative engagement throughout the treatment process.

Table 9.1 An example of a patient symptoms checklist of John

Patient symptoms checklist						
Problems	Sessions	Diagnosed (yes/no)	Patient rated—Impact on quality of life (0–100)	Clinician rated—Impact on quality of life (0–100)	Average rate	Speed efficacy
Psychopathology						
Insomnia	4	Y	100	90	95	23.75
Depression	8	Y	100	100	100	12.5
Specific Phobia	5	Y	5	1	3	0.6
Social Anxiety	14	Y	5	100	52.5	3.75
General Anxiety Disorder	12	Y	10	50	30	2.5
Panic Disorder	7	N	0	0	0	0
OCD	10	Y	50	100	75	7.5
Eating Disorder	16	N	0	0	0	0
Body Dysmorphic Disorder	8	N	0	0	0	0
Substance use	12	Y	0	100	50	4.17
Tic	8	N	0	0	0	0
Impulsivity	8	N	0	0	0	0
Protective factors						
Emotional regulation	13	N/A	100	50	75	5.77
Negative schema	16	N/A	100	60	80	5
Positive schema	16	N/A	100	70	85	5.31
Improving relationship	8	N/A	50	70	60	7.5
Improving reasons for living	1	N/A	50	80	65	65
Self-compassion	1	N/A	5	50	27.5	27.5

References

Hilker, R., Helenius, D., Fagerlund, B., Skytthe, A., Christensen, K., Werge, T. M., & Nordentoft, M. (2018). Heritability of schizophrenia and schizophrenia spectrum based on the nationwide Danish twin register. *Biological Psychiatry, 83*(6), 492–498. https://doi.org/10.1016/j.biopsych.2017.08.017

McGrath, J. J., Saha, S., Al-Hamzawi, A., Alonso, J., Bromet, E. J., Bruffaerts, R., Caldas-de-Almeida, J. M., Chiu, W. T., de Jonge, P., Fayyad, J., Florescu, S., Gureje, O., Haro, J. M., Hu, C., Kovess-Masfety, V., Lepine, J. P., Lim, C. C., Mora, M. E., Navarro-Mateu, F., Ochoa, S., Kessler, R. C., et al. (2015). Psychotic experiences in the general population: A cross-national analysis based on 31, 261 respondents from 18 countries. *JAMA Psychiatry, 72*(7), 697–705. https://doi.org/10.1001/jamapsychiatry.2015.0575

Murray, R. M., Englund, A., Abi-Dargham, A., Lewis, D. A., Di Forti, M., Davies, C., Sherif, M., McGuire, P., & D'Souza, D. C. (2017). Cannabis-associated psychosis: Neural substrate and clinical impact. *Neuropharmacology, 124*, 89–104. https://doi.org/10.1016/j.neuropharm.2017.06.018

Schizophrenia Working Group of the Psychiatric Genomics Consortium. (2014). Biological insights from 108 schizophrenia-associated genetic loci. *Nature, 511*(7510), 421–427.

References

Part IV
Treatment Modules: Stage 1 Reduction of Psychopathology

Chapter 10
Treating Insomnia in Psychosis

Abstract This chapter presents a comprehensive CBT protocol for treating insomnia within the context of psychotic disorders. It begins with the rationale for addressing sleep disturbance as an early-stage therapeutic priority, given its contribution to exacerbating hallucinations, delusions, affective instability, and cognitive impairment. Assessment tools such as the ISI, PSQI, and Epworth Sleepiness Scale are reviewed to establish baseline severity and track progress. The chapter then details core CBT-I components—including sleep hygiene, stimulus control, relaxation techniques, sleep restriction therapy, and cognitive restructuring—adapted for individuals with psychosis to ensure safety and feasibility. A full clinical vignette illustrates how these techniques can be sequenced to reduce insomnia, stabilize the patient, and create downstream improvement in global psychopathology.

Keywords Sleep disturbance • CBT for insomnia • Sleep hygiene • Stimulus control • Sleep restriction

10.1 Goals of Treating Insomnia for Psychosis

The main goal in treating insomnia for psychosis is to reduce the factors that trigger psychotic symptoms and empower patients to manage their symptoms through aspects they can control. Insomnia has been shown to be related to psychotic symptoms (Freeman et al., 2009; Laskemoen et al., 2019), and psychotherapy for insomnia has been shown to improve psychotic symptoms (Freeman et al., 2017). The recommended duration of CBT for insomnia is typically 4–8 sessions (Riemann et al., 2017). Psychotherapists are free to choose the insomnia measurement and techniques relevant to the patient.

10.2 Measuring Insomnia

Comprehensive measurement of insomnia requires tools like polysomnography, sleep electroencephalogram, and actigraphy. However, here we will focus on self-report measures for insomnia, which are more readily available in most psychotherapy offices.

E. S. Jaya, *Cognitive Behavioral Therapy for Psychosis as a Syndrome*,
https://doi.org/10.1007/978-981-95-9203-6_10

10.2.1 Insomnia Severity Index

The Insomnia Severity Index (Morin et al., 2011) is a 7-item self-report questionnaire that assesses the nature, severity, and impact of insomnia within the last month. It evaluates several aspects, including the severity of difficulties with sleep onset and sleep maintenance, early morning awakening problems, dissatisfaction with sleep, interference of sleep difficulties with daytime functioning, the noticeability of sleep problems by others, and the distress caused by these difficulties. Responses are measured on a 5-point Likert scale, ranging from 0 (no problem) to 4 (very severe problem). The total score ranges from 0 to 28, which can be interpreted as absence of insomnia (0–7), subthreshold insomnia (8–14), moderate insomnia (15–21), and severe insomnia (22–28).

10.2.2 Pittsburgh Sleep Quality Index

The Pittsburgh Sleep Quality Index (PSQI) is a 19-item questionnaire that evaluates sleep quality and disturbances over the past month (Buysse et al., 1989). Items 1 to 4 are open-ended questions, while items 5 to 19 are rated on a 4-point Likert scale. These items yield 7 components, which can be summed to form a total score ranging from 0 to 21. A total score greater than 5 suggests poor sleep quality. Furthermore, there are 5 extra questions evaluated by the participant's roommate or sleeping partner, which are included for clinical purposes and are not assigned scores.

10.2.3 Epworth Sleepiness Scale

The Epworth Sleepiness Scale (ESS) is a short, easy-to-administer questionnaire that subjectively measures sleepiness in everyday situations (Johns, 1991). Respondents rate their likelihood of falling asleep in eight situations on a 4-point scale, with a minimum score of 4 and a maximum of 24. A normal score ranges between 0 and 10, while a score above 10 indicates the need for further medical assessment. However, a retrospective review of 268 patients diagnosed with obstructive sleep apnea (OSA) found that at the suggested cut-off of 10, ESS score had low sensitivity (66%) in identifying apnea–hypopnea index of ≥5, which increased to 76% at a lower cut-off of 8. Thus, reducing the cut-off to 8 is suggested as more effective in identifying sleep disorders in the general clinic population (Rosenthal & Dolan, 2008).

10.3 Sleep Hygiene

Sleep hygiene has been shown to contribute to improvements in insomnia, particularly when delivered as part of cognitive behavioral therapy for insomnia (CBT-I), including in individuals with psychosis (Irish et al., 2015; Freeman et al., 2017;

Trauer et al., 2015). Here, we use a sleep hygiene approach similar to those in other treatment manuals, suggesting strategies to patients selectively and assessing what may be missing from the patient's sleep habits.

Sleep Hygiene Guidelines

Good dental hygiene such as brushing your teeth in the morning and evening is important in keeping the health of your teeth and gums. Similarly, good sleep hygiene is important in keeping the quality of your sleep.

Review the guidelines and check the ones you might be breaking:

- Screen Time: Turn Off TV, Computers, Tablets, and Smartphones 1 Hour Before Bedtime
  - The short waves of blue light (emitted from screens) mimic daylight, suppressing melatonin and preventing sleepiness.
  - If screen time is your relaxing activity, try to move it earlier and use low-blue-light settings or screen protectors.
- Caffeine: Avoid Caffeine 6–8 Hours Before Bedtime
  - Caffeine disturbs sleep, even for those not sensitive to it.
  - It can cause micro-awakenings.
  - Caffeine is in coffee, tea, soda, chocolate, and some medications.
  - It should be avoided by 1 p.m. or earlier in the day.
  - The half-life of caffeine is 5 h; 70 mg takes 30 h to reduce to 1 mg.
- Nicotine: Avoid Nicotine Before Bedtime
  - Although some think smoking is relaxing, nicotine is a stimulant.
  - Nicotine should be avoided near bedtime and during the night.
- Alcohol: Avoid Alcohol After Dinner
  - Alcohol helps with sleep onset but causes disturbed, fragmented sleep later.
  - Limit alcohol to 1 drink for women and 2 for men.
- Sleeping Pills: Sleep Medications Are Effective Only Temporarily
  - Sleep medications lose effectiveness after 2–4 weeks.
  - Long-term use can worsen sleep problems and lead to insomnia rebound.
  - Use them sparingly, but don't worry about occasional use. Always consult your doctor.
- Regular Exercise
  - Exercise aids sleep but can take several weeks to show an effect.
  - Avoid exercise within 2 h of bedtime.
- Hot Baths
  - A 20-min hot bath 1–2 h before bed may help sleep.
- Bedroom Environment: Moderate Temperature, Quiet, and Dark
  - Extremes of temperature can disrupt sleep.
  - Noise can be masked with white noise or earplugs.

- Use blackout shades or sleep masks for darkness.
- Keep clocks out of sight.

- Eating
  - A light snack before bed can promote sleep (e.g., warm milk, cheese, cereal).
  - Avoid heavy, spicy meals and caffeine before bed.
  - Avoid midnight snacks to prevent associating hunger with waking up.
- Avoid/Reduce Naps
  - Daytime sleep reduces sleep quality at night.
  - If needed, keep naps brief (no more than 15 min).
- Limit Your Time in Bed
  - Restrict sleep time to your average hours slept over the past week.
  - Don't lie in bed awake. Get up if not asleep within 15–20 min and engage in a relaxing activity outside the bedroom.
- Regular Sleep Schedule
  - Wake up at the same time every day, even on weekends, to set your circadian rhythm.
  - Light exposure in the morning helps regulate your sleep-wake cycle.

10.4 Stimulus Control

Stimulus Control Therapy (SCT) for the treatment of insomnia was proposed by Bootzin (1973). SCT for insomnia is based on a learning analysis of sleep in which falling asleep is conceptualized as an instrumental behavior aimed at achieving reinforcement (i.e., sleep). Difficulty falling asleep may occur due to inadequate stimulus control because strong discriminative stimuli for sleep may not have been established (e.g., never feel sleepy in the bedroom) or discriminative stimuli for activities that interfere with sleep may be present (e.g., feeling anxious or tense in bed, worrying about sleep, or working in bed). The goal of SCT is to reduce cues associated with arousal as well as cues that are discriminative stimuli for activities incompatible with sleep. SCT was designed to help individuals suffering from insomnia to strengthen the bed and bedroom as cues for sleep, weaken the bed and bedroom as cues for arousal, and develop a consistent sleep-wake schedule to help maintain improvements. In other words, SCT is designed to help people who cannot sleep well in their bedroom, similar to how a typical student struggles to study in the bedroom for an exam because of sleepiness.

Here are the instructions for SCT (Bootzin & Perlis, 2011):

1. *Lie down to go to sleep only when you are sleepy.*
2. *Do not use your bed for anything except sleep; that is, do not read, watch television, eat, or worry in bed. Sexual activity is the only exception to this rule. On*

such occasions, the instructions are to be followed afterward when you intend to go to sleep.

3. *If you find yourself unable to fall asleep, get up and go into another room. Stay up as long as you wish and then return to the bedroom to sleep. Although we do not want you to watch the clock, we want you to get out of bed if you do not fall asleep immediately. Remember, the goal is to associate your bed with falling asleep quickly! If you are in bed more than about 10 min without falling asleep and have not gotten up, you are not following this instruction.*
4. *If you still cannot fall asleep, repeat step (3). Do this as often as is necessary throughout the night.*
5. *Set your alarm and get up at the same time every morning irrespective of how much sleep you got during the night. This will help your body acquire a consistent sleep rhythm.*
6. *Do not nap during the day.*

10.5 Relaxation Techniques in the Context of Insomnia

The aim of relaxation techniques is to achieve physical and mental relaxation. They are meant to reduce physical tension and reduce the probability of anxious thoughts that are affecting sleep. There are different types of relaxation techniques. Not all techniques work for everyone. The therapists should consider the number of sessions, practicality, and ease of implementation before teaching a relaxation technique. Here are some relaxation technique suggestions in order of ease of implementation:

10.5.1 4–7–8 Breathing

In short, the therapists teach the patient to breathe for four counts, hold the breath for seven counts and exhale for eight counts. The patient is to do these four breaths at a time in the beginning, and later eight breaths at a time. Specifically, the therapist can give the following instruction:

> Prepare for the practice by resting the tip of your tongue against the roof of your mouth, right behind your top front teeth. You will need to keep your tongue in place throughout the practice. It takes practice to keep from moving your tongue when you exhale. Exhaling during 4–7–8 breathing can be easier for some people when they purse their lips.
>
> The following steps should all be carried out in the cycle of one breath:
>
> 1. First, let your lips part. Make a whooshing sound, exhaling completely through your mouth.
> 2. Next, close your lips, inhaling silently through your nose as you count to four in your head.
> 3. Then, for seven seconds, hold your breath.
> 4. Make another whooshing exhale from your mouth for eight seconds.

When you inhale again, you initiate a new cycle of breath. Practice this pattern for four full breaths.

The held breath (for seven seconds) is the most critical part of this practice. It is also recommended that you only practice 4–7–8 breathing for four breaths when you are first starting out. You can gradually work your way up to eight full breaths.

10.5.2 Progressive Muscle Relaxation

Also called Jacobson's or deep muscle relaxation, this technique involves tensing groups of muscles all over the body one by one and then consciously relaxing them again. One session may take 15–20 min. Specifically, here is the instruction:

1. *Start by lying or sitting down. Relax your entire body. Take five deep, slow breaths.*
2. *Lift your toes upward. Hold, then let go. Pull your toes downward. Hold, then let go.*
3. *Next, tense your calf muscles, then let go.*
4. *Move your knees toward each other. Hold, then let go.*
5. *Squeeze your thigh muscles. Hold, then let go.*
6. *Clench your hands. Pause, then let go.*
7. *Tense your arms. Hold, then let go.*
8. *Squeeze your buttocks. Pause, then let go.*
9. *Contract your abdominal muscles. Pause, then let go.*
10. *Inhale and tighten your chest. Hold, then exhale and let go.*
11. *Raise your shoulders to your ears. Pause, then let go.*
12. *Purse your lips together. Hold, then release.*
13. *Open your mouth wide. Hold, then let go.*
14. *Close your eyes tightly. Pause, then release.*
15. *Lift your eyebrows. Hold, then release.*

10.5.3 Autogenic Training (AT)

Autogenic training involves focusing awareness on different parts of the body and consciously relaxing them. At an advanced level, even involuntary bodily functions like pulse and breathing can be influenced to achieve deep physical relaxation.

Repeat the instructions below four times, saying it slowly and silently to yourself. You can choose the sets that relate best to you, and repeat it after finishing the whole set (e.g. Heavy, Warm, and then back to Heavy again). Try to maintain passive concentration and a relaxed pace. Take about 5 s to make each self-statement (e.g. *My right arm is heavy*). Then, pause for 3 s before beginning the next statement. Practice this once a day, and you can modify the practice to suit your needs. Here is a template:

Set 1: Heavy

My right arm is heavy. My left arm is heavy. Both of my arms are heavy. My right leg is heavy. My left leg is heavy. Both of my legs are heavy. My arms and my legs are heavy.

Set 2: Warmth

My right arm is warm. My left arm is warm. Both of my arms are warm. My right leg is warm. My left leg is warm. Both of my legs are warm. My arms and my legs are warm.

Set 3: A Calm Heart

My arms are heavy and warm. My legs are heavy and warm. My arms and legs are heavy and warm. I feel calm. My heart feels warm and pleasant. My heartbeat is calm and regular.

Set 4: Breathing

My arms are heavy and warm. My legs are heavy and warm. My arms and legs are heavy and warm. I feel calm. My heartbeat is calm and regular. My breathing breathes me.

Set 5: Stomach

My arms are heavy and warm. My legs are heavy and warm. My arms and legs are heavy and warm. I feel calm. My heart feels calm and regular. My breathing breathes me. My stomach is soft and warm.

Set 6: Cool Forehead

My arms are heavy and warm. My legs are heavy and warm. My arms and legs are heavy and warm. I feel calm. My heartbeat is calm and regular. My breathing breathes me. My stomach is soft and warm. My forehead is cool.

Formula for Calming the Mind: I am calm and relaxed. I feel quite quiet. I feel quiet, relaxed, and comfortable. My mind is quiet. I am at peace. I feel an inward quietness. I am at ease. My mind is serene and still.

10.5.4 Imagery (Visualizations)

Another common type of relaxation training is imagery, where you visualize peaceful, pleasant scenes or imagine yourself breathing quietly, gently falling asleep and having a good night's sleep. There are many ways to do imagery relaxation. Here is a template:

Start with breathing deeply and getting into a relaxed state. The imagery technique starts here. Try to imagine yourself amid the most relaxing environment you can imagine. This is very individual. For example, floating in cool water on a remote tropical island, sitting alone by the fire in a cabin deep in the woods, or walking along the beach with the sound of the sea. After you have the scene in mind, try to involve all your senses. Fill in the blanks for each sense: What can you see? What can you smell? What can you hear? The more details, the better.

10.6 Sleep-Restrictive Therapy

This approach aims to restrict the time you spend in bed to the time when you are actually asleep. For example, if you usually lie in bed for 8 h but only sleep for six, then the idea is that you should not spend more than 6 h in bed.

First, track how much sleep you get on average over about 2 weeks. It may help to keep a sleep diary. Another half an hour of time spent falling asleep is added to the average sleeping time. That is the time between "lights out" and actually falling asleep. The best time for you to go to sleep is then calculated "backward," using your wake-up time as the starting point. For instance, if your alarm is set for 6:00 a.m., and you need 6 h of sleep as well as half an hour to fall asleep, you would go to bed at 11:30 p.m. Adjustments like these can help you find the optimal amount of time to spend in bed for a good night's sleep.

10.7 Cognitive Therapy for Insomnia

Cognitive behavioral therapy (CBT) aims to change thought patterns that may be keeping you from sleeping. This is not the same as "positive thinking." It is about changing exaggerated and unrealistic beliefs about sleep. For example, if someone believes that they will always wake up at three in the morning and then not be able to go back to sleep, it may turn into a self-fulfilling prophecy.

Another example of a negative thought that can affect sleep is: "If I don't fall asleep now, I definitely won't make it through tomorrow." A more realistic thought might be: "This happens from time to time. But I might still get some sleep. And it's no big deal if I don't."

A more realistic attitude toward sleep also includes not worrying about how much sleep you end up getting. It's more important that your sleep is restful enough for you to feel good the next day.

10.8 Case Vignette of Application of Treating Insomnia in a Patient with Schizophrenia

Sarah, a 28-year-old woman diagnosed with schizophrenia, sat nervously in her therapy session. Dark circles underlined her eyes as she described her struggle with sleep. Living alone in a supported housing facility, she had been stable on antipsychotic medication but continued to experience persistent insomnia, sleeping only 2–3 h per night. Despite her medication compliance, paranoid thoughts regularly disrupted her nights.

During the first session, Sarah spoke in a hushed voice about her sleep difficulties. "I try to go to bed, but I can't stop thinking someone might break in," she explained, fidgeting with her sleeve. "I check the windows and doors maybe fifteen, twenty times a night. When I finally get to bed, I use my phone to distract myself from the scary thoughts, but then hours pass, and I'm still awake."

The therapist began with a gentle exploration of her typical day. Sarah described consuming six to seven cups of coffee "to stay alert" (*which is related to her paranoid delusion*), taking irregular naps, and using her phone until the early hours of the morning. Her bedroom, she admitted, was cluttered with electronics that stayed on throughout the night, their lights and sounds providing what she called "comfort."

A pivotal moment came during the third session when Sarah and her therapist engaged in a collaborative discussion about making environmental changes according to sleep hygiene principles (no electronics before bed):**Therapist**: I notice you mentioned the lights from your electronics help you feel safe. What makes nighttime feel particularly threatening?

Sarah: When it's dark and quiet, the thoughts get louder. The lights remind me I'm not alone… but I guess they're also keeping me awake.

Therapist: That makes sense. You've found a way to feel safer, though it might be affecting your sleep (*notice how the therapist is indifferent to the psychotic symptoms, "thoughts get louder", mentioned by Sarah*). What if we worked together to find ways to feel secure while helping you sleep better?

Sarah: I don't know if I can change anything. Last time I tried sleeping without checking everything, I had a panic attack.

Therapist: I hear how scary that was. What if we started with very small changes? You're the expert on what feels manageable for you.

Together, they developed a graduated approach to modifying her sleep environment. Rather than eliminating safety checks entirely, they created a structured "security routine" that felt containing but limited. The housing facility's support staff agreed to do one final check before Sarah's bedtime, which helped her reduce her own checking behavior.

Here is an example of implementing the screen time reduction principle of sleep hygiene. Notice how the therapist does not follow-up and is non-reactive to the auditory hallucination symptom that the patient mentioned, and stays focused on the agenda of screen time reduction:**Sarah**: My phone helps distract me from the voices when they get bad at night.

Therapist: What kind of content do you usually look at?

Sarah: Mostly funny videos, sometimes the news. But then I keep scrolling and scrolling…

Therapist: Would you be willing to experiment with something different? We could find audio content that's engaging but less stimulating for your eyes.

Sarah: Like what?

Therapist: Some people find audiobooks or relaxation recordings helpful. We could practice using them here first, where you feel safe.

By week 5, Sarah had developed a modified evening routine. She would have her final cup of coffee before noon, complete her security check with staff at 10:30 PM, then transition to listening to audiobooks with her phone's night mode activated. She learned a modified progressive muscle relaxation technique that focused on her hands and feet, avoiding full-body tension that had previously triggered paranoid sensations.

Here is an example of how focusing on sleep improvement can have an effect on psychotic symptoms, particularly paranoid thoughts:**Sarah**: Something strange happened last night. I woke up and actually felt rested. I can't remember the last time that happened.
Therapist: What do you think contributed to that?
Sarah: I stuck to the routine we planned. And having the staff check helped me not do it so many times myself. The audiobook was interesting enough to distract me, but I wasn't staring at the screen. I still had some thoughts about intruders, but they didn't feel as powerful.

References

Bootzin, R. R. (1973). Stimulus control treatment for insomnia. *Proceedings of the American Psychological Association, 8*, 395–396.

Bootzin, R. R., & Perlis, M. L. (2011). Nonpharmacologic treatments of insomnia. *Journal of Clinical Psychiatry, 72*(9), e36. https://doi.org/10.4088/JCP.10128tx1c

Buysse, D. J., Reynolds, C. F., Monk, T. H., Berman, S. R., & Kupfer, D. J. (1989). The Pittsburgh Sleep Quality Index: A new instrument for psychiatric practice and research. Psychiatry Research, 28(2), 193–213. https://doi.org/10.1016/0165-1781(89)90047-4

Freeman, D., Pugh, K., Vorontsova, N., & Southgate, L. (2009). Insomnia and paranoia. *Schizophrenia Research, 108*(1–3), 280–284. https://doi.org/10.1016/j.schres.2008.12.001

Freeman, D., Sheaves, B., Goodwin, G. M., Yu, L. M., Nickless, A., Harrison, P. J., … Espie, C. A. (2017). The effects of improving sleep on mental health (OASIS): A randomised controlled trial with mediation analysis. *The Lancet Psychiatry, 4*(10), 749–758. https://doi.org/10.1016/S2215-0366(17)30328-0

Irish, L. A., Kline, C. E., Gunn, H. E., Buysse, D. J., & Hall, M. H. (2015). The role of sleep hygiene in promoting public health: A review of empirical evidence. *Sleep Medicine Reviews, 22*, 23–36. https://doi.org/10.1016/j.smrv.2014.10.001

Johns, M. W. (1991). A new method for measuring daytime sleepiness: The Epworth Sleepiness Scale. *Sleep, 14*(6), 540–545. https://doi.org/10.1093/sleep/14.6.540

Laskemoen, J. F., Simonsen, C., Büchmann, C., Barrett, E. A., Bjella, T., Lagerberg, T. V., Vedal, T. J., Andreassen, O. A., Melle, I., & Aas, M. (2019). Sleep disturbances in schizophrenia spectrum and bipolar disorders—A transdiagnostic perspective. *Comprehensive Psychiatry, 91*, 6–12. https://doi.org/10.1016/j.comppsych.2019.02.006

Morin, C. M., Belleville, G., Bélanger, L., & Ivers, H. (2011). The Insomnia Severity Index: Psychometric Indicators to Detect Insomnia Cases and Evaluate Treatment Response. *Sleep, 34*(5), 601–608. https://www.ncbi.nlm.nih.gov/pmc/articles/PMC3079939/

Riemann, D., Baglioni, C., Bassetti, C., Bjorvatn, B., Dolenc Groselj, L., Ellis, J. G., Espie, C. A., Garcia-Borreguero, D., Gjerstad, M., Gonçalves, M., Hertenstein, E., Jansson-Fröjmark, M., Jennum, P. J., Leger, D., Nissen, C., Parrino, L., Paunio, T., Pevernagie, D., Verbraecken, J., Weeß, H. G., Spiegelhalder, K., et al. (2017). European guideline for the diagnosis and treatment of insomnia. *Journal of Sleep Research, 26*(6), 675–700. https://doi.org/10.1111/jsr.12594

Rosenthal, L. D., & Dolan, D. C. (2008). The Epworth Sleepiness Scale in the identification of obstructive sleep apnea. *Journal of Nervous and Mental Disease, 196*(5), 429–431. https://doi.org/10.1097/NMD.0b013e31817108d8

Trauer, J. M., Qian, M. Y., Doyle, J. S., Rajaratnam, S. M. W., & Cunnington, D. (2015). Cognitive behavioral therapy for chronic insomnia: A systematic review and meta-analysis. *Annals of Internal Medicine, 163*(3), 191–204. https://doi.org/10.7326/M14-2841.

Chapter 11
Treating Depression in Psychosis

Abstract This chapter sets out a structured approach to treating depression in people with psychosis, with the dual aim of reducing triggers of psychotic episodes and improving quality of life and treatment motivation. It begins by clarifying why depression is often prioritized in schizophrenia treatment and reviews core assessment tools, including the Calgary Depression Scale for Schizophrenia, PHQ-9, IDS, and DASS. The chapter then presents two main intervention components: behavioral activation tailored to psychotic presentations and cognitive therapy for depression in psychosis. A detailed case vignette illustrates how these methods are applied in a patient with schizophrenia and how improvements in mood can create a foundation for further psychotherapeutic work.

Keywords Behavioral activation · Depressive symptoms · Cognitive therapy · Mood regulation · Functional recovery

11.1 Goals of Treating Depression for Psychosis

The main goals of treating depression in individuals with psychosis are multifaceted: 1) reduce triggers of psychosis, 2) improve quality of life, 3) improve optimism, including motivation for treatment, and 4) provide a basis for other psychotherapeutic works. Depression has been shown to precede an episode of psychosis and precede psychotic symptoms in a community sample (Häfner et al., 2005; Jaya et al., 2018). Psychotherapy for depression has been found to reduce psychotic symptoms in people with psychosis (Singer et al., 2014). Patients with psychosis when surveyed are often keener to have their experiences similar to depressive symptoms lifted, such as improved energy and mood, rather than their psychotic symptoms (Freeman et al., 2019; Rosenheck et al., 2005). Therefore, depression is often a priority in the treatment of schizophrenia within this psychotherapy manual. According to the NICE guidelines (2022), individuals with less severe depression are advised to undergo 8 regular sessions of CBT or behavioral activation, while 16 sessions of CBT or 12–16 sessions of behavioral activation are

E. S. Jaya, *Cognitive Behavioral Therapy for Psychosis as a Syndrome*,
https://doi.org/10.1007/978-981-95-9203-6_11

recommended for more severe cases. Psychotherapists are free to choose the depression measurement and techniques relevant to the patient.

11.2 Measuring Depression

11.2.1 Calgary Depression Scale for Schizophrenia (CDSS)

The Calgary Depression Scale for Schizophrenia (CDSS), developed by Addington et al. (1993), is a clinician-rated instrument developed to evaluate depressive symptomatology in individuals with schizophrenia while minimizing contamination from primary negative symptoms or medication-related motor side effects. Unlike general depression scales, it was constructed with the recognition that diminished affect, psychomotor slowing, or avolition may arise from illness processes other than mood disturbance. The scale consists of nine interview-based items scored using both reported experience and observed presentation, allowing the assessor to estimate the presence and severity of affective disturbance in this population with greater specificity.

11.2.2 Patient-Health-Questionnaire-9 (PHQ-9)

The Patient Health Questionnaire 9 (PHQ-9) (Kroenke, 2021; Kroenke et al., 2001) is a self-administered questionnaire to assess the severity of depressive symptoms in the last 2 weeks. The PHQ-9 consists of nine questions corresponding to the DSM-IV diagnosis of depressive disorders (e.g., little interest or pleasure in doing things, feeling depressed, feeling tired or having little energy over the last 2 weeks). Each question is answered using a scale from 0 (not at all) to 3 (nearly every day) ranging from 0 to 27 (0–4: minimal, 5–9: mild, 10–14: moderate, 15–19: moderately severe, 20–27: severe). The PHQ-9 has been shown to be reliable and valid to measure the severity of depression with published cut-offs ranging from 8 to 13 (Jaya et al., 2024; Manea et al., 2012; Sucitra et al., 2024).

11.2.3 Inventory of Depressive Symptomatology (IDS)

The Inventory of Depressive Symptomatology (IDS) is a widely used measure for assessing the severity of depressive symptoms, developed by Rush et al. (Rush et al., 1986, 1996, 2000). IDS is available in two versions: a clinician-administered version (IDS-C) and a self-report version (IDS-SR). The IDS includes 30 items evaluating a broad range of depressive symptoms, including mood, cognitive changes, sleep, and appetite. Responses are rated on a 4-point Likert scale. The IDS is used in clinical and research settings for monitoring symptom severity and treatment outcomes.

11.2.4 Depression Anxiety Stress Scale (DASS)

The Depression Anxiety Stress Scale (DASS) is a self-report questionnaire measuring the negative emotional state of depression, anxiety, and stress by using a 4-point Likert scale (from 0 to 3) based on their experience over the last week. The full version of DASS consists of 42 items, with 14 items on each scale (Lovibond & Lovibond, 1995). The short version of DASS comprises 21 items, with 7 items on each scale. The depression scale measures dysphoria, hopelessness, devaluation of life, self-deprecation, lack of interest, anhedonia, and inertia. The anxiety scale evaluates autonomic arousal, skeletal muscle effects, situational anxiety, and subjective experience of anxious affect. The stress scale measures difficulty relaxing, nervous arousal, and being easily upset, irritable, and impatient. A higher sum score in each subscale indicates a higher severity of depression, anxiety, or stress.

11.3 Behavioral Activation for Depression in Psychosis

Within psychotic disorders, depressive withdrawal frequently reinforces threat-based interpretations of the social environment and limits opportunities for corrective experiential learning. Behavioral Activation may therefore be conceptualized not solely as a mood-enhancement strategy, but as a graded method of increasing contact with environmental contingencies that are inconsistent with defeatist or danger-related beliefs. By systematically reintroducing manageable patterns of activity into daily life, individuals can encounter alternative sources of reinforcement that are often inaccessible during periods of marked inactivity or avoidance. In this context, therapeutic emphasis is placed on identifying patterns of disengagement that maintain low mood and collaboratively developing feasible actions that promote engagement with meaningful roles or routines.

Behavioral activation (BA) is described extensively in the behavioral therapy literature, including its historical development and proposed mechanisms of action (e.g., Dimidjian et al., 2011). In the present context, emphasis is placed on (a) activity monitoring and structuring, in congruence with (b) the scheduling of behaviors that are in line with personal values and associated with pleasure or mastery, as central mechanisms for achieving the therapeutic objectives of BA.

Scheduling activities that align with values, pleasure, mastery, and goals is described in standard behavioral activation treatment models (e.g., Lejuez et al., 2011; Lewinsohn, 1974; Lewinsohn & Graf, 1973; Martell et al., 2021). The following overview highlights selected elements relevant to its application in individuals with psychosis.

Values refer to personally endorsed directions that give coherence to behavior across time, particularly in situations where motivation may be compromised by low mood or anticipatory anxiety. Clarifying such directions can assist individuals in making activity choices that are not exclusively driven by short-term emotional states but instead reflect broader priorities in areas such as relationships, health, learning, or contribution to others.

Pleasure, referring to experiences associated with enjoyment, may serve as important counterweights to anhedonia by providing immediate sensory or interpersonal reward.These activities need not be elaborate; even brief or routine forms of engagement can contribute to emotional stabilization when undertaken consistently.

Mastery refers to actions that involve effort, skill acquisition, or completion of tasks that extend beyond one's habitual comfort zone. Successful engagement in mastery activities may enhance perceived competence and foster incremental shifts in self-efficacy over time.

When helping individuals clarify what truly matters to them, it can be useful to explore values across several key life areas and set goals based on them. These areas provide a structured way to reflect on how one would like to live, rather than focusing solely on what one wants to feel or avoid. Here are some areas of life psychotherapists can explore with patients, drawing from the Acceptance and Commitment Therapy framework (Hayes & Pierson, 2005). A more complete and thorough value exploration can be found in standard Acceptance and Commitment Therapy manuals.

In the area of *physical well-being*, individuals may value living in safe and secure surroundings, engaging in regular exercise, maintaining a steady income to meet their physical needs, eating food that nourishes their body, balancing rest with activity, or getting sufficient sleep. For example, a person might describe taking care of their health by exercising regularly, preparing balanced meals, maintaining a consistent sleep schedule, or ensuring that their work supports their basic physical needs.

In the area of *mental and emotional health*, individuals may value maintaining psychological balance and resilience by seeking enjoyable experiences, setting aside free time, maintaining independence, challenging negative thinking patterns, making their own decisions, attending therapy when needed, taking prescribed medications, or remaining mentally active through meaningful engagement with life.

In the area of *family relationships*, individuals may value working on improving current relationships, spending meaningful time with family members, taking an active role in raising children, or maintaining open and healthy communication. For example, someone might value being a present parent, resolving conflicts respectfully, checking in regularly with relatives, or providing support to family members during difficult times.

In the area of *intimate relationships*, individuals may value establishing safety and trust, giving and receiving affection, spending quality time together, or expressing appreciation toward their partner. For example, this might involve setting aside time for shared activities, communicating openly about needs, offering emotional support, or acknowledging one another's efforts.

In the area of *friendships and social relationships*, individuals may value ending destructive or harmful relationships, reaching out to form new connections, cultivating a sense of belonging, maintaining close friendships, spending time with peers, or engaging in shared activities. For example, this could include reconnecting with old friends, joining social groups, or making time for regular social interaction.

In the area of *employment or career*, individuals may value being able to influence others, taking on leadership roles, making meaningful decisions within an organization, earning financial rewards, gaining respect, achieving recognition, working productively, reaching significant goals, enjoying one's work, or following established rules and responsibilities.

In the area of *education, training, and personal growth*, individuals may value engaging in personally meaningful pursuits, trying new experiences, learning new skills, seeking adventure, or taking on challenging tasks that promote development. For example, this might include enrolling in courses, learning a new language, or developing technical or creative abilities.

In the area of *citizenship and community involvement*, individuals may value contributing to society, helping those in need, improving their communities, committing to meaningful causes, or making sacrifices for the benefit of others. For example, volunteering, participating in advocacy efforts, or supporting community initiatives may reflect these values.

In the area of *spirituality*, individuals may value following traditions, living according to spiritual principles, practicing religious or philosophical beliefs, reflecting on their purpose, seeking meaning in life, developing a personal philosophy, spending time in nature, or focusing on the greater good.

In the area of *recreation and leisure*, individuals may value engaging in hobbies, pursuing creative interests, relaxing through play, or participating in enjoyable activities that help restore energy.

In the area of *pleasure*, individuals may value engaging in activities that are pursued primarily for enjoyment, such as spending time with family or friends, attending social gatherings, caring for pets, reading, watching films, listening to music, cooking, traveling, playing games, gardening, or engaging in sports. Sensory experiences—such as pleasant smells, sounds, tastes, physical touch, or relaxing baths—may also contribute to enjoyment when engaged in moderation.

In the area of *mastery*, individuals may value engaging in activities that promote the development of competence and skill, such as participating in meaningful work, pursuing creative projects, building or repairing things, practicing music, learning new subjects, developing artistic skills, or participating in sports. These activities often provide a sense of accomplishment and increase confidence when balanced appropriately with pleasurable pursuits.

Encouraging individuals to reflect on both pleasurable and mastery-oriented activities may help them develop a more balanced and fulfilling daily life—one that includes both enjoyment and growth.

The aim of goal setting is to create the larger context of doing the scheduled activities. Also, please remember to set the bar low because sometimes getting up and getting a shower is already an achievement of its own.

11.4 Cognitive Therapy for Depression in Psychosis

Cognitive therapy for depression is a widely used and evidence-based psychotherapy approach designed to help individuals overcome depression by addressing and modifying negative thought patterns and behaviors that contribute to their feelings of distress.

Here are two cognitive therapy techniques for depression, ABCDE and cognitive restructuring. ABCDE sequence is often described within rational-emotive and cognitive-behavioral traditions in many standard cognitive therapy and rational-emotive behavioral therapy texts and is therefore not reproduced. It provides a systematic method for evaluating the evidentiary basis of distress-related interpretations and generating more adaptive alternatives.

In cognitive restructuring as described in standard cognitive therapy frameworks (e.g., Beck et al., 1979, 2024; Burns, 1999), the psychotherapist works with the patient to identify and challenge negative automatic thoughts or cognitive distortions. The psychotherapist encourages the patient to examine evidence for and against negative thoughts to develop more balanced and realistic perspectives. The psychotherapist can start by teaching the patients about common cognitive distortions that may lead to depressive symptoms. Cognitive distortions are patterns of thinking that can lead to negative emotions and behaviors.

However, patients are not introduced to maladaptive thinking patterns solely as abstract psychoeducational material. Instead, the psychotherapists operationalize recurrent appraisal errors into a finite set of recognizable interpretive habits that can be actively identified during therapy. Within this framework, distorted interpretations are conceptualized as predictable inferential shortcuts that systematically bias perception, memory, and threat estimation, particularly under conditions of heightened emotional arousal or uncertainty.

To support real-time detection, the psychotherapists may introduce brief descriptive tags that serve as metacognitive prompts during belief evaluation. These tags are not presented as formal diagnostic constructs but function as heuristic markers that assist patients in determining whether a given interpretation reflects externally verifiable observation or an internally generated appraisal habit. Examples of such tags include: *Black–White* (binary or absolutistic evaluation; e.g., concluding that one workplace mistake will inevitably result in termination); *One = All* (generalization from limited instances; e.g., assuming that one unsuccessful interaction means that all future interactions will also fail); *Negative Zoom* (selective attention to adverse details; e.g., focusing exclusively on a single criticism while disregarding multiple positive comments); *Mind Guessing* (attribution of unobservable mental states; e.g., believing that others are intentionally judging or disliking oneself without direct evidence); *Disaster Mode* (inflation of threat probability or severity; e.g., assuming that a minor health symptom indicates a life-threatening condition); *Self-Blame* (excessive internal causal attribution; e.g., assuming personal responsibility for another person's distress or conflict); *Snap Conclusion* (premature inference without adequate evidence; e.g., deciding that an outcome will be negative before relevant information is available); *Total Control* (globalized assumptions of agency or helplessness; e.g., believing that one has either complete responsibility for events or none at all); *Feeling = Fact* (affective states treated as epistemic evidence; e.g., assuming that feeling anxious necessarily means that danger is present); *Rule Lock* (rigid prescriptive demands; e.g., insisting that one must perform perfectly in all circumstances); Name Calling (identity-level negative labeling; e.g., interpreting a single mistake as evidence of being fundamentally incompetent); *Positive Doesn't Count* (dismissal of favorable disconfirming evidence; e.g., attributing success to luck while accepting failure as personal inadequacy); *Scorekeeping* (hierarchical self–other comparison; e.g., evaluating self-worth solely based on perceived superiority or inferiority relative to others); *Fault Finder* (externalized causal attribution; e.g., attributing personal setbacks entirely to others' actions); and *They Must Change* (outcome dependency on others' behavior; e.g., believing that personal well-being depends on others behaving differently).

Patients are subsequently encouraged to examine spontaneously arising beliefs by collaboratively determining whether the interpretation corresponds to observable evidence or reflects one of these cognitive distortions. This classification procedure provides a structured means of differentiating externally corroborated perceptions from internally generated interpretive shortcuts, thereby supporting cognitive flexibility and reducing conviction in maladaptive appraisals during periods of elevated threat perception.

Tips for treating depression in psychosis:

1. Do your best to avoid putting delusions and hallucinations in a bad light. Here the target is to improve the patient's mood (i.e., reduction of depressive symptoms). Hopefully, by doing this, the patient comes to the realization that holding on to the psychotic symptoms provides a false sense of safety and makes the patient feel depressed.
2. People with schizophrenia often have very negative schemas. Try not to be overwhelmed by this. Instead, focus on the specific event on which we try to improve his perception. Try to tackle a very micro level of the negative automatic thoughts. Small progress goes a long way.

11.5 Case Vignette of Application of Treating Depression in Patient with Schizophrenia

Michael, a 32-year-old man diagnosed with major depressive disorder and schizophrenia with paranoid delusion, slumped in his chair during the initial therapy session. His unwashed hair and wrinkled clothes suggested weeks of minimal self-care.

Living with his elderly mother, he had increasingly isolated himself over the past 8 months, spending most days in his basement bedroom. Despite taking antidepressants, his mood remained low, and he expressed persistent concerns about being "watched" when outdoors.

During the first session, Michael spoke in monotone about his daily routine. "I mostly stay in my room where it's safe," he explained, staring at the floor. "Sometimes I don't get up until 3 PM. I know I should do more, but…" he paused, glancing nervously at the window, "there are people out there who notice everything you do. They judge you."

The therapist began by exploring his typical day. Michael described sleeping 12–14 h, spending most waking hours playing video games, and eating irregular meals, usually microwaved convenience foods. He admitted to not having left the house in 3 weeks, except for therapy appointments.

A significant breakthrough occurred in the second session when the therapist introduced the concept of morning walks:**Therapist**: What memories do you have of times you felt more energetic?
Michael: I used to have a job at the grocery store. Had to get there early to help with deliveries.
Therapist: Tell me about that morning routine. What time was that?
Michael: 6:30 AM. Almost nobody was out then…
Therapist: What did you notice about that time of day?
Michael: It was peaceful. The sun was just coming up. Before the streets got busy.

Notice how the therapist didn't address his implicit concern about other people, instead focusing on the positive aspects of early morning activity:**Therapist**: Would you be interested in exploring what a morning routine might look like now?
Michael: I don't know… It's been so long.
Therapist: What if we started really small? You're the expert on what would feel manageable.
Michael: Maybe just stepping outside? For a few minutes?
Therapist: That sounds like a thoughtful place to start. What time would work best for you?

Together, they developed a graduated approach to morning activity. Rather than jumping into full walks, they created a "morning stepping out" routine that began with simply standing on his front porch for 2 min. His mother agreed to join him initially, which provided additional support.

Here's an example of implementing behavioral activation while working around paranoid thoughts:**Michael**: Yesterday I noticed a car parked across the street. They might have been watching.
Therapist: What time did you step outside yesterday?
Michael: 6:45 AM, like we planned.
Therapist: How did your body feel during those few minutes outside?
Michael: Actually… the morning air felt nice. Cool on my face.
Therapist: Would you be interested in trying 3 min tomorrow, same early time?

By week 4, Michael had established a morning routine. He would wake at 6:30 AM, wash his face, and step outside by 6:45 AM. The duration gradually increased to 10 min, and he began walking to the end of his driveway and back. The therapist noticed how focusing on physical activity improved his overall presentation:**Michael**: I've started looking forward to it, kind of. The sunrise was beautiful today.

Therapist: What changes have you noticed since starting this morning routine?

Michael: I'm actually getting tired earlier at night. And sometimes I want breakfast after being outside. Yesterday I had toast instead of just coffee.

Therapist: You're noticing changes in your sleep and appetite. What else?

Michael: The rest of the day feels… I don't know… more possible? Like if I can do this one thing, maybe I can do other things too.

The case illustrates how behavioral activation can be implemented gradually, working with rather than against the patient's paranoid symptoms by choosing times and approaches that feel safer to them. The therapist consistently redirected attention to physical sensations, practical achievements, and small improvements rather than engaging with paranoid thoughts, while maintaining validation of the patient's experience.

References

Addington, D., Addington, J., & Maticka-tyndale, E. (1993). Assessing depression in schizophrenia: The Calgary depression scale. *The British Journal of Psychiatry, 163*(S22), 39–44. https://doi.org/10.1192/S0007125000292581

Beck, A. T., Rush, A. J., Shaw, B. F., & Emery, G. (1979). *Cognitive therapy of depression.* Guildford.

Beck, A. T., Rush, A. J., Shaw, B. F., Emery, G., DeRubeis, R. J., & Hollon, S. D. (2024). *Cognitive therapy of depression*. Guilford Publications.

Burns, D. D. (1999). *Feeling good: The new mood therapy* (Rev. and updated). Avon.

Dimidjian, S., Barrera, M., Martell, C., Muñoz, R. F., & Lewinsohn, P. M. (2011). The Origins and Current Status of Behavioral Activation Treatments for Depression. Annual Review of Clinical Psychology, 7(1), 1–38. https://doi.org/10.1146/annurev-clinpsy-032210-104535.

Freeman, D., Taylor, K. M., Molodynski, A., & Waite, F. (2019). Treatable clinical intervention targets for patients with schizophrenia. *Schizophrenia Research, 211*, 44–50. https://doi.org/10.1016/j.schres.2019.07.016

Häfner, H., Maurer, K., Trendler, G., an der Heiden, W., Schmidt, M., & Könnecke, R. (2005). Schizophrenia and depression: Challenging the paradigm of two separate diseases—A controlled study of schizophrenia, depression and healthy controls. *Schizophrenia Research, 77*(1), 11–24. https://doi.org/10.1016/j.schres.2005.01.004

Hayes, S. C., & Pierson, H. (2005). Acceptance and commitment therapy. In A. Freeman, S. H. Felgoise, C. M. Nezu, A. M. Nezu, & M. A. Reinecke (Eds.), *Encyclopedia of cognitive behavior therapy* (pp. 1–4). Springer US. https://doi.org/10.1007/0-306-48581-8_1

Jaya, E. S., Ascone, L., & Lincoln, T. M. (2018). A longitudinal mediation analysis of the effect of negative-self-schemas on positive symptoms via negative affect. *Psychological Medicine, 48*(8), 1299–1307. https://doi.org/10.1017/S003329171700277X

Jaya, E. S., Novrianto, R., Pillny, M., & Wiguna, T. (2024). Indonesian patient health questionnaire's clinical utility in psychiatric outpatients: Ruling out conditions per ICD-11 criteria. *Asian Journal of Psychiatry, 100*, 104184. https://doi.org/10.1016/j.ajp.2024.104184

Kroenke, K. (2021). PHQ-9: Global uptake of a depression scale. *World Psychiatry, 20*(1), 135–136. https://doi.org/10.1002/wps.20821

Kroenke, K., Spitzer, R. L., & Williams, J. B. W. (2001). The PHQ-9: Validity of a brief depression severity measure. *Journal of General Internal Medicine, 16*(9), 606–613. https://doi.org/10.1046/j.1525-1497.2001.016009606.x

Lejuez, C. W., Hopko, D. R., Acierno, R., Daughters, S. B., & Pagoto, S. L. (2011). Ten year revision of the brief Behavioral activation treatment for depression: Revised treatment manual. *Behavior Modification, 35*(2), 111–161. https://doi.org/10.1177/0145445510390929

Lewinsohn, P. M. (1974). A behavioral approach to depression. In *The psychology of depression: Contemporary theory and research* (p. xvii, 318–xvii, 318). John Wiley & Sons.

Lewinsohn, P. M., & Graf, M. (1973). Pleasant activities and depression. *Journal of Consulting and Clinical Psychology, 41*(2), 261–268. https://doi.org/10.1037/h0035142

Lovibond, P. F., & Lovibond, S. H. (1995). The structure of negative emotional states: Comparison of the depression anxiety stress scales (DASS) with the Beck depression and anxiety inventories. *Behaviour Research and Therapy, 33*(3), 335–343. https://doi.org/10.1016/0005-7967(94)00075-U

Manea, L., Gilbody, S., & McMillan, D. (2012). Optimal cut-off score for diagnosing depression with the patient health questionnaire (PHQ-9): A meta-analysis. *CMAJ, 184*(3), E191–E196. https://doi.org/10.1503/cmaj.110829

Martell, C. R., Dimidjian, S., & Herman-Dunn, R. (2021). *Behavioral activation for depression: A clinician's guide*. Guilford Publications.

Rosenheck, R., Stroup, S., Keefe, R. S. E., McEvoy, J., Swartz, M., Perkins, D., Hsiao, J., Shumway, M., & Lieberman, J. (2005). Measuring outcome priorities and preferences in people with schizophrenia. *The British Journal of Psychiatry, 187*(6), 529–536. https://doi.org/10.1192/bjp.187.6.529

Rush, A. J., Carmody, T., & Reimitz, P.-E. (2000). The inventory of depressive symptomatology (IDS): Clinician (IDS-C) and self-report (IDS-SR) ratings of depressive symptoms. *International Journal of Methods in Psychiatric Research, 9*(2), 45–59. https://doi.org/10.1002/mpr.79

Rush, A. J., Giles, D. E., Schlesser, M. A., Fulton, C. L., Weissenburger, J., & Burns, C. (1986). The inventory for depressive symptomatology (IDS): Preliminary findings. *Psychiatry Research, 18*(1), 65–87.

Rush, A. J., Gullion, C. M., Basco, M. R., Jarrett, R. B., & Trivedi, M. H. (1996). The inventory of depressive symptomatology (IDS): Psychometric properties. *Psychological Medicine, 26*(3), 477–486.

Singer, A. R., Addington, D. E., Dobson, K. S., & Wright, C. (2014). A pilot study of cognitive behavior therapy for depression in early psychosis. *Cognitive and Behavioral Practice, 21*(3), 323–334. https://doi.org/10.1016/j.cbpra.2013.08.004

Sucitra, E., Novrianto, R., Pasaribu, Y. T., Lincoln, T. M., & Jaya, E. S. (2024). *An analysis of measurement invariance of the Patient Health Questionnaire-9 between Indonesia, Germany, and the USA*.

Chapter 12
Treating Specific Phobia in Psychosis

Abstract This chapter describes how to treat specific phobia in the context of psychosis, with the goal of showing patients that pathological fear can be reduced and that this learning can generalize to other irrational fears. It outlines key assessment procedures, including the use of a DSM-aligned Severity Measure for Specific Phobia to quantify frequency, avoidance, and impairment. The core of the intervention is exposure therapy, complemented by cognitive therapy techniques that target distorted threat appraisals. A case vignette of a patient with schizophrenia demonstrates how graded work with a circumscribed phobia can build confidence, model fear habituation, and indirectly support later work on paranoid and psychotic fears.

Keywords Phobia · Fear avoidance · Exposure therapy · Anxiety reduction · Behavioral experiments

12.1 Goals of Treating Specific Phobia for Psychosis

The main goal in treating specific phobia in individuals with psychosis is to demonstrate the impact of pathological anxiety on psychosis and psychological well-being. When a patient overcomes their phobia, they gain self-confidence and tacit knowledge on how to tackle other irrational fears. For example, a common and mild phobia, such as arachnophobia, can be identified, and the patient can be taught tools on how to get better at conquering their fear of spiders. After significant progress—e.g., from only being able to look at toy spiders to playing with them—the psychotherapist can explain to the patient that, neurologically, the fear response to spiders and to other fears is the same, and that the patient has control to reduce their fear. Here the psychotherapist should not choose a difficult specific phobia that the patient finds hard to overcome, such as a blood phobia.

Following phobia treatment, the idea is to make the patient more motivated to proceed to the next module, which addresses social anxiety disorder or social phobia.

The tacit knowledge gained from overcoming a specific phobia can serve as an analogy in the context of delusion and hallucination, where the patient can learn not

E. S. Jaya, *Cognitive Behavioral Therapy for Psychosis as a Syndrome*,
https://doi.org/10.1007/978-981-95-9203-6_12

to fear psychotic symptoms as well. For example, the therapist might say, "Look, you have managed to no longer be frightened by spiders. You can even go to the insect aquarium full of spiders now. So, this concern about the FBI is similar to the spiders. We do not go around touching spiders, and we would not go around making problems with the FBI either. But our reaction to spiders is okay now, while our reaction to the FBI isn't yet. Let's do some exposure techniques. Let's say this out loud together ten times: FBI (10x)."

A meta-analysis by Wolitzky-Taylor et al. (2008) suggested that five sessions of exposure-based treatment can effectively improve phobic symptoms. Psychotherapists are free to choose the specific phobia measurement and techniques relevant to the patient.

12.2 Measuring Phobia

12.2.1 Severity Measures for Specific Phobia

The Severity Measure for Specific Phobia (Craske et al., 2013) is a self-report questionnaire designed to assess the severity of specific phobias. It consists of ten items that evaluate how often an individual experiences fear or avoidance of specific objects or situations (e.g., heights, animals, flying), as well as the distress and impairment caused by the phobia over the past 2 weeks. The items align with DSM-5 criteria for specific phobias, addressing fear intensity, avoidance behavior, and the impact on daily functioning.

Respondents rate the severity of their symptoms on a scale from 0 (never) to 4 (all of the time). The total score ranges from 0 to 40, with higher scores indicating greater severity. The severity of the phobia is categorized as follows: 0–9 (minimal), 10–19 (mild), 20–29 (moderate), and 30–40 (severe). The Severity Measure for Specific Phobia has shown good reliability and validity in clinical settings (Craske et al., 2013).

12.3 Exposure Therapy

There are several variations of exposure therapy, including:

- In vivo exposure: Directly facing a feared object, situation, or activity in real life. For example, someone with a fear of snakes might be instructed to handle a snake, or someone with social anxiety might be instructed to give a speech in front of an audience.
- Imaginal exposure: Vividly imagining the feared object, situation, or activity. For example, someone with Posttraumatic Stress Disorder might be asked to recall and describe his or her traumatic experience in order to reduce feelings of fear.

- Virtual reality exposure: In some cases, virtual reality technology can be used when in vivo exposure is not practical. For example, someone with a fear of flying might take a virtual flight in the psychologist's office, using equipment that provides the sights, sounds, and smells of an airplane.
- Interoceptive exposure: Deliberately bringing on physical sensations that are harmless, yet feared. For example, someone with Panic Disorder might be instructed to run in place in order to make his or her heart speed up, and therefore learn that this sensation is not dangerous.

Exposure therapy can also be paced in different ways, including:

- Graded exposure: The psychologist helps the client in creating an exposure fear hierarchy, in which feared objects, activities, or situations are ranked according to their difficulty. The process begins with mildly or moderately difficult exposures, then progresses to harder ones.
- Flooding: Using the exposure fear hierarchy to begin with the most difficult tasks, exposing the client to their highest level of fear from the start.
- Systematic desensitization: In some cases, exposure can be combined with relaxation exercises, making the process feel more manageable and helping the client associate the feared objects, activities, or situations with a sense of relaxation.

The mechanism through which exposure therapy works on phobias includes several processes:

- Habituation: Over time, people find that their reactions to feared objects or situations naturally decrease.
- Extinction: Exposure can help weaken the previously learned associations between feared objects, activities, or situations and negative outcomes.
- Self-efficacy: Exposure can help show the client that he/she is capable of confronting his/her fears and managing feelings of anxiety.
- Emotional processing: During exposure, the client can develop new, more realistic beliefs about feared objects, activities, or situations and become more comfortable with the experience of fear.

12.4 Cognitive Therapy for Phobia

Cognitive therapy for phobia can help patients understand and reshape their perceptions and reactions to feared stimuli. A valuable aspect of this process involves identifying patients' perceptions of anxiety before and after exposure therapy, which can help them realize that their initial expectations may have been exaggerated.

Additionally, therapists should collaborate with patients to identify cognitive distortions that contribute to their phobias. Often, individuals exhibit a set of cognitive distortions that manifest across multiple disorders, and addressing these patterns can enhance the effectiveness of therapy.

It is also important to teach patients that not fearing spiders does not imply that one must touch them or engage in extreme behaviors concerning spiders. Psychotherapists should mention to the patient that they can still actively avoid spiders (or FBI, if their delusion or hallucination concerns FBI)—after all, some can be poisonous. Importantly, the therapist should emphasize that those without arachnophobia consciously avoid spiders out of free will and agency, whereas those with arachnophobia do so without free will and agency.

12.5 Case Vignette of Application of Treating Phobia in Patient with Schizophrenia

Tom, a 35-year-old man diagnosed with paranoid schizophrenia, had been stable on antipsychotic medication for the past year but continued to experience significant paranoid thoughts about government surveillance. During his initial assessment, he unexpectedly revealed an intense fear of spiders that significantly impacted his daily functioning. "I know it sounds silly," he said, looking embarrassed, "with everything else going on in my head. But spiders terrify me more than anything. I can't even look at pictures of them."

The therapist recognized an opportunity to use exposure therapy for his specific phobia as a concrete, manageable starting point that could later inform work with his paranoid symptoms. Unlike his complex surveillance fears, the spider phobia presented a clearer target for intervention.

During the assessment session, Tom described his spider-related behaviors: "I get really anxious when I see spiders in my apartment. If I spot one, I either have to get someone else to remove it or I use half a can of bug spray from a distance. I always check behind the shower curtain before using the bathroom, and I get really nervous about the dark corners in my basement storage room. I've missed a few appointments when I've found spiders near my front door."

The therapist noticed similarities between these safety behaviors and those related to his paranoid symptoms (checking for surveillance devices, keeping windows covered, feeling watched), but initially maintained focus solely on the spider phobia:**Therapist**: Would you be interested in learning some techniques that might help with the spider fear first?
Tom: Maybe… but I don't want to see any real spiders.
Therapist: We'd start with whatever feels manageable to you. You'd be in control of each step.
Tom: Like what?
Therapist: There are many possible steps before ever encountering a real spider. We could begin with just talking about them, then maybe look at cartoon drawings when you're ready.

They developed a hierarchy of spider-related exposures, starting with the least anxiety-provoking:

1. Saying the word "spider".
2. Looking at cartoon drawings.

3. Viewing stylized logos/symbols of spiders.
4. Looking at realistic drawings.
5. Viewing photographs of small spiders.
6. Watching videos of spiders behind glass.
7. Being in the same room as a contained spider.
8. Looking at a contained spider up close.

Here's an example of a session focusing on the first exposure exercise, demonstrating how the therapist validated fear while encouraging approach behavior:

Tom: Even just saying the word makes my heart race.
Therapist: That's a normal response when we face something scary. What's happening in your body right now?
Tom: My palms are sweaty. My chest feels tight.
Therapist: Would you be willing to notice those sensations while we sit here together? They tend to decrease on their own with time.
Tom: I can try… it's different than my other fears. I know exactly what I'm afraid of.
Therapist: What makes this fear different?
Tom: With sp…spiders, I can point to them. My other fears are harder to pin down.

By week 4, Tom had progressed to viewing photographs of small spiders. A pivotal moment occurred during this session:**Tom**: Something weird happened. The first photo still scared me, but by the fifth one, my heart wasn't racing as much.
Therapist: What do you make of that change?
Tom: I guess… fear can get tired? Like it runs out of steam if you face it enough?
Therapist: That's an interesting observation about how fear works. What are your thoughts about that?
Tom: It makes me wonder… about my other fears…

The therapist noticed this organic connection but maintained focus on the spider work:**Therapist**: Shall we try one more spider photo today?
Tom: Yeah. It's still scary, but now I'm curious about what happens to the fear.

By week 8, Tom had progressed to watching videos of spiders. During one session, he made another connection:**Tom**: You know how we talked about fear of getting tired? Yesterday, I was sure someone had planted a camera on my TV. Usually, I'd unplug it and cover it up. But I remembered what we learned about the spider photos—how the fear gets less intense if you sit with it. So I tried just sitting with that fear too. Just watching it, like we do with the spider videos.
Therapist: What did you notice when you tried that?
Tom: It was hard. Really hard. But after about 20 min, the fear did get a little quieter. Not gone, but… manageable.

The case illustrates how treating a specific phobia can serve as a concrete demonstration of fear habituation principles. The therapist maintained focus on the spider phobia work, allowing the patient to make his own connections to paranoid symptoms. This approach provided Tom with first-hand experience of exposure principles in a less threatening context, building his confidence in applying these insights to other fears.

By week 12, Tom had successfully progressed to being in the same room as a contained spider and had begun independently applying the principles of exposure to some of his

paranoid fears:**Tom**: The spider work taught me something important. Fear is just fear—whether it's about spiders or surveillance. It follows the same rules. If you run, it grows. If you face it, it eventually gets tired.
Therapist: You've learned a lot about how fear works.
Tom: Yeah. I'm not saying all my fears are like the spider fear. But knowing how to work with fear itself… that helps with everything.

The success with the spider phobia treatment served as both a confidence builder and a practical demonstration of how facing fears leads to their reduction. The therapist allowed these insights to emerge naturally from Tom's experience rather than drawing explicit parallels, maintaining the patient's agency in applying these learnings to his paranoid symptoms.

References

Craske, M. G., Wittchen, U., Bogels, S., Stein, M. B., Andrews, G., & Lebeu, R. (2013). *Severity measure for specific phobia*. American Psychiatric Association.

Wolitzky-Taylor, K. B., Horowitz, J. D., Powers, M. B., & Telch, M. J. (2008). Psychological approaches in the treatment of specific phobias: A meta-analysis. *Clinical Psychology Review, 28*(6), 1021–1037. https://doi.org/10.1016/j.cpr.2008.02.007

Chapter 13
Treating Social Anxiety Disorder in Psychosis

Abstract This chapter explains why treating social anxiety disorder is central in managing psychosis, given its strong links with paranoid ideation and the vicious cycle of negative social experiences and avoidance. It reviews assessment using the Social Phobia Inventory and Liebowitz Social Anxiety Scale, then summarizes a Clark and Wells-based CBT program adapted for psychosis. Core components include psychoeducation, video feedback, reduction of self-focused attention and safety behaviors, Attention Training Technique, behavioral experiments, imagery rescripting, and in vivo exposure. A case vignette with a patient with schizophrenia illustrates how remission of social anxiety expands the range of feasible interventions for paranoid delusions and other socially driven psychotic symptoms.

Keywords Social anxiety · Safety behaviors · Attention training · Imagery rescripting · In vivo exposure

13.1 Goals of Treating Social Anxiety Disorder for Psychosis

Treating social anxiety disorder is one of the most important goals in the treatment of psychosis. Paranoia and social anxiety have been shown to be well correlated (Horton et al., 2014). The main goal in treating social anxiety disorder in the context of psychosis is to reduce the social anxiety component of paranoid symptoms. A maintenance factor of paranoid delusions is the negative feedback loop created by negative social experiences, negative appraisals of situations, and a lack of positive social experiences, due to low motivation to seek social interactions following a history of negative social experience.

With social anxiety disorder in remission, the management of paranoid delusions and other psychotic disorders related to social anxiety will be much easier. Without it being in remission, our treatment tools become limited. For example, we cannot conduct behavioral experiments because the patient may feel anxious even at the thought of doing the experiment. The NICE guidelines (2013) recommend CBT for treating social anxiety disorder, specifying 14 sessions of 90 min each for the Clark

E. S. Jaya, *Cognitive Behavioral Therapy for Psychosis as a Syndrome*,
https://doi.org/10.1007/978-981-95-9203-6_13

and Wells model or 16 sessions total (15 sessions of 60 min plus one 90-min exposure session) for the Heimberg model. Psychotherapists are free to choose the social anxiety disorder measurement and techniques relevant to the patient.

13.2 Measuring Social Anxiety Disorder

13.2.1 Social Phobia Inventory (SPIN)

The Social Phobia Inventory (SPIN) (Connor et al., 2000) is a self-report questionnaire used to assess the severity of social anxiety disorder (social phobia). The SPIN consists of 17 items that measure fear, avoidance, and physical discomfort related to social situations. Respondents rate how much these symptoms have bothered them in the past week on a scale from 0 (not at all) to 4 (extremely).

The total score ranges from 0 to 68, with higher scores indicating greater severity of social anxiety. SPIN scores can be interpreted as follows: 0–20 (mild), 21–30 (moderate), 31–40 (severe), and 41–68 (very severe). The SPIN has been shown to have good internal consistency, test-retest reliability, and validity, making it a widely used tool for both clinical and research purposes (Connor et al., 2000).

13.2.2 Liebowitz Social Anxiety Scale (LSAS)

The Liebowitz Social Anxiety Scale (LSAS) (Liebowitz, 1987) is a clinician-administered or self-report questionnaire used to assess social anxiety disorder. It consists of 24 items, with 13 items focusing on performance situations (e.g., public speaking) and 11 items addressing social interaction situations (e.g., meeting strangers). Respondents rate both their fear and avoidance of these situations over the past week on two separate scales: one for fear (0 = none to 3 = severe) and one for avoidance (0 = never to 3 = usually).

The total score ranges from 0 to 144, with higher scores reflecting more severe social anxiety. Severity categories are typically defined as follows: 55–65 (moderate), 65–80 (marked), 80–95 (severe), and over 95 (very severe). The LSAS has demonstrated strong psychometric properties, including high internal consistency and good convergent validity, making it a robust tool for assessing social anxiety in both clinical and research settings (Liebowitz, 1987).

13.3 Clark and Well's CBT for Social Anxiety Disorder

13.3.1 Psychoeducation

Psychoeducation serves as the foundation of CBT for Social Anxiety Disorder (SAD), providing individuals with comprehensive information about the nature of social anxiety, its triggers, and maintenance factors. This phase aims to enhance awareness of the cognitive and behavioral aspects of social anxiety, normalizing the experience and fostering a better understanding of the cognitive model underlying SAD. Psychoeducation also includes information about the treatment rationale, focusing on the role of cognitive biases and safety behaviors in maintaining social anxiety (Clark & Wells, 1995).

13.3.2 Video Feedback

Video Feedback constitutes a vital component of CBT for SAD. This technique involves recording social interactions or performances and subsequently reviewing these recordings with the therapist. Video Feedback aims to increase self-awareness by identifying negative self-perceptions, safety behaviors, and cognitive distortions exhibited during social situations. Through this process, individuals gain a more objective perspective, enabling them to challenge and modify their negative self-evaluations (Clark et al., 2003).

13.3.3 Self-Focused Attention and Safety Behaviors

Addressing self-focused attention and safety behaviors is essential within CBT for SAD. This stage involves identifying and challenging the habit of self-focused attention, where individuals excessively monitor themselves during social situations, often leading to increased self-criticism. Therapists help individuals reduce self-focused attention and eliminate safety behaviors, such as avoiding eye contact or constantly checking one's appearance, by encouraging more external and less self-referential focus during social interactions (Clark & Wells, 1995).

13.3.4 Attention Training Technique (ATT)

The Attention Training Technique (ATT) is a central component of CBT for SAD. ATT involves redirecting attention externally, away from internal self-focused attention. The technique includes attention-shifting exercises and attention-focusing tasks during social situations, helping individuals reduce their self-focused attention and self-monitoring tendencies. Through practice, individuals learn to allocate attention externally, fostering more adaptive perceptions of social situations (Clark & Wells, 1995).

13.3.5 Behavioral Experiments

Behavioral experiments are integral within CBT for SAD and involve conducting structured tasks or role-plays in social situations to test negative beliefs and predictions. These experiments aim to challenge and modify maladaptive beliefs related to social interactions. Individuals are guided to test their assumptions systematically, leading to the collection of evidence that contradicts negative self-beliefs. Through these experiments, individuals gain more realistic and less threatening perspectives on social situations (Clark & Wells, 1995).

13.3.6 Imagery Rescripting

Imagery Rescripting is a technique targeting traumatic or aversive memories related to social situations in SAD. This method involves modifying negative images or memories linked to social experiences by creating new positive mental images or altering the existing negative images. The goal is to diminish the emotional impact of past experiences, reducing the emotional distress and negative self-beliefs associated with those memories (Wild et al., 2008).

13.3.7 In Vivo Exposure

In Vivo Exposure is a fundamental component of CBT for SAD, involving gradual exposure to feared social situations. Individuals systematically confront anxiety-provoking situations or scenarios that they typically avoid due to social anxiety. Through exposure and habituation, individuals learn to tolerate and manage anxiety in real-life situations, leading to a reduction in avoidance behaviors and increased confidence in social interactions (Clark & Wells, 1995).

13.4 Case Vignette of Application of Treating Social Anxiety Disorder in Patient with Schizophrenia

David, a 25-year-old man with paranoid schizophrenia, had achieved stability on antipsychotic medication but continued to experience significant social anxiety alongside his paranoid beliefs. While he believed that certain organizations were monitoring him, he also displayed marked fear of social interactions that went beyond his paranoid concerns. "Even when I'm feeling okay about the surveillance stuff," he explained, "I still can't talk to people. I get so nervous I might say something stupid or weird."

During the assessment, David described avoiding most social situations, particularly interactions with strangers. He ordered groceries online, used self-checkout when he had to shop in person, and had declined several job opportunities that would require customer interaction. His therapist noted that while some avoidance stemmed from paranoid beliefs, he also showed classic social anxiety symptoms like fear of judgment, excessive self-consciousness, and worry about appearing awkward.

The therapist introduced the concept of attention training:**Therapist**: When you're talking to someone, where does your attention usually go?
David: Everywhere. Their face to see if they think I'm weird. My hands to make sure they're not shaking. The exit in case I need to leave. My thoughts to check if what I'm about to say sounds normal.
Therapist: That's a lot to track. What if we practiced putting our attention somewhere specific?
David: Like where?
Therapist: We could start here. When we talk, try focusing just on what I'm saying, rather than monitoring yourself.

They practiced this during sessions, with David gradually learning to redirect his attention outward rather than maintaining hypervigilant self-focus. The therapist would deliberately include pauses or mild jokes in the conversation, giving David opportunities to notice when his attention drifted inward.

Here's an example of setting up a behavioral experiment:**Therapist**: What do you predict would happen if you asked the coffee shop barista how their day is going?
David: They'd probably think I'm weird for asking. Or they might be suspicious about why I want to know.
Therapist: Would you be willing to test that prediction? We could watch other customers first, see how baristas typically respond to small talk.
David: Maybe... but what if they're actually part of—(referring to his paranoid beliefs)
Therapist: Let's focus on the social interaction part first. What's the shortest, simplest question you could ask?
David: I guess just 'How's your day going?' That's pretty normal, right?
Therapist: Exactly. Would you be willing to observe how many customers ask similar questions?

They developed a series of behavioral experiments, starting with observation tasks:

1. Sit in the coffee shop and count how many customers engage in small talk.
2. Note the typical length and content of customer-barista interactions.
3. Observe barista responses to simple questions.
4. Practice ordering while making brief eye contact.
5. Ask one simple question beyond the coffee order.

During an observation session, David made an important discovery:**David**: I watched for an hour. At least half the customers chat with the baristas. And the baristas seem… happy about it?
Therapist: What surprised you about what you saw?
David: Nobody got rejected or looked stupid. Even when people fumbled their words, the baristas just acted normal.
Therapist: What might that tell us about social interactions?
David: Maybe… people are more focused on their own stuff than judging others?

This insight began to influence his broader thought patterns. During a later session:**David**: Something interesting happened. I tried asking the barista about their day, like we practiced. She smiled and actually seemed happy to answer. Then I realized—if she's just a normal person who enjoys quick chats with customers, maybe she's not gathering information about me either.
Therapist: What was it like to have that experience?
David: Kind of… freeing? Like, maybe not everyone is as focused on me as I thought.

They continued building on these experiences with more behavioral experiments:**Therapist**: Would you be willing to try something new this week? We could explore how people typically respond when asked for simple directions.
David: That seems scary… but like the coffee shop, maybe I could watch others do it first?
Therapist: Good thinking. What would you want to observe?
David: How many people stop to help. If they seem annoyed. The normal length of these conversations.

By week 10, David had successfully completed several behavioral experiments, each providing evidence that contradicted both his social anxiety and paranoid beliefs:**David**: The more I talk to strangers, the more I realize most people are just… people. They're not analyzing everything I do. They're not reporting on me. They're usually just trying to get through their day, like me.
Therapist: How has this affected your comfort with social interactions?
David: I'm still nervous, but it's different now. I'm more focused on the actual conversation instead of all my fears about it. And when I'm focused outward like we practiced, the paranoid thoughts don't grab me as much.

The case illustrates how treating social anxiety through attention training and behavioral experiments can naturally lead to reality-testing of paranoid beliefs. The therapist maintained focus on social anxiety techniques while allowing David to make his own connections about the true nature of social interactions. This approach provided both concrete social skills and a new framework for understanding human behavior, gradually reducing both social anxiety and paranoid ideation.

The success with social anxiety treatment served as a practical demonstration that people are generally focused on their own concerns rather than scrutinizing or monitoring others. The therapist allowed these insights to emerge naturally from David's experiences rather than directly challenging paranoid beliefs, maintaining the patient's agency in developing new understandings of social interactions.

References

Clark, D. M., & Wells, A. (1995). A cognitive model of social phobia. In R. G. Heimberg, M. R. Liebowitz, D. A. Hope, & F. R. Schneier (Eds.), *Social phobia: Diagnosis, assessment, and treatment* (pp. 69–93). Guilford Press.

Clark, D. M., et al. (2003). Video feedback in the treatment of social phobia. *Behavior Research and Therapy, 41*(2), 179–187.

Connor, K. M., Davidson, J. R., Churchill, L. E., Sherwood, A., Foa, E., & Weisler, R. H. (2000). Psychometric properties of the social phobia inventory (SPIN): New self-rating scale. *The British Journal of Psychiatry, 176*(4), 379–386. https://doi.org/10.1192/bjp.176.4.379

Horton, L. E., Barrantes-Vidal, N., Silvia, P. J., & Kwapil, T. R. (2014). Worries about being judged versus being harmed: Disentangling the association of social anxiety and paranoia with schizotypy. *PLoS ONE, 9*(6), e96269. https://doi.org/10.1371/journal.pone.0096269

Liebowitz, M. R. (1987). Social phobia. *Modern Problems of Pharmacopsychiatry, 22*, 141–173. https://doi.org/10.1159/000414022

National Institute for Health and Care Excellence. (2013). *Social anxiety disorder: Recognition, assessment and treatment* (clinical guideline CG159). https://www.nice.org.uk/guidance/cg159

Wild, J., et al. (2008). Changing views of imagery rescripting: A qualitative study of patients' experience. *Behavioural and Cognitive Psychotherapy, 36*(2), 129–147.

References

Chapter 14
Treating General Anxiety Disorder in Psychosis

Abstract This chapter presents a module for treating generalized anxiety disorder in psychosis, focused on lowering the patient's baseline anxiety level to stabilize psychotic symptoms. It begins with the rationale for targeting worry and outlines assessment using the GAD-7. The treatment sequence consists of anxiety management training (e.g., relaxation and physiological regulation skills), cognitive restructuring of worry-based thoughts, and situational exposure to avoided contexts. A case vignette shows how these components are implemented with a patient with schizophrenia and how reduction in generalized anxiety can lead to improvements in psychotic symptom burden and day-to-day functioning.

Keywords Generalized anxiety · Cognitive restructuring · Worry management · Situational exposure · Anxiety training

14.1 Goals of Treating General Anxiety Disorder for Psychosis

The main goal in treating generalized anxiety disorder (GAD) for psychosis is to make sure that the basal anxiety rate of the patient is good. Research suggests that generalized anxiety is linked to psychotic symptoms (Hartley et al., 2013; Jaya et al., 2018), and psychotherapy targeting worry has been effective in reducing these symptoms (Freeman et al., 2015). The NICE guidelines (2020) recommend 12–15 weekly sessions of either CBT or applied relaxation for the treatment of generalized anxiety disorder. Psychotherapists are free to choose the GAD measurement and techniques relevant to the patient.

E. S. Jaya, *Cognitive Behavioral Therapy for Psychosis as a Syndrome*,
https://doi.org/10.1007/978-981-95-9203-6_14

14.2 Measuring General Anxiety Disorder

14.2.1 Generalized Anxiety Disorder Scale-7 (GAD-7)

The Generalized Anxiety Disorder Scale-7 (GAD-7) (Spitzer et al., 2006) is a self-report screening questionnaire for generalized anxiety disorder (GAD) and its severity. It consists of seven items that assess how the subject has been feeling nervous, worrying too much, having trouble relaxing, and feeling restless in the last 2 weeks. These symptoms correlate with the DSM-IV diagnostic criteria for GAD. Subjects are asked to rate the frequency and severity of their symptoms on a scale from 0 (not at all) to 3 (nearly every day). The severity of the anxiety is determined by the sum score of the items, which ranges from 0 to 21, categorized as follows: 0–4 (minimal), 5–9 (mild), 10–14 (moderate), and 15–21 (severe). The GAD-7 has demonstrated good reliability and validity (Spitzer et al., 2006).

14.3 Anxiety Management Training (Suinn, 1977)

Anxiety Management Training is a foundational phase in Cognitive Behavioral Therapy (CBT) that emphasizes teaching individuals a wide array of strategies and techniques to effectively manage and alleviate symptoms of anxiety. This crucial stage involves educating clients about the physiological and psychological aspects of anxiety, including its triggers and the body's stress response. Drawing from Suinn's pioneering work (1977) in behavioral rehearsal combined with relaxation methods, this phase often includes various relaxation techniques, such as diaphragmatic breathing, progressive muscle relaxation (PMR), autogenic training, and mindfulness practices. These techniques aim to help individuals recognize the physical manifestations of anxiety and develop tools to reduce immediate anxiety symptoms.

Furthermore, Anxiety Management Training involves psychoeducation about anxiety-inducing situations and common anxiety-provoking thoughts. It delves into identifying personal stressors and anxious triggers, helping individuals to recognize patterns that exacerbate anxiety symptoms. By fostering an understanding of the mind-body connection and the role of stress in triggering anxiety, clients learn practical skills to self-regulate and intervene during heightened anxiety states.

14.4 Cognitive Restructuring

Cognitive Restructuring, a cornerstone of CBT, focuses on recognizing and modifying maladaptive thought patterns associated with anxiety. This phase, initially introduced by Beck (1976), involves in-depth exploration of cognitive distortions, including catastrophizing, overgeneralization, black-and-white thinking, and personalization. Through guided exploration, clients learn to identify and challenge these irrational beliefs, examining evidence that supports or refutes their anxious thoughts. Therapists use various cognitive techniques, such as Socratic questioning, thought records, and cognitive restructuring worksheets, to assist individuals in reframing irrational beliefs. This process aids in developing more realistic, balanced, and adaptive thinking patterns, enabling clients to reduce anxiety by altering their interpretations of situations.

Cognitive restructuring aims to enhance clients' awareness of the connections between thoughts, emotions, and behaviors. It involves identifying automatic negative thoughts associated with anxiety-provoking situations and replacing them with rational, evidence-based alternatives. By recognizing and challenging cognitive distortions, individuals gradually shift their perspective, reducing the intensity and frequency of anxious feelings and responses.

14.5 Situational Exposure

Situational exposure is a pivotal and systematic component of CBT for anxiety disorders, designed to help individuals confront and overcome their fears in a controlled manner. This gradual and hierarchical exposure approach, based on Öst's paradigm (1996), involves creating an anxiety hierarchy, which consists of feared situations ranked from least to most anxiety-provoking. The process initiates with exposure to less distressing scenarios and progressively advances toward more challenging situations.

Therapists work collaboratively with clients to devise exposure exercises tailored to their specific fears, ensuring a systematic and graded exposure process. These exercises may involve real-life exposures or virtual reality-based simulations, depending on the client's comfort level and the nature of their anxiety triggers. Through repeated and prolonged exposures to feared stimuli or situations, individuals learn that their anticipated catastrophic outcomes are less likely to occur. This process facilitates habituation, enabling clients to develop a more accurate perception of the feared situations, ultimately reducing anxiety responses.

14.6 Case Vignette of Application of Treating General Anxiety Disorder in Patient with Schizophrenia

Linda, a 30-year-old woman with paranoid schizophrenia, worked part-time as a data entry clerk. While her psychotic symptoms were relatively stable on medication, she struggled with constant worry and tension. Her anxiety manifested in both typical GAD symptoms and increased paranoid thinking throughout the workday. "I worry about everything," she explained during assessment. "Bills, health, making mistakes at work… and then I start thinking my coworkers are documenting my errors to build a case against me."

Her therapist noticed that Linda's baseline anxiety seemed to fuel her paranoid thoughts, particularly at work. "The more tense I get about deadlines, the more I notice people walking past my desk," she said. "By afternoon, my shoulders are so tight, and I'm convinced the FBI is watching me mess up." The therapist introduced Progressive Muscle Relaxation (PMR) as a concrete skill for managing physical tension:**Therapist**: Before we address any specific worries, would you be interested in learning a technique to help your body feel calmer?
Linda: I've tried deep breathing, but it's hard to remember when I'm stressed.
Therapist: This is a bit different. It's about noticing and releasing tension systematically. Would you like to try a short version right now?
Linda: As long as I can keep my eyes open. (*referring to her paranoid concerns*)
Therapist: Of course. You're in control of how we do this.

They started with a modified PMR routine focusing on muscles that could be tensed and released discreetly at work:

1. Hands: making and releasing fists.
2. Arms: pressing and releasing arms against chair.
3. Shoulders: gentle shrug and release.
4. Feet: pressing and releasing against floor.
5. Facial muscles: brief tension and release.

During the learning process, the therapist emphasized how PMR could be broken down into subtle movements suitable for the workplace:**Therapist**: How might you practice this at your desk without drawing the coworkers' attention?
Linda: I could do the hand part while pretending to stretch. Maybe the shoulders too.
Therapist: Good thinking. When would be the best times to practice?
Linda: Maybe during my scheduled breaks? That's when I'm supposed to pause anyway.

They developed a routine that fit naturally into her workday:

- Morning: Full PMR session before leaving for work.
- Mid-morning break: Focus on hands and shoulders.
- Lunch: Brief full-body sequence in her car.
- Afternoon break: Focus on facial muscles and feet.
- Evening: Complete PMR session at home.

By week 3, Linda noticed initial changes:**Linda**: I tried the hand exercise during my morning break. It was the first time I noticed how tense I'd gotten just from typing.
Therapist: What happened when you released that tension?
Linda: It was easier to focus on the actual work instead of worrying about mistakes.
Therapist: Would you be willing to track when you notice tension and when you use PMR this week?

Week 5 brought an important observation:**Linda**: Something interesting happened. Usually by lunch, I'm convinced the coworkers are talking about my work. But yesterday, I did the PMR in my car first, and I realized I was just hearing normal office chatter. They are not talking about me at all or anything close to my work.

Therapist: What do you make of that difference?
Linda: I think… when I'm really tense, everything seems more threatening.

The therapist encouraged this insight while maintaining focus on the physical relaxation practice:**Therapist**: Would you be interested in experimenting with adding another brief practice time?
Linda: Maybe right when I get back from lunch? That's when things usually start feeling more… suspicious.

By week 8, Linda had established a consistent relaxation routine and noticed broader changes:**Linda**: The PMR is becoming automatic now. Sometimes I catch myself doing the hand exercise without even thinking about it.
Therapist: What changes have you noticed since establishing this routine?
Linda: Well, my shoulders don't hurt anymore. But also… it's easier to stay focused on my tasks. When I'm physically relaxed, I don't get so caught up in wondering what others are thinking.

Week 12 brought evidence of how reduced physical tension affected both her anxiety and paranoid thoughts:**Linda**: My supervisor gave me more responsibilities last week. Usually, that would convince me they were setting me up to fail. But I've been doing my relaxation exercises, and I can think about it differently now.
Therapist: What's different in how you're thinking about it?
Linda: When I'm not so tense, it's easier to see it as a normal work thing. Like maybe they actually trust me to do more?

The case illustrates how regular PMR practice can create a positive cycle: reduced physical tension leads to clearer thinking, which enables better reality testing, which in turn reduces both anxiety and paranoid ideation. The therapist maintained focus on the concrete skill of physical relaxation while allowing Linda to discover the broader impacts herself. By week 16, Linda reported significant improvements in her work functioning:**Linda**: I was able to join a team project last week. I still get nervous, but now I have tools for managing it. When I keep my body calm, my mind doesn't jump to the worst conclusions.
Therapist: You've developed quite a consistent practice.
Linda: Yes. I've learned that anxiety builds up in my body throughout the day. If I keep releasing the tension, everything else feels more manageable—the worries, the suspicious thoughts, all of it.

The success with PMR served as both a practical coping strategy and a demonstration of how physical state affects mental state. The therapist allowed these insights to emerge naturally from Linda's experience rather than making explicit connections, maintaining the patient's agency in applying these learnings to her paranoid symptoms.

References

Beck, A. T. (1976). *Cognitive therapy and the emotional disorders*. Penguin.
Freeman, D., Dunn, G., Startup, H., Pugh, K., Cordwell, J., Mander, H., Černis, E., Wingham, G., Shirvell, K., & Kingdon, D. (2015). Effects of cognitive behaviour therapy for worry on

persecutory delusions in patients with psychosis (WIT): A parallel, single-blind, randomised controlled trial with a mediation analysis. *The Lancet Psychiatry, 2*(4), 305–313. https://doi.org/10.1016/S2215-0366(15)00039-5

Hartley, S., Barrowclough, C., & Haddock, G. (2013). Anxiety and depression in psychosis: A systematic review of associations with positive psychotic symptoms. *Acta Psychiatrica Scandinavica, 128*(5), 327–346. https://doi.org/10.1111/acps.12080

Jaya, E. S., Ascone, L., & Lincoln, T. M. (2018). A longitudinal mediation analysis of the effect of negative-self-schemas on positive symptoms via negative affect. *Psychological Medicine, 48*(8), 1299–1307. https://doi.org/10.1017/S003329171700277X

National Institute for Health and Care Excellence. (2020). *Generalised anxiety disorder and panic disorder in adults: Management* (clinical guideline CG113). https://www.nice.org.uk/guidance/cg113

Öst, L. G. (1996). One-session group treatment of spider phobia. *Behaviour Research and Therapy, 34*(9), 707–715. https://doi.org/10.1016/0005-7967(96)00022-8

Spitzer, R. L., Kroenke, K., Williams, J. B., & Löwe, B. (2006). A brief measure for assessing generalized anxiety disorder: The GAD-7. *Archives of Internal Medicine, 166*(10), 1092–1097.

Suinn, R. M. (1977). Behavioral rehearsal with relaxation in treating test anxiety. *Journal of Counseling Psychology, 24*(5), 414–422.

Chapter 15
Treating Panic Disorder and Agoraphobia in Psychosis

Abstract This chapter details the treatment of panic disorder and agoraphobia in psychosis, highlighting how mastery over panic sensations can reduce overall fear and support psychosis management. After stating the treatment goals, it introduces the Panic Disorder Severity Scale for assessment. The intervention includes psychoeducation about panic, breathing retraining, progressive muscular relaxation, cognitive restructuring of catastrophic misinterpretations, interoceptive exposure to feared bodily sensations, and in vivo exposure to avoided situations. A case vignette illustrates how this structured program is delivered to a patient with schizophrenia and how gains in panic control can indirectly weaken paranoid beliefs and functional avoidance.

Keywords Panic disorder · Interoceptive exposure · Breathing retraining · Agoraphobia · Anxiety sensitivity

15.1 Goals of Treating Panic Disorder for Psychosis

The main goal in treating panic disorder for psychosis is to improve the quality of life of the patient and prevent psychotherapy progress stagnation in the later stage particularly if there is agoraphobia that limits social interaction. Panic disorder has been shown to be associated with psychotic symptoms (Buckley et al., 2009; Freeman et al., 2019), and psychotherapy targeting panic disorder has been effective in improving these symptoms (Hofmann et al., 2000). The NICE guidelines (2020) recommend 7–14 h of CBT, delivered as weekly sessions lasting 1 to 2 h, for the treatment of panic disorder. Psychotherapists are free to choose the panic disorder measurement and techniques relevant to the patient.

E. S. Jaya, *Cognitive Behavioral Therapy for Psychosis as a Syndrome*,
https://doi.org/10.1007/978-981-95-9203-6_15

15.2 Measuring Panic Disorder

15.2.1 Panic Disorder Severity Scale

The Panic Disorder Severity Scale (PDSS) (Shear et al., 1997) is a 7-item standardized interview administered by clinicians to measure various dimensions of panic disorder and its associated symptoms. The seven dimensions include: 1) frequency of panic attacks; 2) distress during panic attacks; 3) anticipatory anxiety (worry about future panic attacks); 4) agoraphobic fear and avoidance; 5) interoceptive fear and avoidance (i.e., apprehension and avoidance of bodily sensations); 6) impairment or interference in work functioning; and 7) impairment or interference in social functioning. Depending on the answers of the patient, clinicians rate the severity of each aspect on a 0 to 4 scale, with higher ratings reflecting a greater symptom severity. The total score is the average of the scores on the seven items. The PDSS offers a simple and efficient way to monitor the severity of panic disorder in those with an existing diagnosis, rather than serving as a diagnostic tool. It has shown excellent interrater reliability, as well as good convergent and discriminant validity (Shear et al., 1997).

15.3 Psychoeducation

Psychoeducation plays a pivotal role in the comprehensive treatment approach for panic disorder within the Cognitive Behavioral Therapy (CBT) framework. This foundational step involves imparting essential knowledge about panic symptoms, their physiological underpinnings, and the cognitive behavioral model that underscores panic attacks. This phase educates patients about the fight-or-flight response, cognitive biases, and the perpetuating cycle of panic. The primary aim is to normalize the symptoms experienced during panic attacks and reinforce the understanding that these sensations, although distressing, are not harmful. Psychoeducation also involves empowering patients with tools to recognize and cope with panic symptoms effectively in their daily lives (Barlow, 2002).

15.4 Breathing Retraining

Breathing retraining constitutes a crucial aspect of managing panic attacks. It focuses on correcting hyperventilation, a common phenomenon during panic episodes that can exacerbate symptoms. Techniques such as diaphragmatic breathing and paced breathing are introduced to restore normal respiration patterns. The goal is to reduce hyperventilation-induced symptoms like dizziness, chest tightness, and breathlessness by guiding individuals to adopt controlled, slower breathing techniques (Meuret et al., 2010).

15.5 Progressive Muscular Relaxation (PMR)

Progressive Muscular Relaxation (PMR) serves as an effective relaxation technique employed in panic disorder treatment. This systematic method involves tensing and relaxing muscle groups, progressively inducing a state of deep relaxation. PMR aims to alleviate the physical tension and discomfort often associated with panic attacks, thereby enabling individuals to recognize and manage their physical responses to stress and anxiety (Öst, 1987).

15.6 Cognitive Restructuring

Cognitive restructuring is a core therapeutic strategy that targets the modification of distorted or catastrophic thoughts associated with panic attacks. This cognitive intervention aims to challenge and reframe maladaptive beliefs about the consequences of physical sensations. Through structured exercises and guided inquiry, individuals learn to identify, evaluate, and modify these negative thought patterns, fostering more adaptive and realistic interpretations of bodily sensations (Beck, 2011).

15.7 Interoceptive Exposure

Interoceptive exposure constitutes a fundamental technique within CBT for panic disorder. It involves systematically inducing physical sensations akin to those experienced during panic attacks in a controlled environment. By repeatedly exposing individuals to these sensations, the goal is to reduce their fear and sensitivity to bodily cues, promoting habituation and desensitization to feared bodily sensations (Barlow & Craske, 2007).

15.8 In Vivo Exposure (Suinn 1977)

In vivo exposure, as outlined by Suinn (1977), represents a critical component in the treatment of panic disorder. This therapeutic technique involves real-life exposure to feared situations, environments, or activities that individuals tend to avoid due to their association with panic attacks. Through graded exposure and systematic confrontation, individuals gradually confront their fears, allowing for habituation and a reduction in anxiety responses when encountering previously feared situations. This process assists individuals in reclaiming a sense of control over their lives (Suinn, 1977).

15.9 Case Vignette of Application of Treating Panic Disorder in Patient with Schizophrenia

James, a 27-year-old man with paranoid schizophrenia, had been experiencing frequent panic attacks alongside his psychotic symptoms. While his paranoid beliefs about being pursued were stable on medication, his panic attacks severely limited his mobility. "Sometimes I can't tell what's worse," he admitted during assessment, "thinking someone's after me, or the feeling that I'm about to have a heart attack when I try to leave my apartment."

His most frightening panic symptom was heart palpitations, which he interpreted as signs of impending cardiac arrest. This fear had led to multiple emergency room visits, where medical examinations always came back normal. The panic attacks had severely restricted his life—he avoided public transportation, couldn't go grocery shopping alone, and had recently quit his part-time job at a library.

The therapist introduced the concept of interoceptive exposure, focusing specifically on his fear of heart-related sensations:**Therapist**: Would you be interested in learning more about these physical sensations you're experiencing?
James: You mean the heart problems?
Therapist: The scary sensations in your chest. What if we could practice experiencing them in a safe environment?
James: Practice them? Wouldn't that be dangerous?
Therapist: These sensations can feel very frightening, but they're actually not harmful. Would you be willing to try a small experiment?

They started with psychoeducation about the body's alarm system and the role of the autonomic nervous system. The therapist explained how certain exercises could safely produce similar sensations to those experienced during panic:**Therapist**: What happens to your heart rate when you climb stairs?
James: It speeds up... but that's different. That's normal.
Therapist: Exactly. Today we could try something similar—running in place for 30 seconds. Would you be willing to try that?

They developed a hierarchy of heart-related exposures:

1. Running in place for 30 s.
2. Climbing one flight of stairs.
3. Doing 10 jumping jacks.
4. Spinning in a chair for 30 s.
5. Breathing through a thin straw (to create mild chest discomfort).

During the first exposure session:**James**: My heart is beating faster...

Therapist: That's exactly what we want. Can you stay with that sensation? What number would you give your fear right now, 0 to 10?
James: Seven… but it's not getting worse.
Therapist: Notice that. The sensation is there, but you're handling it.

By week 3, James made an important observation:**James**: Something weird happened at home. I felt my heart racing, but instead of calling 911, I remembered our exercises. I realized it felt just like when we do the jumping jacks.
Therapist: What did you do?
James: I just… let it happen. It was scary, but it passed, just like in our sessions.

Week 5 brought an unexpected insight:**James**: You know what I noticed? When I'm not so scared of the heart stuff, I can think more clearly about other things too. Like yesterday, I heard footsteps behind me on the street. Usually, that would trigger both paranoia and panic. But I was able to focus on managing the physical symptoms, and somehow that made the paranoid thoughts less intense.
Therapist: What do you think about that connection?
James: Maybe when I'm not fighting the panic, I have more energy to deal with other fears?

The therapist encouraged continued practice while letting James make his own connections. By week 8, he reported significant changes:**James**: I took the bus yesterday. First time in months.
Therapist: How did you manage that?
James: I told myself it's just body sensations—like our exercises. My heart might race, and that's okay. It's not an emergency.
Therapist: What else did you notice during the bus ride?
James: Actually… I was so focused on managing the panic that I didn't have much room for other thoughts. Usually, I'd be convinced other passengers were watching me, but I was too busy practicing what we've learned.

By week 12, the improvements in his panic symptoms had led to substantial functional gains:**James**: I went back to the library job. Part-time for now. My heart still races sometimes, but I know what to do. And you know what's really interesting? When I'm busy at work, focused on tasks and managing any panic symptoms that come up, the paranoid thoughts don't grab me as much.
Therapist: You've made some important discoveries about how different symptoms interact.
James: Yeah. It's like… when I learned I could handle the panic, it gave me confidence to handle other fears too. And being more active leaves less time for paranoid thoughts.

The case illustrates how mastery over panic symptoms through interoceptive exposure can create a foundation for managing other fears. The reduction in panic attacks allowed for increased activity and engagement, which in turn provided natural evidence against paranoid beliefs. The therapist maintained focus on the concrete work of managing panic while allowing James to discover these broader impacts himself.

By week 16, James had expanded his world considerably:**James**: Last week I did something really big—I took the bus to a shopping center. Had some heart racing, used our techniques, got through it. Then I realized… I was out in public, around strangers, and

I was okay. Not just the panic, but the paranoid thoughts too. Being able to handle the physical symptoms somehow makes everything else more manageable.

The success with panic disorder treatment served as both a practical coping strategy and a demonstration that feared sensations could be tolerated. The therapist allowed these insights to emerge naturally from James's experience rather than making explicit connections, maintaining the patient's agency in applying these learnings to his paranoid symptoms.

References

Barlow, D. H. (2002). *Anxiety and its disorders: The nature and treatment of anxiety and panic* (2nd ed.). Guilford Press.

Barlow, D. H., & Craske, M. G. (2007). *Mastery of your anxiety and panic: Workbook* (4th ed.). Oxford University Press.

Beck, J. S. (2011). *Cognitive behavior therapy: Basics and beyond* (2nd ed.). Guilford Press.

Buckley, P. F., Miller, B. J., Lehrer, D. S., & Castle, D. J. (2009). Psychiatric comorbidities and schizophrenia. *Schizophrenia Bulletin, 35*(2), 383–402. https://doi.org/10.1093/schbul/sbn135

Freeman, D., Taylor, K. M., Molodynski, A., & Waite, F. (2019). Treatable clinical intervention targets for patients with schizophrenia. *Schizophrenia Research, 211*, 44–50. https://doi.org/10.1016/j.schres.2019.07.016

Hofmann, S. G., Bufka, L. F., Brady, S. M., Du Rand, C., & Goff, D. C. (2000). Cognitive-behavioral treatment of panic in patients with schizophrenia: Preliminary findings. *Journal of Cognitive Psychotherapy, 14*(4), 381–392.

Meuret, A. E., Rosenfield, D., Seidel, A., Bhaskara, L., & Hofmann, S. G. (2010). Respiratory and cognitive mediators of treatment change in panic disorder: Evidence for intervention specificity. *Journal of Consulting and Clinical Psychology, 78*(5), 691–704. https://doi.org/10.1037/a0019552

National Institute for Health and Care Excellence. (2020). *Generalised anxiety disorder and panic disorder in adults: Management* (clinical guideline CG113). https://www.nice.org.uk/guidance/cg113

Öst, L.-G. (1987). Applied relaxation: Description of a coping technique and review of controlled studies. *Behaviour Research and Therapy, 25*(5), 397–409. https://doi.org/10.1016/0005-7967(87)90017-9

Shear, M. K., Brown, T. A., Barlow, D. H., Money, R., Sholomskas, D. E., Woods, S. W., Gorman, J. M., & Papp, L. A. (1997). Multicenter collaborative panic disorder severity scale. *The American Journal of Psychiatry, 154*(11), 1571–1575. https://doi.org/10.1176/ajp.154.11.1571

Suinn, R. M. (1977). Behavioral rehearsal with relaxation in treating test anxiety. *Journal of Counseling Psychology, 24*(5), 414–422.

Chapter 16
Treating Obsessive-Compulsive Disorder in Psychosis

Abstract This chapter outlines a CBT program for obsessive–compulsive disorder in patients with psychosis, focusing on cases where severe, low-insight OCD symptoms may overlap with or mimic psychotic phenomena. It begins with treatment goals and assessment using instruments such as the Yale–Brown Obsessive-Compulsive Scale, Obsessive-Compulsive Inventory-Revised, and Florida Obsessive-Compulsive Inventory. The core intervention is Exposure and Response Prevention, broken down into exposure control, in vivo and in sensu exposure, choice of gradual versus flooding strategies, and decisions about the degree of response prevention. A case vignette of a patient with schizophrenia demonstrates how ERP is implemented and how successful treatment of OCD can also improve psychotic symptoms that were partly driven by compulsive processes.

Keywords Obsessive–compulsive symptoms • Exposure and response prevention • Intrusive thoughts • Compulsive behavior • ERP

16.1 Goals of Treating Obsessive-Compulsive Disorder for Psychosis

The main goal to treat obsessive-compulsive disorder (OCD) for psychosis is to improve psychotic symptoms that may actually be a manifestation of severe, lacking insight, obsessive-compulsive symptoms. OCD is associated with psychotic symptoms (Buckley et al., 2009), and psychotherapy for OCD has been shown to improve these symptoms (Tundo & Necci, 2016). The NICE guidelines (2005) recommend up to 10 h of CBT, including Exposure and Response Prevention (ERP), for mild functional impairment, and more than 10 h for moderate or severe impairment. Psychotherapists are free to choose the OCD measurement and techniques relevant to the patient.

E. S. Jaya, *Cognitive Behavioral Therapy for Psychosis as a Syndrome*,
https://doi.org/10.1007/978-981-95-9203-6_16

16.2 Measuring Obsessive-Compulsive Disorder

16.2.1 Yale-Brown Obsessive-Compulsive Scale (Y-BOCS)

The Yale-Brown Obsessive-Compulsive Scale (Y-BOCS) (Goodman et al., 1989) is a clinician-administered assessment used to measure the severity of obsessive-compulsive disorder (OCD) symptoms. The Y-BOCS consists of ten core items divided into two subscales: obsessions and compulsions. Each item assesses the time spent on obsessions and compulsions, associated distress, interference with functioning, resistance, and control over symptoms. Respondents rate these items on a scale from 0 (no symptoms) to 4 (extreme symptoms). The total score ranges from 0 to 40 and is categorized as follows: 0–7 (subclinical), 8–15 (mild), 16–23 (moderate), 24–31 (severe), and 32–40 (extreme). The Y-BOCS is widely used for assessing OCD severity due to its strong psychometric properties, including high internal consistency, inter-rater reliability, and sensitivity to treatment effects (Goodman et al., 1989).

16.2.2 Obsessive-Compulsive Inventory-Revised (OCI-R)

The Obsessive-Compulsive Inventory-Revised (OCI-R) (Foa et al., 2002) is a self-report questionnaire designed to assess the presence and severity of obsessive-compulsive symptoms. The OCI-R consists of 18 items across six subscales: washing, checking, ordering, obsessing, hoarding, and neutralizing. Respondents rate their level of distress caused by these symptoms over the past month on a scale from 0 (not at all) to 4 (extremely). The total score ranges from 0 to 72, with higher scores indicating more severe symptoms. Scores of 21 or above suggest a likely presence of OCD. The OCI-R has demonstrated good internal consistency, test-retest reliability, and convergent validity, making it a reliable tool for both clinical assessment and research purposes (Foa et al., 2002).

16.2.3 Florida Obsessive-Compulsive Inventory (FOCI)

The Florida Obsessive-Compulsive Inventory (FOCI) (Storch et al., 2007) is a self-report questionnaire designed to assess the presence and severity of obsessive-compulsive disorder (OCD) symptoms. The FOCI has two sections: the Symptom Checklist, consisting of 20 items that assess specific obsessions and compulsions (e.g., contamination fears, checking behaviors, hoarding), and the Severity Scale, which includes five items evaluating distress, time interference, functional impairment, avoidance, and resistance over the past week. Respondents rate these items on a scale from 0 (none) to 4 (extreme). The total score for the Severity Scale ranges from 0 to 20, with higher scores indicating greater severity of OCD symptoms. The FOCI has shown strong internal consistency and convergent validity, making it a useful tool for both clinical and research purposes in assessing OCD severity (Storch et al., 2007).

16.3 Exposure-Response Prevention

Exposure-Response Prevention involves systematic exposure to anxiety-provoking stimuli while simultaneously preventing the associated compulsive or avoidance behaviors.

16.3.1 Exposure Control

Exposure can be controlled by the therapist, the individual, or through a collaborative approach (shared control). Therapists often guide and structure exposure exercises, providing support and ensuring safety during challenging exposures. Alternatively, individuals may conduct self-directed exposures after receiving guidance and instructions. Shared control allows for joint decision-making and collaborative planning between therapist and individual, fostering autonomy and active involvement in the therapeutic process.

16.3.2 In Vivo and in Sensu Exposure

ERP employs two main exposure modalities: in vivo (real-life exposure to feared objects or situations) and in sensu (imaginal exposure involving vivid mental imagery of anxiety-inducing scenarios). Co-exposure, combining both in vivo and in sensu techniques, offers a comprehensive approach to exposure and enhances treatment efficacy (De Araujo et al., 1995).

16.3.3 The Exposure Strategy: Gradual or Flooding

A critical consideration in ERP is the exposure strategy. Some studies advocate for "flooding," where individuals are exposed to highly anxiety-provoking stimuli immediately. Conversely, "gradual exposure" involves a step-by-step approach, increasing exposure intensity systematically over sessions. Flooding aims for rapid habituation to fear-inducing stimuli, while gradual exposure allows for a more tolerable and controlled progression, catering to individual tolerance levels (Boersma et al., 1976; Emmelkamp & Kuipers, 1980).

16.3.4 Degree of Response Prevention

The extent of response prevention required during ERP varies across studies. Treatment protocols may involve complete, gradual, or no response prevention. Complete response prevention strictly prohibits engagement in compulsive behaviors or avoidance actions. Studies have shown that combining complete response prevention with exposure significantly reduces OCD symptoms (Abramowitz, 1996; Foa et al., 1984), while gradual or partial response prevention strategies also exhibit effectiveness in managing symptoms (Emmelkamp et al., 1990; Emmelkamp & de Lange, 1983). The efficacy of ERP lies in strategically combining controlled exposure to anxiety triggers with the prevention of ritualistic or avoidance behaviors, facilitating symptom reduction and fostering adaptive coping strategies in individuals grappling with anxiety-related disorders.

16.4 Case Vignette of Application of Obsessive-Compulsive Disorder in Patient with Schizophrenia

Alex, a 31-year-old man with schizophrenia and OCD, sought treatment. While he experienced paranoid beliefs about being monitored, he also has intrusive thoughts about being humiliated or rejected. He would spend hours checking social media for signs that people were mocking him, reviewing past conversations for mistakes he might have made, and repeatedly seeking reassurance from his family that people weren't secretly angry at him.

During assessment, Alex described his daily rituals, "I have to review every conversation I have, word by word. I spend hours at night going through everything I said that day, checking if I might have offended someone or if they were dropping hints that they hate me. I screenshot all my text messages as proof. Sometimes I miss work because I'm stuck reviewing yesterday's interactions."

The therapist noticed the intertwining of OCD and psychotic symptoms but maintained focus on the behavioral components of the OCD:**Therapist**: What happens if you don't review the conversations?
Alex: The thoughts get louder. The anxiety becomes unbearable. I'm convinced I've ruined everything.
Therapist: Would you be interested in learning a different way to handle these thoughts and checking behaviors?
Alex: I've tried to stop checking, but the signs get clearer… (referring to his delusions)
Therapist: Let's start with understanding your current routine. Walk me through exactly how you review conversations.

They began developing an ERP hierarchy, focusing strictly on the behavioral aspects:

1. Letting one brief "good morning" interaction go unreviewed.
2. Deleting one screenshot of a neutral conversation.
3. Waiting 30 min before checking social media.
4. Having a short conversation without asking for reassurance.
5. Waiting 2 h before reviewing a conversation.
6. Deleting screenshots older than 1 week.
7. Going a full day without reviewing past conversations.
8. Engaging in casual conversations without mental review.

Here's an example of an early exposure session:**Therapist**: Today we're going to practice not checking your phone for 30 min after a conversation. What's your anxiety level from 0 to 10?
Alex: Eight… they might be talking about me right now… (referring to delusions)
Therapist: Let's focus on your anxiety number. Can you stay with that feeling even though it's at an eight?
Alex: I really need to check my messages right now…
Therapist: That's the urge we're working with. Can you sit with that urge for just two more minutes?

The therapist consistently redirected focus to the exposure task:**Alex**: But what if they're sending hidden messages—
Therapist: What's your anxiety number right now?
Alex: Nine.
Therapist: Let's watch if that number changes while we sit here without checking.

By week 4, Alex noticed something during an exposure:**Alex**: I waited 15 min before checking my messages. The anxiety was really high, but then it started to drop a little.
Therapist: What did you learn from that?
Alex: That maybe the anxiety doesn't keep climbing forever?

Progress was gradual and nonlinear. Week 6:**Alex**: I had a setback. Spent 4 h reviewing conversations yesterday.
Therapist: What would you like to work on in today's exposure?
Alex: Could we try the 30-min delay again? Even though I failed yesterday?
Therapist: Each exposure stands on its own. What's your anxiety number right now?

By week 10, some behavioral changes emerged:**Alex**: I was able to have lunch with a coworker this week. Still reviewed the conversation afterwards, but only for 30 min instead of 3 h.
Therapist: How did you manage the anxiety during lunch?
Alex: It was high, maybe an eight, but I remembered what we practiced about letting the feelings be there.

The therapist maintained focus on practical goals while acknowledging ongoing challenges:**Alex**: The feeling that people are sending me hidden messages is still there, but sometimes I can have brief conversations anyway.
Therapist: What's your anxiety number when you're talking to someone now?
Alex: Usually starts at eight, drops to maybe a six. Before, it stayed at ten the whole time.

By week 14, Alex reported modest functional improvements:**Alex**: I'm spending less time checking social media. I set a timer for 15 min of review time, and sometimes I can actually stop when it rings.
Therapist: What exposure practice would help you build on that progress?

Progress continued with basic social interactions, though some avoidance remained. Week 16:**Alex**: I can handle short conversations better now. Long ones are still scary, and I still think people might be mocking me… but I'm spending less time reviewing everything.
Therapist: What's different about how you handle the anxiety now?
Alex: I'm learning it can go down on its own. Doesn't mean I'm comfortable, but I can sometimes participate anyway.

The therapist consistently brought focus back to the exposure tasks and response prevention, allowing Alex to build tolerance for anxiety and uncertainty without directly addressing his psychotic symptoms. This focused behavioral approach led to modest but meaningful functional improvements in daily living skills.

The success with ERP demonstrated that anxiety tolerance could improve even while other symptoms remained. The therapist maintained focus on concrete behavioral goals rather than attempting to address all symptoms simultaneously, allowing Alex to develop specific skills for managing his OCD symptoms even in the presence of ongoing psychotic symptoms.

References

Abramowitz, J. S. (1996). Variants of exposure and response prevention in the treatment of obsessive-compulsive disorder: A meta-analysis. *Behavior Therapy, 27*(4), 583–600. https://doi.org/10.1016/S0005-7894(96)80045-1

Boersma, F. J., Den Hengst, S., Dekker, A. J., & Emmelkamp, P. M. (1976). Flooding in vivo versus imaginal systematic desensitization in the treatment of phobic patients. *Behaviour Research and Therapy, 14*(1), 63–70. https://doi.org/10.1016/0005-7967(76)90037-6

Buckley, P. F., Miller, B. J., Lehrer, D. S., & Castle, D. J. (2009). Psychiatric comorbidities and schizophrenia. *Schizophrenia Bulletin, 35*(2), 383–402. https://doi.org/10.1093/schbul/sbn135

De Araujo, L. A., Ito, L. M., & Marks, I. M. (1995). Comparative efficacy of matching and mismatching imaginal and in vivo exposure for obsessive-compulsive disorder. *Journal of Consulting and Clinical Psychology, 63*(1), 331–341. https://doi.org/10.1037/0022-006X.63.2.331

Emmelkamp, P. M., & de Lange, R. (1983). Agoraphobia: A comparative study of self-exposure in vivo and intensive exposure in vivo plus cognitive restructuring and exposure in sensu. *Behavior Modification, 7*(4), 489–501. https://doi.org/10.1177/01454455830074003

Emmelkamp, P. M., & Kuipers, A. C. (1980). Flooding vs. gradual desensitization in vivo: A case study. *Behaviour Research and Therapy, 18*(5), 429–435. https://doi.org/10.1016/0005-7967(80)90003-2

Emmelkamp, P. M., Kwee, M. G., & Muris, P. (1990). Symptom-specific effects of cognitive and behavioral interventions in the treatment of obsessive-compulsive disorder. *Behaviour Research and Therapy, 28*(2), 153–162. https://doi.org/10.1016/0005-7967(90)90023-M

Foa, E. B., Huppert, J. D., Leiberg, S., Langner, R., Kichic, R., Hajcak, G., & Salkovskis, P. M. (2002). The obsessive-compulsive inventory: Development and validation of a short version. *Psychological Assessment, 14*(4), 485–496. https://doi.org/10.1037/1040-3590.14.4.485

Foa, E. B., Liebowitz, M. R., Kozak, M. J., Davies, S., Campeas, R., Franklin, M. E., & Tu, X. (1984). Randomized, placebo-controlled trial of exposure and ritual prevention, clomipramine, and their combination in the treatment of obsessive-compulsive disorder. *The American Journal of Psychiatry, 141*(5), 581–585. https://doi.org/10.1176/ajp.141.5.581

Goodman, W. K., Price, L. H., Rasmussen, S. A., Mazure, C., Fleischmann, R. L., Hill, C. L., Heninger, G. R., & Charney, D. S. (1989). The Yale-Brown obsessive-compulsive scale: I. Development, use, and reliability. *Archives of General Psychiatry, 46*(11), 1006–1011. https://doi.org/10.1001/archpsyc.1989.01810110048007

National Institute for Health and Care Excellence. (2005). *Obsessive-compulsive disorder and body dysmorphic disorder: Treatment* (clinical guideline CG31). https://www.nice.org.uk/guidance/cg31

Storch, E. A., Bagner, D. M., Merlo, L. J., Shapira, N. A., Geffken, G. R., Murphy, T. K., & Goodman, W. K. (2007). Florida obsessive-compulsive inventory: Development, reliability, and validity. *Journal of Clinical Psychology, 63*(9), 851–859. https://doi.org/10.1002/jclp.20394

Tundo, A., & Necci, R. (2016). Cognitive-behavioural therapy for obsessive-compulsive disorder co-occurring with psychosis: Systematic review of evidence. *World Journal of Psychiatry, 6*(4), 449–455. https://doi.org/10.5498/wjp.v6.i4.449

Chapter 17
Treating Eating Disorder in Psychosis

Abstract This chapter addresses eating disorders co-occurring with psychosis, with aims that include ruling out malnutrition and metabolic disturbances as causes of psychotic symptoms, differentiating body image distortions from delusional beliefs, and managing binge-type problems linked to antipsychotic medication. It reviews screening and monitoring using SCOFF, EAT-26, EDE-Q, PHQ-ED, BMI/body weight, and broader physical monitoring. The chapter then presents CBT-ED applications for anorexia nervosa, binge eating disorder, and bulimia nervosa, describing typical components such as nutrition education, regular eating patterns, cognitive restructuring, mood regulation, body image work, and relapse prevention. These interventions are framed as part of an integrated plan that stabilizes physical health, supports ongoing pharmacotherapy, and reduces psychopathology in psychosis.

Keywords Eating pathology · Body image disturbance · CBT-ED · Nutritional monitoring · Disordered eating

17.1 Goals of Treating Eating Disorder for Psychosis

The main goals in treating eating disorder co-occurring with psychosis are to: 1) ensure that none of the psychotic symptoms observed is due to malnutrition, starvation, fluid/electrolyte imbalances, or abnormal heart rates; 2) address psychotic symptoms, such as hallucinations, delusions, and distorted cognitive functions that may overlap with eating disorder symptoms (e.g., believing oneself to be obese despite a low BMI); and 3) manage eating disorder, such as binge eating disorder, that may arise as a side effect of antipsychotic medications, thereby supporting continued pharmacotherapy for psychosis.

Starvation, electrolyte imbalances, and metabolic disturbances are known to provoke transient psychotic symptoms. Certain antipsychotics, particularly olanzapine and clozapine, have been associated with medication-induced binge eating. Clinicians can find it difficult to distinguish the firm belief that one is fat (when that is clearly

E. S. Jaya, *Cognitive Behavioral Therapy for Psychosis as a Syndrome*,
https://doi.org/10.1007/978-981-95-9203-6_17

not the case) from a delusion. The body image disturbance at the heart of anorexia nervosa is a false perception akin to the perceptual disorders found in schizophrenia. Additional psychotic features associated with eating disorders—usually transient—have been attributed to the effects of starvation and electrolyte imbalance.

Comorbidity between eating disorders and psychotic illness is more commonly seen in care settings for psychosis than in treatment programs for eating disorders, even though the self-starvation associated with some types of eating disorder can often result in psychotic symptoms. Therefore, it is possible that treatment for psychosis (i.e., antipsychotic medications) may contribute to this comorbidity to some extent. Psychotherapists are free to choose the eating disorder measurement and techniques relevant to the patient.

17.2 Measuring Eating Disorder

17.2.1 SCOFF Questions

The SCOFF Questionnaire (Morgan et al., 1999) is a screening tool for identifying individuals at risk for eating disorders. This brief, memorable questionnaire consists of five questions:

1. **S**ick: Do you make yourself sick because you feel uncomfortably full?
2. **C**ontrol: Do you worry that you have lost control over how much you eat?
3. **O**ne stone: Have you recently lost more than one stone (14 lb. or approximately 6.4 kg) in a 3-month period?
4. **F**at: Do you believe yourself to be fat when others say you are too thin?
5. **F**ood: Would you say that food dominates your life?

Each "yes" response equals 1 point, and a total score of 2 or more indicates a positive screen, suggesting a higher likelihood of an eating disorder. However, a positive result does not confirm an eating disorder diagnosis; rather, it signals the need for further evaluation by a healthcare professional to assess the presence and severity of an eating disorder. The SCOFF Questionnaire has a positive rate of 12.5%, which presents an acceptable trade-off for very high sensitivity. It is efficient to screen cases of eating disorders in specific populations (e.g., adult women in primary care), but further work is needed to validate it in other populations (Luck et al., 2002).

17.2.2 Eating Attitudes Test-26 (EAT-26)

The Eating Attitudes Test-26 (EAT-26) (Garner et al., 1982) is a widely used self-report measure designed to assess symptoms and concerns related to eating disorders. It consists of 26 items, which are rated on a six-point Likert scale ranging from

1 (never) to 6 (always). The items focus on behaviors and attitudes related to food, eating, and body image, including dieting, bulimia, and preoccupation with food. The total score of the EAT-26 is calculated by summing the responses, with scores of 20 or higher indicating a potential risk of an eating disorder that warrants further clinical evaluation. Additionally, the test includes behavioral questions that assess symptoms such as binge eating, vomiting, and excessive exercise over the past 6 months. The EAT-26 has demonstrated good reliability and validity across various populations, making it an effective screening tool for identifying individuals at risk of eating disorders (Garner et al., 1982).

17.2.3 Eating Disorder Examination Questionnaire (EDE-Q)

The Eating Disorder Examination Questionnaire (EDE-Q) (Fairburn & Beglin, 1994) is a 28-item self-report measure adapted from a semi-structured interview to assess the range, frequency, and severity of eating disorder behaviors. It consists of four subscales: Restraint, Eating Concern, Shape Concern, and Weight Concern. The Restraint subscale measures the attempts to restrict food intake to influence body shape and weight, while the Eating Concern subscale measures preoccupation with food, eating habits, and related emotional distress and anxiety. The Shape and Weight Concern subscales measure concerns regarding body weight and shape. Patients are asked to rate their experiences and behaviors over the past 28 days on a Likert-type scale. A global score can also be calculated, with higher scores indicating more problematic eating problems. This scale is suitable for patients aged 14 and older. Several studies have examined the psychometrics of the EDE-Q and support the reliability and validity of this measurement (Berg et al., 2012).

17.2.4 Patient Health Questionnaire Eating Disorder (PHQ-ED)

The Patient Health Questionnaire Eating Disorder Module (PHQ-ED) is a self-report questionnaire derived from the PHQ series, specifically designed to screen for eating disorders (Spitzer et al., 1999). It assesses behaviors and symptoms associated with eating disorders, such as anorexia nervosa, bulimia nervosa, and binge eating disorder. The PHQ-ED includes items focused on body image, food intake restrictions, and compensatory behaviors like vomiting and excessive exercise. Responses are rated on a frequency scale to determine the presence of eating disorder behaviors within a set timeframe.

The PHQ-ED is part of the broader Patient Health Questionnaire (PHQ), which is a widely used tool for screening psychiatric conditions. The PHQ-ED is effective in both clinical and primary care settings for the early identification of individuals at risk for eating disorders. While it does not diagnose an eating disorder on its own, it serves as a valuable initial screening tool that may prompt further clinical evaluation. The PHQ-ED has demonstrated good reliability and validity in identifying key symptoms of eating disorders (Spitzer et al., 1999).

17.2.5 Body Mass Index (BMI) or Body Weight

Body Mass Index (BMI) measures an individual's body weight relative to their height. It is a simple tool used to categorize individuals as underweight, normal weight, overweight, or obese. BMI does not directly measure body fat, but it provides an estimation of body fatness and helps identify potential health risks associated with weight. The formula to calculate BMI is as follows:

BMI = weight (in kilograms) / (height (in meters) x height (in meters))

BMI categories are as follows:

- Underweight = < 18.5
- Normal weight = 18.5–24.9
- Overweight = 25–29.9
- Obesity = BMI of 30 or greater

17.2.6 Physical Monitoring

When working with individuals with eating disorders, it is crucial to incorporate regular physical monitoring as part of their care plan. This is especially important for clients who may be engaging in compensatory behaviors such as vomiting, laxative or diuretic use, or water loading. These behaviors can lead to significant fluid and electrolyte imbalances, which require medical assessment and intervention.

Referral to a medical doctor for the evaluation of fluid and electrolyte balance is essential for clients presenting with these behaviors. In cases where there are concerns about potential medical complications, such as those related to rapid weight loss, excessive exercise, or severe purging behaviors, further physical assessment may be necessary.

Particularly, consider whether ECG (electrocardiogram) monitoring is appropriate. ECG monitoring should be prioritized for clients presenting with any of the following risk factors: bradycardia (slow heart rate), hypotension (low blood pressure), excessive caffeine intake (including energy drinks), prescribed or non-prescribed medication use, muscular weakness, electrolyte imbalances, or a history of abnormal heart rhythms. Proper assessment and referral can help prevent serious medical complications associated with eating disorders.

17.3 CBT-ED for Anorexia Nervosa

CBT-ED programs for adults with anorexia nervosa encompass up to 40 sessions delivered over 40 weeks. In the initial treatment phase, sessions are conducted twice a week for the first 2–3 weeks. The core objective of this therapy is multifaceted, aiming to reduce physical health risks and associated symptoms while simultaneously promoting healthy eating behaviors and achieving a sustainable, healthy body weight.

This treatment protocol involves a comprehensive range of therapeutic components, including:

- Nutrition Education: Educating individuals about nutrition and balanced eating patterns.
- Cognitive Restructuring: Addressing and reshaping maladaptive thought patterns related to body image, self-esteem, and food.
- Mood Regulation: Teaching skills to manage emotions related to eating behaviors.
- Social Skills Development: Assisting in fostering healthy social interactions and communication.
- Body Image Concerns: Targeting distorted perceptions of body image and promoting a realistic self-perception.
- Relapse Prevention Strategies: Equipping individuals with tools to prevent relapse.

Additionally, the therapeutic approach is personalized, taking into account the specific factors that perpetuate the eating problem. It emphasizes self-monitoring of dietary intake, associated thoughts, and emotions, while assigning homework exercises to help individuals apply learned skills in their daily lives, thereby enhancing self-efficacy.

17.4 CBT-ED for Binge Eating Disorder

For individuals with binge eating disorder, CBT-ED generally spans 16–20 sessions. The treatment plan includes a comprehensive psychological formulation to identify how dietary and emotional factors contribute to binge eating behaviors. The treatment approach involves:

- Structured Eating Patterns: Advising individuals to adopt regular meal plans and avoid prolonged periods of hunger.

- Cognitive Restructuring: Addressing emotional triggers through cognitive restructuring, behavioral experiments, and exposure techniques.
- Weekly Monitoring: Regular monitoring of binge eating behaviors, dietary intake, and weight to track progress.
- Body Image Issues: Addressing body image concerns, if present, within the therapeutic context.

While the primary goal of CBT-ED is not weight loss, the cessation of binge eating may lead to weight changes in the long term. The approach advises against deliberate attempts to lose weight during treatment, as this can potentially trigger binge eating episodes.

17.5 CBT-ED for Bulimia Nervosa

For individuals with bulimia nervosa, CBT-ED involves up to 20 sessions delivered over 20 weeks, with considerations for twice-weekly sessions during the initial phase. The treatment initially focuses on engagement, psychoeducation, and establishing regular eating patterns. Subsequently, it addresses the psychopathology associated with the disorder and works toward maintaining positive changes while minimizing the risk of relapse. Additionally, involving significant others may enhance the effectiveness of individual therapy sessions.

References

Berg, K. C., Peterson, C. B., Frazier, P., & Crow, S. J. (2012). Psychometric evaluation of the eating disorder examination and eating disorder examination-questionnaire: A systematic review of the literature. *International Journal of Eating Disorders, 45*(3), 428–438.

Fairburn, C. G., & Beglin, S. J. (1994). Assessment of eating disorders: Interview or self-report questionnaire? *International Journal of Eating Disorders, 16*(4), 363–370.

Garner, D. M., Olmsted, M. P., Bohr, Y., & Garfinkel, P. E. (1982). The eating attitudes test: Psychometric features and clinical correlates. *Psychological Medicine, 12*(4), 871–878. https://doi.org/10.1017/S0033291700049163

Luck, A. J., Morgan Luck, J. F., Reid, F., O'Brien, A., Brunton, J., Price, C., Perry, L., & Lacey, J. H. (2002). The SCOFF questionnaire and clinical interview for eating disorders in general practice: Comparative study. *BMJ, 325*(7367), 755–756. https://doi.org/10.1136/bmj.325.7367.755

Morgan, J. F., Reid, F., & Lacey, J. H. (1999). The SCOFF questionnaire: Assessment of a new screening tool for eating disorders. *BMJ, 319*(7223), 1467–1468. https://doi.org/10.1136/bmj.319.7223.1467

Spitzer, R. L., Kroenke, K., Williams, J. B. W., & Löwe, B. (1999). Patient health questionnaire (PHQ). In *Pfizer* (pp. 1–9). https://doi.org/10.1007/s11606-006-0098-0

Chapter 18
Treating Body Dysmorphic Disorder in Psychosis

Abstract This chapter focuses on body dysmorphic disorder in psychosis, emphasizing delusional conviction about appearance as a key psychotic feature. It discusses debates about delusional versus nondelusional variants of BDD and their relationship to schizophrenia, then sets treatment goals for this population. Assessment includes the BDD-modified Yale–Brown Obsessive Compulsive Scale, the Body Dysmorphic Disorder Questionnaire, and the Body Dysmorphic Disorder Symptom Scale. The treatment module combines Exposure and Response Prevention with mirror retraining techniques and provides guidance on integrating these methods into a unified protocol. The chapter highlights how targeting appearance-related delusional beliefs and compulsive checking can reduce distress and improve functioning in psychotic patients with BDD features.

Keywords Body dysmorphic disorder • Appearance concerns • Mirror retraining • Exposure therapy • Cognitive distortions

18.1 Goals of Treating Body Dysmorphic Disorder for Psychosis

A debated and clinically significant question during the DSM-IV era revolved around the connection between delusional and nondelusional variants of Body Dysmorphic Disorder (BDD) (Phillips & Hollander, 1996). The debate questioned whether these variants constituted distinct disorders or were part of the same disorder, differing in the spectrum of insight they exhibited. This scrutiny raised concerns about whether the DSM accurately captured the nature of this condition. Additionally, it prompted exploration into how these variants responded to various psychological and pharmacological treatments.

The primary feature of psychosis in BDD manifests as a strong delusional conviction regarding one's appearance. Despite their physical appearance aligning with societal norms, patients often harbor beliefs of being unattractive, deformed, or disfigured. In severe cases, they may perceive themselves as resembling a monstrous

E. S. Jaya, *Cognitive Behavioral Therapy for Psychosis as a Syndrome*,
https://doi.org/10.1007/978-981-95-9203-6_18

figure, the Elephant Man, or the wife of Frankenstein (Phillips, 1996). This delusional conviction regarding appearance has been acknowledged in clinical literature for some time (Phillips, 1991). In earlier times, many authors even considered BDD to be either a precursor to or a variant of schizophrenia (Zaidens, 1950; Phillips, 1991).

Randomized controlled trials have shown that 8–12 sessions of CBT lead to significant improvements in BDD symptoms (Khemlani-Patel et al., 2011; Rosen et al., 1995; Veale et al., 1996). Complementing this evidence, a case study conducted in Indonesia reported that both online and in-person CBT interventions were associated with substantial symptom reduction, with response rates ranging from 40% to 100% as measured by the BDD-YBOCS (Adelheid et al., 2025). Psychotherapists are free to choose the BDD measurement and techniques relevant to the patient.

18.2 Measuring Body Dysmorphic Disorder

18.2.1 Yale-Brown Obsessive Compulsive Scale Modified for Body Dysmorphic Disorder (BDD-YBOCS)

The Yale-Brown Obsessive Compulsive Scale Modified for Body Dysmorphic Disorder (BDD-YBOCS) is a clinician-administered scale adapted from the original Y-BOCS to specifically assess the severity of Body Dysmorphic Disorder (BDD) symptoms. The scale consists of 12 items that measure both obsessional preoccupation with perceived physical defects and the compulsive behaviors (e.g., mirror checking, camouflaging) aimed at addressing these concerns. Each item is rated on a scale from 0 (no symptoms) to 4 (extreme symptoms), with total scores ranging from 0 to 48. The BDD-YBOCS provides insight into symptom severity and is used to monitor treatment progress. It has demonstrated high reliability and validity for individuals diagnosed with BDD (Phillips et al., 1997).

18.2.2 Body Dysmorphic Disorder Questionnaire (BDDQ)

The Body Dysmorphic Disorder Questionnaire (BDDQ) is a brief self-report screening tool for Body Dysmorphic Disorder (BDD) based on DSM-IV diagnostic criteria. The first two questions must be answered with a "yes" to continue the questionnaire. These questions ask if respondents worry about some parts of their body that they categorize as unattractive and if these concerns preoccupy them. The third question assesses the distress and impairment caused by preoccupation. The fourth question evaluates the duration criteria needed for a DSM-IV BDD diagnosis. An important exclusion criterion for the differential diagnosis of eating disorder is assessed with the question if the patient thinks they are not thin enough or too fat.

In a Swedish population, the BDDQ has shown good concurrent validity, with 94% sensitivity and 90% specificity (Brohede et al., 2013).

18.2.3 Body Dysmorphic Disorder Symptom Scale (BDD-SS)

The Body Dysmorphic Disorder Symptom Scale (BDD-SS) (Wilhelm et al., 2016) is a self-report measure designed to assess the severity of Body Dysmorphic Disorder (BDD) symptoms. The scale evaluates the extent of preoccupation with perceived appearance flaws and the distress and functional impairment caused by these concerns. It consists of items that measure the frequency of BDD-related behaviors, such as mirror checking, seeking reassurance, and attempts to camouflage or alter perceived defects. Items are rated on a Likert scale, with higher scores indicating greater symptom severity. The BDD-SS has demonstrated strong psychometric properties, including good reliability and validity for assessing BDD symptoms across different clinical settings.

18.3 Exposure-Response Prevention

ERP is a cornerstone of CBT for BDD, serving to confront and reduce avoidance behaviors and ritualistic responses triggered by appearance concerns. The ERP protocol begins with a careful assessment of individual triggers and the distress levels related to perceived flaws. A fear hierarchy is then established, ranking situations or stimuli from least to most anxiety-provoking.

Subsequently, exposure tasks are systematically designed, starting with less distressing situations and gradually progressing to more challenging scenarios. These exposures aim to facilitate habituation to feared situations while preventing the engagement of compulsive behaviors or avoidance strategies. Over time, individuals learn to tolerate distress without engaging in rituals, thus breaking the cycle of avoidance and reducing anxiety associated with appearance concerns.

18.4 Mirror Retraining Techniques in BDD Treatment

Mirror Retraining represents an innovative technique integrated into CBT for BDD, focusing on altering individuals' habitual perception of themselves in mirrors. The primary objective is to modify obsessive checking and scrutinizing behaviors, encouraging a more realistic self-perception.

Therapeutic exercises in Mirror Retraining involve controlled periods of mirror viewing without engaging in habitual checking or scrutinizing behaviors. Therapists guide individuals in redirecting their attention away from perceived flaws, encouraging a more balanced and less distorted view of their appearance. By emphasizing positive attributes and practicing self-compassion during mirror exercises, individuals gradually reduce their avoidance of mirrors and alleviate distress associated with perceived flaws.

18.5 Integrating ERP and Mirror Retraining

The collaborative use of ERP and Mirror Retraining in CBT for BDD enhances treatment outcomes synergistically. While ERP targets avoidance behaviors and reduces distress linked to feared situations, Mirror Retraining complements this process by promoting a shift in the habitual perception of appearance. This integrated approach fosters adaptive coping strategies, diminishes distress, and contributes to an improved quality of life for individuals grappling with BDD.

References

Adelheid, T., Ramadhani, A. P., Novrianto, R., & Jaya, E. S. (2025). Case series of body dysmorphic disorder treatment using exposure and response prevention psychotherapy. *Asian Journal of Psychiatry, 108*, 104505. https://doi.org/10.1016/j.ajp.2025.104505.

Brohede, S., Wingren, G., Wijma, B., & Wijma, K. (2013). Validation of the body dysmorphic disorder questionnaire in a community sample of Swedish women. *Psychiatry Research, 210*(2), 647–652.

Khemlani-Patel, S., Neziroglu, F., & Mancusi, L. M. (2011). Cognitive-behavioral therapy for body dysmorphic disorder: A comparative investigation. *International Journal of Cognitive Therapy, 4*(4), 363–380. https://doi.org/10.1521/ijct.2011.4.4.363

Phillips, K. A. (1996). Body dysmorphic disorder: Diagnosis and treatment of imagined ugliness. *The Journal of Clinical Psychiatry, 57*(Suppl 8), 61–65.

Phillips, K. A. (1991). Body dysmorphic disorder: The distress of imagined ugliness. *The American Journal of Psychiatry, 148*(9), 1138–1149. https://doi.org/10.1176/ajp.148.9.1138

Phillips, K. A., & Hollander, E. (1996). Body dysmorphic disorder. In T. A. Widiger, A. J. Frances, H. A. Pincus, R. Ross, M. B. First, & W. W. Davis (Eds.), *DSM-IV sourcebook* (Vol. 2). American Psychiatric Association.

Phillips, K. A., Hollander, E., Rasmussen, S. A., Aronowitz, B. R., DeCaria, C., & Goodman, W. K. (1997). A severity rating scale for body dysmorphic disorder: Development, reliability, and validity of a modified version of the Yale-Brown obsessive-compulsive scale. *Psychopharmacology Bulletin, 33*(1), 17–22.

Rosen, J. C., Reiter, J., & Orosan, P. (1995). Cognitive-behavioral body image therapy for body dysmorphic disorder. *Journal of Consulting and Clinical Psychology, 63*(2), 263–269. https://doi.org/10.1037/a0022-006x.63.2.263

Veale, D., Gournay, K., Dryden, W., Boocock, A., Shah, F., Willson, R., & Walburn, J. (1996). Body dysmorphic disorder: A cognitive behavioural model and pilot randomised controlled trial. *Behaviour Research and Therapy, 34*(9), 717–729. https://doi.org/10.1016/0005-7967(96)00025-3

Wilhelm, S., Greenberg, J. L., Fama, J. M., & Rosenfield, E. (2016). Development and validation of the body dysmorphic disorder symptom scale. *Body Image, 17*, 82–87. https://doi.org/10.1016/j.bodyim.2016.02.002

Zaidens, S. H. (1950). Dermatologic hypochondriasis; A form of schizophrenia. *Psychosomatic Medicine, 12*(4), 250–253. https://doi.org/10.1097/00006842-195007000-00006

Chapter 19
Management of Substance Use in Psychosis

Abstract This chapter presents a CBT-based framework for managing substance use among people with psychosis. It defines treatment goals and describes assessment using TAPS, general physical examination, and urine testing to identify substance types, severity, and medical complications. The chapter then outlines how to choose appropriate techniques based on patient profile and substance, with specific sections on contingency management, habit reversal, and the use of Exposure and Response Prevention approach to work with substance-related cues and cravings. The overall focus is on reducing use, minimizing relapse risk, and stabilizing psychotic symptoms as part of an integrated treatment plan.

Keywords Substance misuse · Contingency management · Habit reversal · Dual diagnosis · Behavioral intervention

19.1 Goals of Treating Substance Usage for Psychosis

The main goal of treating substance use in individuals with psychosis is to reduce possible complications arising from the interactions of substance use and pharmacotherapy. In addition, many substances, such as methamphetamine and cannabis, are known to trigger psychotic symptoms. When a patient intermittently uses substances that may induce psychotic symptoms, it becomes difficult to determine whether the psychotic symptoms observed during consultation are primarily due to substance use or not. Literature indicates that long-term substance use may induce reverse sensitization and desensitization, which trigger symptoms in patients either when taking or not taking the substance. Therefore, the substance's dosage needs to be precisely adjusted at the time of use, as it can vary from day to day. Thus, it becomes imperative for people with psychosis to manage or abstain from substances to help manage their psychotic symptoms. Randomized controlled trials have demonstrated the efficacy of 12 sessions of contingency management in treating various substance use disorders (Angelo et al., 2013; Barry et al., 2009; McDonell et al., 2017).

E. S. Jaya, *Cognitive Behavioral Therapy for Psychosis as a Syndrome*,
https://doi.org/10.1007/978-981-95-9203-6_19

19.2 Measuring Substance Usage

19.2.1 Tobacco, Alcohol, Prescription Medication, and Other Substances (TAPS)

The Tobacco, Alcohol, Prescription Medication, and Other Substances (TAPS) tool (McNeely et al., 2016) is a brief, self-administered or clinician-administered screening measure designed to assess the use of tobacco, alcohol, prescription medications, and other substances in a primary care setting. The TAPS consists of two parts: the first part is a screening questionnaire that assesses recent substance use, while the second part evaluates problematic use, including dependency and misuse, through additional questions based on positive responses from the first part. The TAPS tool is widely used in clinical practice to quickly identify substance use disorders and guide treatment decisions. It has been validated for use in general healthcare settings and shows high sensitivity and specificity.

19.2.2 General Physical Examination

Patients presenting with substance abuse issues may have a variety of physical health concerns. A general physical examination, often conducted by a physician, includes assessing signs of intoxication, withdrawal symptoms, and the long-term effects of substance use. In addition, some important areas to attend to are skin marks that may suggest intravenous drug use, respiratory health to understand stimulant or opioid use, and cardiovascular health such as blood pressure.

19.2.3 Physical Examination: Urine Testing

Urine drug testing is a widely used tool in the management and monitoring of substance use disorders. As a psychotherapist working with substance abuse patients, understanding the principles and techniques of urine drug testing is vital for treatment planning and therapeutic interventions. Urine drug tests are used to:

1. Confirm Recent Substance Use: Urine tests help identify whether a patient has recently used substances, providing objective data to verify self-reports (Levin & Fishman, 2020).
2. Monitor Treatment Compliance: Regular testing helps ensure that patients adhere to prescribed treatments, such as abstinence from substances or adherence to medication-assisted therapies (Levin & Fishman, 2020).

3. Support Relapse Prevention: Urine testing can be an important tool for detecting early signs of relapse, allowing therapists to intervene promptly (Substance Abuse and Mental Health Services Administration [SAMHSA], 2012).

19.2.3.1 Types of Urine Testing

Several methods of urine testing can be employed in substance abuse treatment, depending on the goals of treatment and the specific needs of the patient:

- Random Urine Testing: This is considered the most effective method for monitoring patients with substance use disorders. By conducting tests at random intervals, patients are less likely to anticipate testing and attempt to evade detection through delayed substance use or the use of adulterants. Random testing increases the chances of identifying recent use and provides a more accurate picture of the patient's substance use patterns (DuPont et al., 2017).
- Scheduled Urine Testing: Scheduled testing, where patients know the date and time of the test in advance, can be used to reinforce treatment adherence, though it is generally considered less effective for detecting intermittent or unpredictable substance use (Levin & Fishman, 2020).
- Observed Urine Testing: In some cases, observed urine testing may be necessary to ensure the integrity of the sample. This technique involves having a trained healthcare professional observe the patient as they provide the urine sample, preventing tampering or substitution of the sample (SAMHSA, 2012).
- Point-of-Care Testing (POCT): This is a rapid urine test that can be conducted in the clinic, offering immediate results. It is a useful tool for real-time monitoring, though laboratory confirmation may still be required for accuracy (Levin & Fishman, 2020).

19.2.3.2 Considerations for Urine Testing

When implementing urine testing in a treatment program, several important considerations must be taken into account:

- Frequency of Testing: The frequency of testing should be tailored to the patient's risk of relapse and level of treatment engagement. High-risk patients or those in early stages of recovery may benefit from more frequent, random testing, while patients with demonstrated treatment adherence may require less frequent testing (DuPont et al., 2017).
- Substance Detection Windows: Different substances have varying detection windows, meaning that they can be detected in urine for different lengths of time. For example, cannabis can be detected for weeks after use in chronic users, while substances like alcohol or cocaine have shorter detection periods. Understanding these windows can inform decisions on testing frequency and interpretation of results (Levin & Fishman, 2020).

- Ethical and Therapeutic Considerations: Urine testing can sometimes introduce feelings of mistrust or invasion of privacy, particularly if patients feel they are being monitored excessively. Psychotherapists should work with their patients to explain the rationale for testing, emphasizing that it is a supportive tool for their recovery rather than a punitive measure (Saitz et al., 2014).

19.2.3.3 Limitations and Challenges in Urine Testing

While urine testing is a valuable tool, it is important to acknowledge its limitations. False positives and false negatives can occur, particularly when over-the-counter medications or other factors interfere with the test. Additionally, patients may attempt to tamper with or adulterate samples, underscoring the importance of using techniques such as observed or random testing when necessary (SAMHSA, 2012).

19.3 Choosing Appropriate Techniques

It is important that the clinician, if not a medical doctor, collaborates with a medical doctor who provides pharmacotherapy treatment for substance dependence. Integrating Contingency Management, Habit Reversal, and Exposure-Response Prevention strategies offers a holistic approach to treating Substance Use Disorder. By combining the reinforcement of positive behaviors, modification of maladaptive habits, and desensitization to triggers, individuals gain practical tools to manage cravings and maintain sobriety.

19.4 Contingency Management in CBT

Contingency Management utilizes operant conditioning principles to reinforce abstinence and positive behavioral changes. It involves the use of tangible rewards or incentives to reinforce drug abstinence or adherence to treatment goals. For instance, individuals receive vouchers exchangeable for goods or privileges based on drug-negative urine tests or the achievement of treatment objectives. By reinforcing desired behaviors, such as attending therapy sessions or maintaining sobriety, Contingency Management encourages sustained abstinence and adherence to treatment.

19.5 Habit Reversal

Habit Reversal Techniques aim to identify, challenge, and replace maladaptive habits associated with substance use. For instance, if an individual has a habit of consuming alcohol in response to stress, therapists help in recognizing triggers and developing alternative coping strategies. The individual learns to substitute the habit of drinking with healthier behaviors, such as relaxation exercises or engaging in enjoyable activities. Through awareness training and practice of alternative responses, Habit Reversal Techniques empower individuals to break the cycle of substance-related habits.

19.6 Exposure-Response Prevention

Exposure-Response Prevention (ERP), derived from its success in treating anxiety disorders, helps individuals confront and manage substance-related triggers. In this technique, individuals are gradually exposed to substance cues or situations that trigger cravings, while being prevented from using the substance. For instance, a person with alcohol use disorder might be exposed to a setting where they typically drink but is guided to resist consuming alcohol. Over time, repeated exposure without substance use helps desensitize individuals to triggers, reducing the conditioned response and decreasing cravings.

References

Angelo, F. N., McDonell, M. G., Lewin, M. R., Srebnik, D., Lowe, J., Roll, J., & Ries, R. (2013). Predictors of stimulant abuse treatment outcomes in severely mentally ill outpatients. *Drug and Alcohol Dependence, 131*(1–2), 162–165. https://doi.org/10.1016/j.drugalcdep.2012.11.017

Barry, D., Sullivan, B., & Petry, N. M. (2009). Comparable efficacy of contingency management for cocaine dependence among African American, Hispanic, and white methadone maintenance clients. *Psychology of Addictive Behaviors, 23*(1), 168–174. https://doi.org/10.1037/a0014575

DuPont, R. L., Humphreys, K., Carr, C. J., & Shea, C. L. (2017). Random drug testing: A critical tool for preventing addiction and saving lives. *Journal of Global Drug Policy and Practice, 11*(1), 12–23.

Levin, F. R., & Fishman, M. J. (2020). *Substance use disorders: A practical guide for clinicians* (6th ed.). Wolters Kluwer.

McDonell, M. G., Leickly, E., McPherson, S., Skalisky, J., Srebnik, D., Angelo, F., Ries, R. K., et al. (2017). A randomized controlled trial of ethyl glucuronide-based contingency management for outpatients with co-occurring alcohol use disorders and serious mental illness. *American Journal of Psychiatry, 174*(4), 370–377. https://doi.org/10.1176/appi.ajp.2016.16050627

McNeely, J., Wu, L. T., Subramaniam, G., Sharma, G., Cathers, L. A., Svikis, D., Sleiter, L., Russell, L., Nordeck, C., Sharma, A., O'Grady, K. E., Bouk, L. B., Cushing, C., King, J., Wahle, A., & Schwartz, R. P. (2016). Performance of the tobacco, alcohol, prescription medication, and other substance use (TAPS) tool for substance use screening in primary care patients. *Annals of Internal Medicine, 165*(10), 690–699. https://doi.org/10.7326/M16-0317

Saitz, R., Miller, S. C., Fiellin, D. A., & Rosenthal, R. N. (2014). *The ASAM principles of addiction medicine* (5th ed.). Lippincott Williams & Wilkins.

Substance Abuse and Mental Health Services Administration (SAMHSA). (2012). *Clinical drug testing in primary care: Technical assistance publication series (TAP 32)*. U.S. Department of Health and Human Services.

Chapter 20
Treating Tic in Psychosis

Abstract This chapter describes the treatment of tic disorders in psychosis, where severe tics and poor insight may present with overlapping phenomenology to psychotic symptoms. It starts by clarifying treatment goals and outlines assessment using the Yale Global Tic Severity Scale to evaluate motor tics, vocal tics, overall severity, and impairment. The intervention module combines Exposure and Response Prevention with Habit Reversal Training, explaining how exposure to tic triggers, prevention of tic responses, and the use of competing responses can reduce tic frequency and distress. The chapter frames tic treatment as a way to reduce functional interference and to clarify the boundary between tic-related phenomena and true psychotic symptoms.

Keywords Tic disorders · Habit reversal training · Behavioral therapy · Motor control · Response prevention

20.1 Goals of Treating Tic for Psychosis

The main goal to treat tic disorder for psychosis is to improve psychotic symptoms that may be a manifestation of severe, lacking insight, tic symptoms. It has been shown that Tourette Syndrome shared phenomenology with psychosis (Kerbeshian et al., 2009). A few randomized controlled trials have found that 8–14 sessions of habit reversal training and 12 sessions of ERP are associated with positive outcomes in Tourette Syndrome (Deckersbach et al., 2006; Verdellen et al., 2004; Wilhelm et al., 2012)

E. S. Jaya, *Cognitive Behavioral Therapy for Psychosis as a Syndrome*,
https://doi.org/10.1007/978-981-95-9203-6_20

20.2 Measuring Tic

20.2.1 The Yale Global Tic Severity Scale (YGTSS)

The Yale-Global Tic Severity Scale (YGTSS) (Leckman et al., 1997) is a comprehensive instrument designed to assess the severity and impairment of tic disorders, including Tourette Syndrome. This scale provides a structured and detailed evaluation of both motor and vocal tics, allowing clinicians to track changes over time and measure the impact of tics on daily functioning. The YGTSS is a clinician-administered scale that consists of several key components:

- **Motor Tics**: This section evaluates the severity of motor tics, both simple (e.g., blinking, head jerks) and complex (e.g., touching objects, repeating movements).
- **Vocal Tics**: This section assesses the severity of vocal tics, including simple (e.g., grunting, throat clearing) and complex (e.g., repeating words or phrases).
- **Global Severity**: This component provides an overall severity rating, considering both the frequency and intensity of tics.
- **Impairment**: This section measures the extent to which tics interfere with the individual's daily life, including social, academic, and occupational functioning.

The YGTSS is typically administered during a clinical interview or through self-report, with the clinician rating the severity of tics and the degree of impairment. The severity is scored on a scale from 0 (no tic) to 5 (extreme severity), while impairment is rated from 0 (no impairment) to 5 (extreme impairment). The total score provides an integrated measure of tic severity and its impact on functioning.

20.3 Choosing Appropriate Techniques

The integration of Exposure and Response Prevention and Habit Reversal Training in CBT for Tic Disorder provides a comprehensive framework for reducing tic severity, distress, and interference. By combining exposure to triggers while preventing tic responses and replacing tics with competing responses, individuals can gain better control over their symptoms.

20.4 Exposure and Response Prevention

Exposure and Response Prevention (ERP) aims to reduce the distress and interference caused by tics through exposing individuals to tic-related triggers, while preventing the associated tic response. For instance, a person experiencing distress due to an urge to blink excessively might deliberately face situations that trigger this urge (such as watching bright lights) while refraining from blinking excessively.

Over repeated exposures, individuals habituate to the urge, leading to decreased tic-related distress and a diminished urge to perform the tic.

Example of ERP in Tic Disorder: A person with a vocal tic of throat clearing might deliberately engage in situations that trigger the urge to clear their throat (such as being in a dusty environment) and resist the urge. They may initially experience heightened anxiety, but with repeated exposures, learn to tolerate the discomfort without engaging in the tic.

20.5 Habit Reversal Training

Habit reversal training (HRT) is a behavioral intervention that focuses on increasing awareness of premonitory sensations or urges preceding tics and developing alternative responses incompatible with the tic. It involves three main components: awareness training, competing response training, and social support. By identifying premonitory sensations and substituting a competing response, individuals can effectively reduce or control their tics.

Example of HRT in Tic Disorder: A person with a tic of eye blinking might learn to identify the premonitory sensation leading to the urge to blink. With therapist guidance, they practice a competing response, like gently pressing their eyelids together when they feel the urge. Over time, this competing response replaces the tic, reducing its occurrence.

References

Deckersbach, T., Rauch, S., Buhlmann, U., & Wilhelm, S. (2006). Habit reversal versus supportive psychotherapy in Tourette's disorder: A randomized controlled trial and predictors of treatment response. *Behaviour Research and Therapy, 44*(8), 1079–1090. https://doi.org/10.1016/j.brat.2005.08.007

Kerbeshian, J., Peng, C. Z., & Burd, L. (2009). Tourette syndrome and comorbid early-onset schizophrenia. *Journal of Psychosomatic Research, 67*(6), 515–523. https://doi.org/10.1016/j.jpsychores.2009.08.002

Leckman, J. F., Greene, D. J., & Pauls, D. L. (1997). Yale global tic severity scale (YGTSS): A multi-dimensional measure of tic severity. *Journal of the American Academy of Child and Adolescent Psychiatry, 36*(6), 1004–1013. https://doi.org/10.1097/00004583-199706000-00013

Verdellen, C. W., Keijsers, G. P., Cath, D. C., & Hoogduin, C. A. (2004). Exposure with response prevention versus habit reversal in Tourettes's syndrome: A controlled study. *Behaviour Research and Therapy, 42*(5), 501–511. https://doi.org/10.1016/S0005-7967(03)00154-2

Wilhelm, S., Peterson, A. L., Piacentini, J., Woods, D. W., Deckersbach, T., Sukhodolsky, D. G., Chang, S., Liu, H., Dziura, J., Walkup, J. T., & Scahill, L. (2012). Randomized trial of behavior therapy for adults with Tourette syndrome. *Archives of General Psychiatry, 69*(8), 795–803. https://doi.org/10.1001/archgenpsychiatry.2011.1528

References

Chapter 21
Treating Impulsivity in Psychosis

Abstract This chapter offers a structured intervention for impulsivity in psychosis, aiming to reduce high-risk behaviors and improve self-control. It begins with assessment using the Barratt Impulsiveness Scale, Lifetime History of Impulsive Behaviors, UPPS-P, and the Impulsive Compulsive Behaviors Checklist. The treatment module comprises two main strands: mindfulness-based approaches (mindful breathing, body scan, urge surfing) and attention-training methods, including attention bias modification, cognitive control training, attentional flexibility training, and mindfulness-based attention training. These techniques are presented as practical tools for increasing awareness of impulses, lengthening the pause before action, and supporting safer, more deliberate behavior in people with psychosis.

Keywords Treating impulsivity in psychosis: impulse control · Mindfulness training · Cognitive control · Urge surfing · Attentional bias

21.1 Goals of Treating Impulsivity for Psychosis

The main goal of treating impulsivity in psychosis is to reduce potentially self-destructive behavior that could trigger negative events. These events may lead to negative emotions, increasing the likelihood of psychotic symptoms appearing. For instance, impulsive actions can rupture relationships that provide essential social support for the patient. Suppose a patient hears voices instructing him to throw a glass mug at his mother, with the promise that the voice will go away if he obeys and he will be cured. If he can resist impulsivity, he may choose to negotiate with the voice or distract himself with other activities. However, if he acts impulsively and throws the mug, his mother might become afraid of him and no longer provide him with emotional support out of fear. This loss of relationship may reinforce the patient's belief that everybody is evil, a type of paranoid thinking. Previous randomized controlled trials have found that 8–10 sessions of mindfulness are effective in reducing impulsivity (Carmona i Farrés et al., 2019; Davis et al., 2019).

E. S. Jaya, *Cognitive Behavioral Therapy for Psychosis as a Syndrome*,
https://doi.org/10.1007/978-981-95-9203-6_21

Psychotherapists are free to choose the measurement and techniques relevant to the patient.

21.2 Measuring Impulsivity

21.2.1 Barratt Impulsiveness Scale (BIS-11)

The Barratt Impulsiveness Scale (BIS-11) is a self-report instrument designed to assess impulsiveness across three major facets: attentional, motor, and non-planning impulsiveness. The BIS-11 consists of 30 items rated on a 4-point scale, ranging from 1 (rarely/never) to 4 (almost always/always). Higher total scores reflect greater impulsivity. The scale is used in various research and clinical settings to evaluate impulsive behaviors and traits associated with disorders such as ADHD, substance abuse, and personality disorders (Patton et al., 1995). The BIS-11 has demonstrated strong internal consistency and test-retest reliability (Stanford et al., 2009).

21.2.2 Lifetime History of Impulsive Behaviors (LHIB-Q53)

The Lifetime History of Impulsive Behaviors Questionnaire (LHIB-Q53) is a comprehensive self-report measure designed to assess a broad range of impulsive behaviors across an individual's lifetime. It consists of 53 items that cover various domains of impulsivity, including risky behaviors, aggression, and substance use. Each item is rated based on the frequency and severity of the behavior. The LHIB-Q53 is useful for identifying impulsivity patterns and understanding the impact of impulsive behaviors on an individual's life. The scale has shown good reliability and validity in diverse populations (Wilhelm et al., 2016).

21.2.3 UPPS-P Impulsive Behavior Scale

The UPPS-P Impulsive Behavior Scale is a self-report tool that measures impulsivity across five distinct dimensions: Urgency, Premeditation, Perseverance, Sensation Seeking, and Positive Urgency. This 59-item scale helps in understanding various facets of impulsivity and their relation to behavioral disorders. Responses are rated on a 4-point scale from 1 (agree strongly) to 4 (disagree strongly). The UPPS-P has demonstrated strong psychometric properties and is widely used in research and clinical settings to assess impulsive behaviors (Lynam et al., 2007).

21.2.4 Impulsive Compulsive Behaviors Checklist (ICBC)

The Impulsive Compulsive Behaviors Checklist (ICBC) is a tool designed to assess a range of impulsive and compulsive behaviors that may be associated with various psychiatric conditions. The checklist includes items related to compulsive gambling, shopping, eating, and substance use. Each behavior is rated based on the frequency and severity of its occurrence. The ICBC is useful for clinicians in identifying problematic behaviors and planning interventions. The checklist has shown good reliability and validity in different clinical populations (Verdejo-Garcia et al., 2008).

21.3 Mindfulness

Mindfulness techniques within the framework of CBT have shown promising results in addressing impulsivity by enhancing self-awareness, self-regulation, and emotional control (Linehan, 2014). Mindfulness involves being fully present in the moment without judgment. The purpose is to increase awareness of thoughts, emotions, bodily sensations, and environmental stimuli without reacting impulsively. Here are some exercises that can be provided to the patient.

21.3.1 Mindful Breathing Exercise

The practice of mindful breathing involves concentrating on the natural rhythm of breathing, allowing individuals to ground themselves in the present moment. This exercise encourages observing the breath without attempting to change it. Patients can practice this for a few minutes daily, gradually extending the duration as they become more comfortable.

For example: Instruct the patient to sit comfortably, close their eyes, and direct attention to the sensations of their breath—the rising and falling of the abdomen or the airflow through the nostrils. When the mind drifts, gently guide attention back to the breath.

21.3.2 Body Scan

A body scan meditation involves systematically focusing attention on different parts of the body. The aim is to notice physical sensations, such as tension or discomfort, without judgment. Patients can start at their toes and work their way up, gently observing sensations in each area. This practice helps increase body awareness and promotes relaxation.

For example: Instruct the patient to lie down or sit comfortably. Guide their attention gradually from head to toe, directing them to notice physical sensations in each body part. Encourage them to observe without judgment, acknowledging any discomfort or tension and allowing it to pass without reacting impulsively.

21.3.3 Urge Surfing

Urge surfing involves acknowledging and observing impulses without acting on them. Patients are encouraged to imagine themselves riding a wave, representing the urge, and noticing its rise and fall without giving in. They observe the urge with curiosity, allowing it to diminish naturally.

For example: Instruct the patient to recognize impulsive urges without acting on them. Instruct them to label the thoughts and sensations associated with urges as transient and not requiring immediate action. Emphasize observing the ebb and flow of urges without being carried away by them.

21.4 Attention Training

There are many attention-training exercises. Here are four of the common ones that can be used for managing impulsivity. The psychotherapist can choose the ones that the patient most enjoyed or easily accessible for the patient.

21.4.1 Attention Bias Modification (ABM)

Attention Bias Modification (ABM) targets automatic attentional processes, redirecting attention away from impulsive stimuli by repeatedly training individuals to focus on neutral or non-impulsive cues. In a computer-based task, participants identify target cues while ignoring impulsive or distracting stimuli. Over sessions, the program gradually adjusts to emphasize non-impulsive cues, thereby reducing attentional bias toward impulsive triggers. For instance, the Dot-Probe Task presents pairs of stimuli (e.g., neutral and impulsive images or words) on a screen. A dot then appears in the location previously occupied by one of the stimuli, and participants identify the dot's location. By consistently replacing the neutral stimulus, this task effectively shifts attention away from the impulsive cue.

21.4.2 Cognitive Control Training

Cognitive control exercises enhance inhibitory control, empowering individuals to suppress impulsive responses and make more considered choices. The Stroop Task is an exemplary exercise wherein participants view color words (e.g., "red," "blue") printed in incongruent ink colors (e.g., the word "red" printed in blue ink). Participants are directed to name the ink color while inhibiting the automatic reading of the word. This task effectively strengthens inhibitory control by necessitating individuals to override automatic responses.

21.4.3 Attentional Flexibility Training

Attentional Flexibility Training enhances the ability to shift between different tasks or stimuli, reducing impulsivity associated with rigid attentional focus. For example, Task Switching exercises require participants to rapidly alternate between different activities. For instance, participants might sort shapes by color and then abruptly switch to sorting the same shapes by size. This exercise promotes cognitive flexibility by training individuals to transition attention between distinct tasks, fostering adaptability and reducing impulsivity in fixation.

21.4.4 Mindfulness-Based Attention Training

Mindfulness techniques, including candle gazing and meditation practices, cultivate sustained attention, thereby reducing impulsive reactions. Candle Gazing Meditation, a notable example, involves focusing attention on a candle flame. This practice trains individuals to sustain focus, observe impulses without immediate reactions, and enhance present-moment awareness.

References

Carmona i Farrés, C., Elices, M., Soler, J., Domínguez-Clavé, E., Pomarol-Clotet, E., Salvador, R., & Pascual, J. C. (2019). Effects of mindfulness training on borderline personality disorder: Impulsivity versus emotional dysregulation. *Mindfulness, 10*(7), 1243–1254. https://doi.org/10.1007/s12671-018-1071-4

Davis, J. P., Barr, N., Dworkin, E. R., Dumas, T. M., Berey, B., DiGuiseppi, G., & Rael Cahn, B. (2019). Effect of mindfulness-based relapse prevention on impulsivity trajectories among young adults in residential substance use disorder treatment. *Mindfulness, 10*(10), 1997–2009. https://doi.org/10.1007/s12671-019-01164-0

Linehan, M. M. (2014). *DBT skills training handouts and worksheets* (2nd ed.). The Guilford Press.

Lynam, D. R., Smith, G. T., Cyders, M. A., & Fischer, S. (2007). The UPPS-P impulsive behavior scale: Development and assessment of a new measure of impulsivity. *Psychological Assessment, 19*(1), 55–68. https://doi.org/10.1037/1040-3590.19.1.55

Patton, J. H., Stanford, M. S., & Barratt, E. S. (1995). Factor structure of the Barratt impulsiveness scale. *Journal of Clinical Psychology, 51*(6), 768–774. https://doi.org/10.1002/1097-4679(199511)51:6<768::AID-JCLP2270510607>3.0.CO;2-1

Stanford, M. S., Mathias, C. W., Dougherty, D. M., & Lake, A. M. (2009). Fifty years of the Barratt impulsiveness scale: An update and review. *Personality and Individual Differences, 47*(5), 385–395. https://doi.org/10.1016/j.paid.2009.01.061

Verdejo-Garcia, A., Lawrence, A. J., & Clark, L. (2008). Impulsivity as a vulnerability marker for substance-use disorders: Recent findings and clinical implications. *Current Drug Abuse Reviews, 1*(3), 207–221. https://doi.org/10.2174/1874473710801030207

Wilhelm, S., Berman, N. C., Keshaviah, A., Schwartz, R. A., & Steketee, G. (2016). Development and psychometric evaluation of the Lifetime History of Impulsive Behaviors Interview (LHIB). *Psychological Assessment, 28*(11), 1405–1417. https://doi.org/10.1037/pas0000266

Part V
Treatment Modules: Stage 2 Improvement of Risk and Protective Factors

Chapter 22
Improving Emotional Regulation in Psychosis

Abstract This chapter outlines a structured emotion regulation module adapted for individuals with psychosis. It begins by defining therapeutic goals and reviewing validated assessment instruments such as the SEK-27, ERQ, DERS, CERQ, SRES, and BERI to establish baseline regulatory capacity. The chapter then introduces DBT-based skills tailored for psychosis, including identifying and labeling emotions, recognizing emotional vulnerabilities, validating emotional experience, applying targeted regulation strategies, and building distress-tolerance skills. These components are presented as a cohesive framework to strengthen emotional stability, reduce symptom reactivity, and improve overall functioning.

Keywords Improving emotional regulation in psychosis: emotion regulation • Distress tolerance • DBT skills • Emotional awareness • Adaptive coping

22.1 Goals of Improving Emotional Regulation for Psychosis

The main goal of improving emotional regulation skills for psychosis is to reduce psychotic symptoms triggered by unnecessarily strong emotional response. Ecological momentary studies have shown that emotions like sadness and anxiety often precede increases in psychotic symptoms (Ben-Zeev et al., 2011; Ludwig et al. 2020; Orth et al., 2022). It is also well known that our emotional responses to environmental triggers can sometimes be inappropriate, either too strong or too weak. For example, a traumatized individual might freeze and not react upon receiving unwanted sexual advance (too weak of a response) or a perfectionist individual can shout in extreme anger when the margin of a document is not the same on every page (too strong of a response). Here, we also aim to reduce non-adaptive emotional regulation strategies, such as suppression. It has been shown that suppressing emotions, negative or positive, increases the intensity of the emotions. Since we know that negative emotions can precede psychotic symptoms, it is important to make

E. S. Jaya, *Cognitive Behavioral Therapy for Psychosis as a Syndrome*,
https://doi.org/10.1007/978-981-95-9203-6_22

sure that negative emotions are well-regulated to prevent triggering psychotic symptoms. Some randomized controlled trials have found that 13–16 sessions of dialectical behavior therapy (DBT) can help improve emotion regulation (Neacsiu et al., 2014; Soler et al., 2009).

22.2 Measuring Emotional Regulation Skills

22.2.1 Emotion Regulation Skills Questionnaire (SEK-27)

The Emotion Regulation Skills Questionnaire (SEK-27), developed by Berking and Znoj (2011), measures emotional regulation abilities across nine domains, such as emotional awareness, acceptance, and resilience. The scale consists of 27 items rated on a Likert scale, assessing an individual's competence in managing emotions. With demonstrated reliability and validity, the SEK-27 is widely used in clinical and research contexts for evaluating emotional skills.

22.2.2 Emotion Regulation Questionnaire (ERQ)

The Emotion Regulation Questionnaire (ERQ), developed by Gross and John (2003), measures two primary strategies of emotion regulation: cognitive reappraisal and expressive suppression. The scale consists of ten items, with six items assessing cognitive reappraisal and four items assessing expressive suppression. Respondents rate the frequency of their use of these strategies on a 7-point Likert scale, ranging from "almost never" to "almost always." The ERQ is widely used to understand how individuals manage their emotions and its impact on psychological outcomes.

22.2.3 Difficulties in Emotion Regulation Scale (DERS)

The Difficulties in Emotion Regulation Scale (DERS), developed by Gratz and Roemer (2004), assesses various difficulties in regulating emotions. It includes 36 items rated on a 5-point Likert scale. The DERS evaluates domains such as emotional awareness, acceptance, and regulation strategies. High scores indicate greater difficulties in managing emotions, and the scale is frequently used to study emotional dysregulation and related psychological issues.

22.2.4 Cognitive Emotion Regulation Questionnaire (CERQ)

The Cognitive Emotion Regulation Questionnaire (CERQ), developed by Garnefski et al. (2001), assesses cognitive strategies used to manage emotions. It includes 36 items rated on a 5-point Likert scale, covering strategies such as self-blame, rumination, and positive refocusing. The CERQ is used to evaluate how individuals use cognitive processes to handle emotional experiences and is useful in research on coping and adjustment.

22.2.5 Strategies for Regulating Emotions Scale (SRES)

The Strategies for Regulating Emotions Scale (SRES), developed by Thompson (1994), assesses various strategies individuals use to regulate their emotions, including problem-solving, seeking support, and avoidance. It includes multiple subscales and provides insights into the effectiveness of different emotion regulation strategies. The SRES is used to understand individual differences in emotion regulation and its impact on psychological functioning.

22.2.6 Brief Emotion Regulation Inventory (BERI)

The Brief Emotion Regulation Inventory (BERI), created by Waugh et al. (2008), is a shorter measure designed to assess various aspects of emotion regulation, including strategies like suppression, acceptance, and cognitive change. It provides a quick yet comprehensive assessment of emotional regulation abilities, with fewer items than other measures, making it suitable for both clinical and research applications.

22.3 Emotional Regulation Skills DBT

Emotional regulation skills are vital components of therapy for individuals experiencing psychosis. Emotions play a significant role in shaping thoughts and behaviors. The following skills, derived from Linehan's DBT, are essential in assisting individuals in managing their emotional experiences effectively.

22.3.1 Understanding and Identifying Emotions

Help individuals comprehend their emotions by using the DBT Emotion Regulation Skill of "Identifying and Labeling Emotions." Teach them to recognize and label their emotional experiences accurately. This skill enhances self-awareness and contributes to better emotional regulation.

22.3.2 Recognizing Emotional Vulnerabilities

Explore factors contributing to emotional vulnerabilities. Discuss the importance of identifying personal triggers, such as stressors or cognitive distortions, that intensify emotional responses.

22.3.3 Acceptance and Validation of Emotions

Introduce the concept of Radical Acceptance, emphasizing the practice of acknowledging and accepting emotions and situations without judgment or attempting to change them. Encourage individuals experiencing psychosis to accept their emotional experiences as they are, promoting a non-judgmental attitude toward their feelings. This skill facilitates a non-judgmental stance toward emotions, fostering resilience and reducing distress.

22.3.4 Emotion Regulation Strategies

Teach practical strategies including:

- *Opposite Action*: Explain Opposite Action as a skill involving acting in a way that is contrary to the emotional impulse. This technique helps in managing intense emotions effectively. For example, guide individuals to identify intense emotions disproportionate to the situation and encourage them to deliberately engage in actions opposite to those driven by the emotion.
- *Coping Ahead*: Guide individuals to plan and prepare for situations that may evoke intense emotions. This proactive approach assists in regulating emotions before they escalate. For example, assist individuals in foreseeing and planning responses to situations that might elicit intense emotions due to psychotic experiences, thereby managing emotions before they escalate.
- *ABC PLEASE*: Incorporate self-care practices such as activities (Accumulating Positives), maintaining a healthy lifestyle (Balancing Eating), contributing to

physical well-being (Contributing), maintaining mastery and self-respect (Building Mastery), and getting adequate sleep (Balancing Sleep):

- *Accumulating Positives*: Encourage individuals to engage in activities that bring positivity and pleasure to their lives, thereby enhancing their mood and emotional well-being.
- *Balancing Eating*: Emphasize the importance of maintaining a balanced diet to support emotional regulation and stabilize mood.
- *Contributing*: Advocate for activities that enable individuals to make meaningful contributions, fostering a sense of purpose and fulfillment.
- *Building Mastery*: Encourage the pursuit of activities that enhance skills and competence, boosting self-esteem and confidence.
- *Balancing Sleep*: Highlight the significance of adequate sleep in regulating emotions and improving overall well-being.

22.3.5 Distress Tolerance

Introduce distress-tolerance skills to help individuals tolerate intense emotions without resorting to maladaptive behaviors. Teach individuals skills such as distraction, self-soothing, improving the moment, and other coping techniques to manage distress more effectively.

References

Ben-Zeev, D., Ellington, K., Swendsen, J., & Granholm, E. (2011). Examining a cognitive model of persecutory ideation in the daily life of people with schizophrenia: A computerized experience sampling study. *Schizophrenia Bulletin, 37*(6), 1248–1256. https://doi.org/10.1093/schbul/sbq041

Berking, M., & Znoj, H. (2011). *SEK-27. Fragebogen zur standardisierten Selbsteinschätzung emotionaler Kompetenzen*. Open Test Archive. Trier: ZPID. https://doi.org/10.23668/psycharchives.5261

Garnefski, N., Kraaij, V., & Spinhoven, P. (2001). Negative life events, cognitive emotion regulation, and emotional problems. *Personality and Individual Differences, 30*(8), 1311–1327. https://doi.org/10.1016/S0191-8869(00)00113-6

Gratz, K. L., & Roemer, L. (2004). The difficulties in emotion regulation scale: Development and validation of an instrument to assess emotional dysregulation. *Journal of Psychopathology and Behavioral Assessment, 26*(1), 41–54. https://doi.org/10.1023/B:JOBA.0000007455.08539.94

Gross, J. J., & John, O. P. (2003). Individual differences in two emotion regulation processes: Implications for affect, relationships, and Well-being. *Journal of Personality and Social Psychology, 85*(2), 348–362. https://doi.org/10.1037/0022-3514.85.2.348

Ludwig, L., Mehl, S., Schlier, B., Krkovic, K., & Lincoln, T. M. (2020). Awareness and rumination moderate the affective pathway to paranoia in daily life. *Schizophrenia Research, 216*, 161–167. https://doi.org/10.1016/j.schres.2019.12.007

Neacsiu, A. D., Eberle, J. W., Kramer, R., Wiesmann, T., & Linehan, M. M. (2014). Dialectical behavior therapy skills for transdiagnostic emotion dysregulation: A pilot randomized controlled trial. *Behaviour Research and Therapy, 59*, 40–51. https://doi.org/10.1016/j.brat.2014.05.005

Orth, R. D., Hur, J., Jacome, A. M., Savage, C. L. G., Grogans, S. E., Kim, Y. H., Choe, E. K., Shackman, A. J., & Blanchard, J. J. (2022). Understanding the consequences of moment-by-moment fluctuations in mood and social experience for paranoid ideation in psychotic disorders. *Schizophrenia Bulletin Open, 3*(1), sgac 064. https://doi.org/10.1093/schizbullopen/sgac064

Soler, J., Pascual, J. C., Tiana, T., Cebrià, A., Barrachina, J., Campins, M. J., Gich, I., Alvarez, E., & Pérez, V. (2009). Dialectical behaviour therapy skills training compared to standard group therapy in borderline personality disorder: A 3-month randomised controlled clinical trial. *Behaviour Research and Therapy, 47*(5), 353–358. https://doi.org/10.1016/j.brat.2009.01.013

Thompson, R. A. (1994). Emotion regulation: A theme in search of definition. *Monographs of the Society for Research in Child Development, 59*(2–3), 25–52.

Waugh, C. E., & Fredrickson, B. L. (2008). The emotional regulation scale: A brief measure of emotion regulation. *Journal of Personality Assessment, 90*(4), 319–327.

Chapter 23
Reducing Negative Schemas in Psychosis

Abstract This chapter presents CBT methods for identifying and modifying negative schemas that contribute to distress and symptom exacerbation in psychosis. It outlines therapeutic goals and describes assessment approaches for detecting maladaptive core beliefs. Cognitive restructuring techniques are detailed step-by-step, followed by behavioral experiments designed to test schema-driven predictions and generate corrective experiences. The chapter emphasizes how reducing negative schemas improves emotional resilience, interpersonal functioning, and vulnerability to psychotic stressors.

Keywords Reducing negative schemas in psychosis: maladaptive schemas · Core beliefs · Cognitive restructuring · Schema modification · Behavioral experiments

23.1 Goals of Reducing Negative Schemas for Psychosis

The main goal of reducing negative schemas in psychosis is to minimize triggers of psychotic symptoms. Negative schemas have been shown to be a maintenance factor of psychotic symptoms via negative affect (Jaya et al., 2017; Oliver et al., 2012). By addressing and reducing these negative schemas, interventions can have a lasting impact, helping patients remain free of psychotic symptoms for longer periods. A randomized controlled trial found that 16 sessions of CBT for social anxiety disorder led to a clinically significant reduction in negative self-views (Goldin et al., 2013).

23.2 Measuring Negative Schemas

The Brief Core Schema Scales (BCSS) (Fowler et al., 2006) consist of 24 items that assess beliefs about self and others, rated on a five-point scale (0–4). Items examples of beliefs about self are judging oneself to be weak, worthless, useless, and

E. S. Jaya, *Cognitive Behavioral Therapy for Psychosis as a Syndrome*,
https://doi.org/10.1007/978-981-95-9203-6_23

inadequate. Examples of beliefs about others are judging others to be bad, devious, and untrustworthy. The scale provides four subscores: negative-self (six items), positive-self (six items), negative-others (six items), and positive-others (six items). This scale is very brief and takes only about 2 min to complete. In different populations, the BCSS has been shown to have good validity and reliability (Addington & Tran, 2009; Fowler et al., 2006).

23.3 Cognitive Restructuring

Cognitive restructuring involves identifying and challenging maladaptive beliefs and thought patterns that contribute to negative schemas.

- Identifying Negative Beliefs: Assist individuals in recognizing maladaptive beliefs or thought patterns, such as paranoid beliefs or negative views about self-worth, that reinforce negative schemas related to their psychotic experiences.
- Questioning the Validity of Thoughts: Guide individuals to examine the evidence supporting their negative beliefs, encouraging them to challenge the accuracy and rationality of these thoughts.
- Developing Alternative Beliefs: Help individuals generate and adopt alternative, more balanced, and realistic beliefs, facilitating a shift away from negative schemas related to their psychosis.

23.4 Behavioral Experiment to Test Negative Schemas

Behavioral experiments involve designing and conducting activities or tasks to test the validity of negative beliefs and challenge their impact on behavior.

- Designing Experiments: Collaborate with individuals to design behavioral experiments aimed at testing the accuracy and reliability of negative schemas related to their psychotic experiences.
- Implementing Experiments: Encourage individuals to engage in planned activities or tasks that challenge their negative beliefs or predictions associated with their psychosis.
- Reflecting on Outcomes: Support individuals in reflecting on the outcomes of the experiments, helping them evaluate the evidence gathered and encouraging adjustments in their beliefs based on the results.

References

Addington, J., & Tran, L. (2009). Using the brief core schema scales with individuals at clinical high risk of psychosis. *Behavioural and Cognitive Psychotherapy, 37*(2), 227–231.

Fowler, D., Freeman, D., Smith, B. E. N., Kuipers, E., Bebbington, P., Bashforth, H., Garety, P., et al. (2006). The brief Core schema scales (BCSS): Psychometric properties and associations with paranoia and grandiosity in non-clinical and psychosis samples. *Psychological Medicine, 36*(6), 749–759.

Goldin, P. R., Jazaieri, H., Ziv, M., Kraemer, H., Heimberg, R. G., & Gross, J. J. (2013). Changes in positive self-views mediate the effect of cognitive-behavioral therapy for social anxiety disorder. *Clinical Psychological Science, 1*(3), 301–310. https://doi.org/10.1177/2167702613476867

Jaya, E. S., Ascone, L., & Lincoln, T. M. (2017). Social adversity and psychosis: The mediating role of cognitive vulnerability. *Schizophrenia Bulletin, 43*(3), 557–565. https://doi.org/10.1093/schbul/sbw104

Oliver, J. E., O'Connor, J. A., Jose, P. E., McLachlan, K., & Peters, E. (2012). The impact of negative schemas, mood and psychological flexibility on delusional ideation—Mediating and moderating effects. *Psychosis: Psychological, Social and Integrative Approaches, 4*(1), 6–18. https://doi.org/10.1080/17522439.2011.637117

Chapter 24
Improving Positive Schemas in Psychosis

Abstract This chapter focuses on strengthening positive schemas to enhance psychological well-being in psychosis. It begins by clarifying treatment goals and reviewing measures for assessing positive schemas. The chapter outlines cognitive restructuring strategies aimed at reinforcing helpful beliefs about the self and others. It then introduces Compassion-Focused Therapy techniques to cultivate warmth, self-acceptance, and inner safety. Together, these interventions aim to increase protective cognitive patterns that buffer against psychotic vulnerability and support recovery.

Keywords Reducing negative schemas in psychosis: maladaptive schemas · Core beliefs · Cognitive restructuring · Schema modification · Behavioral experiments

24.1 Goals of Improving Positive Schemas for Psychosis

The main goal of improving positive schemas in psychosis is to establish them as protective factors against possible adverse experiences that may trigger psychotic symptoms. For example, an individual with good positive schemas about others may show resilience in the face of discriminatory events, preventing the activation of generalized suspicious thinking. To illustrate, if a person with good positive others schema encounters racial discrimination in a shop and is not served, he will not think that the shop is evil or that the world is against him because of his race (jumping to conclusion bias, paranoid thinking). Instead, he may think that he is a bit unlucky to be served by that particular racist person in the shop. A randomized controlled trial found that 16 sessions of CBT for social anxiety disorder resulted in a clinically significant improvement in positive self-views (Goldin et al., 2013).

E. S. Jaya, *Cognitive Behavioral Therapy for Psychosis as a Syndrome*,
https://doi.org/10.1007/978-981-95-9203-6_24

24.2 Measuring Positive Schemas

The Brief Core Schema Scales (BCSS) (Fowler et al., 2006) consist of 24 items that assess beliefs about self and others, rated on a five-point scale (0–4). Items examples of beliefs about self are judging oneself to be weak, worthless, useless, and inadequate. Examples of beliefs about others are judging others to be bad, devious, and untrustworthy. The scale provides four subscores: negative-self (six items), positive-self (six items), negative-others (six items), and positive-others (six items). This scale is very brief and takes only about 2 min to complete. In different populations, the BCSS has been shown to have good validity and reliability (Addington & Tran, 2009; Fowler et al., 2006).

24.3 Cognitive Restructuring

Cognitive restructuring is a fundamental facet in addressing maladaptive thought patterns, aiming to cultivate positive and adaptive beliefs in individuals experiencing psychosis. This process involves identifying and reinforcing positive beliefs that counterbalance the negative schemas associated with their psychotic encounters. By guiding individuals to actively challenge distressing thoughts, presenting evidence both for and against them, cognitive restructuring fosters the development of more balanced thinking. Moreover, by assisting individuals in reinterpreting their experiences through a positive and realistic lens, this approach supports the cultivation of positive schemas essential for their mental well-being.

Some techniques that can be used include:

- Positive Data Logs: Encourage individuals to maintain logs of positive experiences, accomplishments, or moments of clarity. This exercise helps challenge negative beliefs by providing evidence for positive aspects of their lives.
- Evidence Analysis: Assist individuals in critically evaluating the evidence supporting negative beliefs. Use Socratic questioning to explore counter-evidence or alternative explanations, fostering more balanced perspectives.
- Reframing Interpretations: Guide individuals to reframe distressing or delusional interpretations of events. Encourage consideration of alternative explanations that are less threatening and align more closely with reality.
- Pros and Cons Lists: Engage individuals in constructing lists that compare the positive and negative aspects of their beliefs. This practice aids in identifying the drawbacks of negative schemas while highlighting the benefits of adopting more positive ones.

24.4 Compassion-Focused Therapy Techniques

Compassion-Focused Therapy emphasizes developing self-compassion and positive emotions to build a more compassionate relationship with oneself. Some techniques that can be used include:

- Compassionate Imagery: Guide individuals through compassionate imagery exercises, visualizing a compassionate figure or a safe place that evokes feelings of kindness, safety, and self-acceptance.
- Self-Compassion Journaling: Encourage individuals to keep a journal where they write self-compassionate messages to themselves. They can also write compassionate responses to distressing thoughts or experiences.
- Mindful Self-Compassion Exercises: Practice mindfulness-based exercises combined with self-compassion techniques, emphasizing self-kindness and non-judgmental acceptance of thoughts and emotions.

Letter Writing: Encourage individuals to write a compassionate letter to themselves, expressing understanding, empathy, and encouragement.

References

Addington, J., & Tran, L. (2009). Using the brief core schema scales with individuals at clinical high risk of psychosis. *Behavioural and Cognitive Psychotherapy, 37*(2), 227–231.

Fowler, D., Freeman, D., Smith, B. E. N., Kuipers, E., Bebbington, P., Bashforth, H., Garety, P., et al. (2006). The brief Core schema scales (BCSS): Psychometric properties and associations with paranoia and grandiosity in non-clinical and psychosis samples. *Psychological Medicine, 36*(6), 749–759.

Goldin, P. R., Jazaieri, H., Ziv, M., Kraemer, H., Heimberg, R. G., & Gross, J. J. (2013). Changes in positive self-views mediate the effect of cognitive-behavioral therapy for social anxiety disorder. *Clinical Psychological Science, 1*(3), 301–310. https://doi.org/10.1177/2167702613476867

Chapter 25
Improving Relationships in Psychosis

Abstract This chapter provides a relationship-focused intervention module addressing social functioning difficulties common in psychosis. It reviews assessment tools measuring relational adversity, undermining, discrimination, loneliness, bullying, and attachment-related challenges, including ACE, Social Undermining Scale, Illinois Bully Scale, EDS, and UCLA Loneliness Scale. The chapter then introduces psychoeducational and skills-based components such as understanding communication styles, assertiveness, boundary setting, I-messages, trust-building, and conflict navigation. These techniques aim to enhance interpersonal competence and strengthen protective relational networks.

Keywords Improving relationships in psychosis: interpersonal functioning · Social skills · Assertive communication · Boundary setting · Relationship quality

25.1 Goals of Improving Relationships for Psychosis

The main goal of improving relationships in psychosis is to prevent psychotic symptoms, which are often triggered by relationship problems. Numerous studies have demonstrated a link between adverse relationship experiences and psychotic symptoms (Jaya et al., 2017; Jaya & Lincoln, 2016). Furthermore, according to the social defeat hypothesis, schizophrenia may be caused by long-term adverse social experiences, such as childhood trauma, bullying, discrimination, social undermining, and loneliness. Some studies have found that 8–16 sessions of social skills training can help improve the social functioning of patients with psychosis (Chien et al., 2003; Rus-Calafell et al., 2013; Xiang et al., 2007).

E. S. Jaya, *Cognitive Behavioral Therapy for Psychosis as a Syndrome*,
https://doi.org/10.1007/978-981-95-9203-6_25

25.2 Measuring Relationships

25.2.1 Adverse Childhood Experience (ACE)

The Adverse Childhood Experience (ACE) questionnaire assesses early traumatic experiences, such as abuse, neglect, and household dysfunction, which occurred during childhood. This self-report measure includes ten items that inquire about emotional, physical, and sexual abuse as well as household challenges like parental separation, substance abuse, or mental illness. Each "yes" response scores 1 point, with higher scores indicating a greater risk of negative health outcomes, including mental health issues and chronic diseases (Felitti et al., 1998). The ACE questionnaire has been extensively validated and is widely used in both research and clinical settings to understand the impact of childhood trauma on later life outcomes.

25.2.2 Social Undermining Scale

The Social Undermining Scale, developed by Vinokur and van Ryn (1993), is a five-item measure that assesses the frequency of negative interactions with a spouse or significant other over the past 4 weeks. The scale includes questions such as "How much does your spouse or significant other act in an unpleasant or angry manner toward you?" Responses are rated on a 5-point Likert scale ranging from 1 (not at all) to 5 (a great deal). The scale is widely used in research to explore the impact of social relationships on emotional well-being and stress, particularly in the context of marital or significant-other dynamics.

25.2.3 Illinois Bully Scale (IBS)

The Illinois Bully Scale (IBS) is a self-report measure used to assess bullying behavior and victimization among adolescents. It consists of 18 items that evaluate three dimensions: bullying, victimization, and fighting. Respondents rate the frequency of behaviors, such as being teased, threatened, or engaging in physical altercations, on a 5-point Likert scale (0 = never, 4 = always). The IBS has been validated as a reliable tool for both research and school-based assessments to identify individuals involved in bullying, whether as victims or perpetrators (Espelage & Holt, 2001).

25.2.4 *Everyday Discrimination Scale (EDS)*

The Everyday Discrimination Scale (EDS), developed by Williams et al. (1997), is a widely used self-report measure assessing perceived experiences of routine discrimination. It consists of nine items that inquire about the frequency of subtle, daily discriminatory experiences, such as being treated with less courtesy, receiving poorer service, or being called names. Respondents rate the frequency of such occurrences on a 6-point Likert scale ranging from "never" to "almost every day." The EDS is designed to capture the chronic and pervasive nature of discrimination experienced by minority populations.

25.2.5 *UCLA Loneliness Scale (ULS-6)*

The UCLA Loneliness Scale (ULS-6) is a brief, six-item self-report measure designed to assess subjective feelings of loneliness and social isolation. Each item is rated on a 4-point Likert scale, ranging from 1 (never) to 4 (often), with higher scores indicating greater levels of loneliness. The ULS-6 has demonstrated strong psychometric properties, including good internal consistency and validity across various populations. A recent validation study confirmed its utility in diverse cultural settings, establishing it as a reliable tool for measuring loneliness in both clinical and research settings (Hudiyana et al., 2020).

25.3 Communication Styles

Effective communication styles are pivotal in fostering healthy relationships. Understanding various communication styles helps individuals navigate interactions and resolve conflicts more skillfully. There are four primary communication styles: passive, aggressive, passive-aggressive, and assertive. Passive communication involves avoiding conflict and not expressing one's needs or opinions. Aggressive communication tends to involve dominating others, often at the expense of their feelings. Passive-aggressive communication is indirect, using sarcasm or veiled remarks to express discontent. In contrast, assertive communication balances respecting one's needs while also considering others. It involves expressing thoughts, feelings, and needs honestly and directly while respecting the rights of others.

25.4 Assertive Communication

Assertive communication is a cornerstone for healthy relationships, enabling individuals to express their needs and opinions effectively. Here we encourage individuals to practice assertiveness, emphasizing clear and direct expression without violating the rights of others. It involves understanding personal rights, such as the right to say no, express feelings, and make mistakes. Through assertive communication, individuals can express their thoughts and feelings openly, make requests, and set boundaries, fostering healthy relationships while minimizing conflict and misunderstandings.

25.5 Boundaries

Establishing and maintaining healthy boundaries is essential for fostering respectful relationships. Here we emphasize the importance of setting clear and appropriate boundaries to protect one's physical, emotional, and mental well-being. Boundaries help delineate where one person ends, and another begins, defining permissible behaviors, limits, and responsibilities in relationships. It involves understanding personal limits and communicating them effectively to others. Healthy boundaries enable individuals to assert themselves, protect against exploitation, and foster mutual respect in relationships.

25.6 I-Message

I-messages are a key aspect of effective communication, emphasizing personal responsibility and assertiveness in expressing feelings or concerns without blame or criticism. I-messages involve using assertive statements that convey feelings, thoughts, or opinions without attacking or accusing others. They typically follow a structure of "I feel [emotion] when [specific behavior or situation occurs]," helping individuals express themselves without escalating conflict. Utilizing I-messages fosters open communication, encourages mutual respect, and reduces defensiveness in interpersonal interactions.

25.7 Trusts in Relationship

Trust is fundamental in building and maintaining healthy relationships. Here we emphasize the importance of trust, which forms the foundation for secure and supportive relationships. Trust involves relying on others, believing in their intentions, and feeling safe and secure within the relationship. Establishing trust requires consistent behavior, honesty, reliability, and respect for boundaries. Cultivating trust in relationships encourages vulnerability, deepens connections, and fosters emotional intimacy.

25.8 Navigating Resistance and Conflict

Here are strategies for navigating resistance and managing conflicts in relationships. Resistance can stem from various factors, including fear, discomfort, or a lack of understanding. Here we emphasize validating resistance by acknowledging the person's feelings or concerns without judgment. Managing conflicts effectively involves active listening, empathetic understanding, and using dialectics to reconcile opposing viewpoints. Skills such as DEAR MAN (Describe, Express, Assert, Reinforce, Mindful, Appear confident, Negotiate) assist in resolving conflicts assertively while maintaining the relationship (Linehan, 2014). Recognizing and addressing resistance and conflict skillfully can lead to improved communication and healthier relationships.

References

Chien, H. C., Ku, C. H., Lu, R. B., Chu, H., Tao, Y. H., & Chou, K. R. (2003). Effects of social skills training on improving social skills of patients with schizophrenia. *Archives of Psychiatric Nursing, 17*(5), 228–236. https://doi.org/10.1016/s0883-9417(03)00095-5

Espelage, D. L., & Holt, M. K. (2001). Bullying and victimization during early adolescence: Peer influences and psychosocial correlates. *Journal of Emotional Abuse, 2*(2–3), 123–142. https://doi.org/10.1300/J135v02n02_08

Felitti, V. J., Anda, R. F., Nordenberg, D., Williamson, D. F., Spitz, A. M., Edwards, V., Koss, M. P., & Marks, J. S. (1998). Relationship of childhood abuse and household dysfunction to many of the leading causes of death in adults: The adverse childhood experiences (ACE) study. *American Journal of Preventive Medicine, 14*(4), 245–258. https://doi.org/10.1016/S0749-3797(98)00017-8

Hudiyana, J., Lincoln, T. M., Hartanto, T., & Witvliet, M. (2020). Measuring loneliness in Indonesia: Validating the UCLA loneliness scale version 3 and its six-item short form in Indonesian adolescents. *Assessment, 27*(8), 1540–1551. https://doi.org/10.1177/1073191119828410

Jaya, E. S., & Lincoln, T. M. (2016). Social adversities and psychotic symptoms: A test of predictions derived from the social defeat hypothesis. *Psychiatry Research, 245*, 466–472. https://doi.org/10.1016/j.psychres.2016.09.002

Linehan, M. M. (2014). *DBT skills training handouts and worksheets* (2nd ed.). The Guilford Press.

Rus-Calafell, M., Gutiérrez-Maldonado, J., Ortega-Bravo, M., Ribas-Sabaté, J., & Caqueo-Urízar, A. (2013). A brief cognitive-behavioural social skills training for stabilised outpatients with schizophrenia: A preliminary study. *Schizophrenia Research, 143*(2–3), 327–336. https://doi.org/10.1016/j.schres.2012.11.014

Vinokur, A. D., & van Ryn, M. (1993). Social support and undermining in close relationships: Their independent effects on the mental health of unemployed persons. *Journal of Personality and Social Psychology, 65*(2), 350–359.

Williams, D. R., Yu, Y., Jackson, J. S., & Anderson, N. B. (1997). Racial differences in physical and mental health: Socio-economic status, stress, and discrimination. *Journal of Health Psychology, 2*(3), 335–351.

Xiang, Y. T., Weng, Y. Z., Li, W. Y., Gao, L., Chen, G. L., Xie, L., Chang, Y. L., Tang, W. K., & Ungvari, G. S. (2007). Efficacy of the community re-entry module for patients with schizophrenia in Beijing, China: Outcome at 2-year follow-up. *British Journal of Psychiatry, 190*(1), 49–56. https://doi.org/10.1192/bjp.bp.106.023697

Chapter 26
Increasing Reasons for Living in Psychosis

Abstract This chapter presents a module dedicated to enhancing reasons for living to reduce suicide risk in individuals with psychosis. It identifies treatment goals and uses the Reasons for Living Scale to assess protective beliefs. The chapter introduces counseling and coaching strategies to expand purpose, future orientation, and value-driven behavior. Skills such as distress tolerance through values-based action and differentiating willingness from willfulness are emphasized as practical tools for strengthening motivation to live and reducing self-harm vulnerability.

Keywords Increasing reasons for living in psychosis: values-based action · Suicide prevention · Meaning in life · Psychological resilience · Motivation

26.1 Goals of Increasing Reasons for Living for Psychosis

The main goal of improving reasons for living in psychosis is to enhance motivation for psychological treatment. Psychological treatment can be challenging, and success is difficult without the necessary motivation. This is not idiosyncratic to psychological treatment alone, any treatment that involves changing behavior requires significant motivation. For example, smoking cessation campaigns often remind participants about their children. Here, the aim of the psychologist is to discover significant motivators for the patient to stay engaged throughout the long-term duration of treatment. Sometimes the psychologist is required to create the motivation for the patient to stay in treatment, such as coaching them to get a promotion, repairing relationships, or returning to school. The Teachable Moment Brief Intervention (TMBI), a one-session intervention involving components of Dialectical Behavior Therapy (DBT), was found to increase reasons for living (O'Connor et al., 2015).

E. S. Jaya, *Cognitive Behavioral Therapy for Psychosis as a Syndrome*,
https://doi.org/10.1007/978-981-95-9203-6_26

26.2 Measuring Reasons for Living

26.2.1 Reasons for Living Scale (RFL)

The Reasons for Living Scale (RFL), developed by Linehan et al. (1983), is a self-report measure designed to assess factors that might prevent an individual from attempting suicide. It consists of 48 items across several domains, including survival and coping beliefs, responsibility to family, fear of suicide, moral objections, and fear of social disapproval. Respondents rate the importance of each reason for staying alive on a 6-point Likert scale, ranging from "not at all important" to "extremely important." The RFL has been used widely in both clinical and research settings to explore protective factors against suicidal behavior.

26.3 Counseling/Coaching

Counseling and coaching serve as pivotal tools in uncovering and nurturing motivations for life while elevating one's overall well-being. Individuals grappling with severe mental illnesses like schizophrenia often arrive at our doorstep having experienced a substantial loss in various facets of life. For instance, they might seek guidance from a psychotherapist in their 30 s without educational credentials, lacking a social circle, and devoid of romantic experiences. Our responsibility lies in cultivating optimism within them, illuminating the path forward and emphasizing that despite past challenges, a fulfilling life remains within their grasp. It may not entail winning prestigious accolades or gracing magazine covers but rather encompasses achievements significant enough to imbue their lives with purpose and contentment.

As psychotherapists, our role involves sitting with them, nurturing their aspirations, and guiding them toward ambitious yet attainable goals. These objectives may include fostering independence, pursuing a fulfilling career, seeking a meaningful romantic relationship, attaining a healthy body mass index, and other similar aspirations. Moreover, it is imperative to understand the patient's cultural context, enabling us to provide tailored guidance on the goals they should strive for. For example, for religious individuals within a religious environment, introducing goals related to volunteering within their faith community or committing to memorizing significant religious texts might resonate deeply.

Counseling provides a secure haven for individuals to delve into their thoughts, emotions, and behaviors, fostering self-discovery and introspection. Through compassionate guidance, individuals can unravel the core reasons propelling their existence, identify their strengths, and commence a journey toward meaningful transformation. Conversely, coaching focuses on delineating and accomplishing specific objectives, leveraging motivation to facilitate behavioral changes. Both counseling and coaching converge on a singular objective: empowering individuals to recognize and pursue a life that harmonizes with their values and aspirations.

26.4 Distress Tolerance Skills: Actions Based on Values

Distress tolerance skills help individuals navigate difficult emotions and situations while staying committed to their values and goals. Distress tolerance involves accepting painful emotions and experiences without escalating them. Within this framework, actions based on values are crucial. These skills guide individuals to engage in meaningful activities aligned with their core values, even amidst distress. By focusing on values, individuals can make choices and take actions that contribute to a sense of purpose and fulfillment. Whether experiencing intense emotions or distressing situations, practicing actions based on values allows individuals to stay connected to what is truly meaningful and important to them, enhancing reasons for living and promoting psychological well-being.

26.5 Willingness Vs. Willfulness

Willingness and willfulness are fundamental concepts that influence reasons for living. Willingness involves an open and accepting attitude toward present-moment experiences, including distressing emotions or challenging situations. Being willing means embracing what life offers without judgment or resistance. On the contrary, willfulness refers to a rigid or resistant stance toward experiences, often leading to increased suffering. Embracing willingness allows individuals to remain open to experiences, adapt to life's uncertainties, and take actions aligned with their values, fostering resilience and enhancing reasons for living. Recognizing and cultivating willingness over willfulness promotes psychological flexibility, encouraging individuals to live a more meaningful and fulfilling life despite adversities.

References

Linehan, M. M., Goodstein, J. L., Nielsen, S. L., & Chiles, J. A. (1983). Reasons for staying alive when you are thinking of killing yourself: The reasons for living inventory. *Journal of Consulting and Clinical Psychology, 51*(2), 276–286. https://doi.org/10.1037/0022-006X.51.2.276

O'Connor, S. S., Comtois, K. A., Wang, J., Russo, J., Peterson, R., Lapping-Carr, L., & Zatzick, D. (2015). The development and implementation of a brief intervention for medically admitted suicide attempt survivors. *General Hospital Psychiatry, 37*(5), 427–433. https://doi.org/10.1016/j.genhosppsych.2015.05.001

Chapter 27
Improving Self-Compassion in Psychosis

Abstract This chapter introduces a self-compassion module designed to reduce shame, self-criticism, and internalized stigma in psychosis. It outlines treatment goals, reviews assessment using the Self-Compassion Scale, and describes key therapeutic techniques such as the compassionate break exercise. The module emphasizes developing a kinder internal dialog, increasing emotional warmth toward oneself, and building protective self-schemas that support psychological recovery and resilience.

Keywords Improving self-compassion in psychosis: self-compassion · Compassion-focused intervention · Self-criticism · Emotional resilience · Psychological well-being

27.1 Goals of Improving Self-Compassion for Psychosis

The main goal of improving self-compassion for psychosis is to enhance protective factors that may reduce the likelihood of relapse and vulnerability to being easily triggered. A meta-analysis of self-compassion interventions found that 1–12 sessions led to significant improvements in various outcomes, including increased self-compassion and reduced self-criticism (Ferrari et al., 2019).

27.2 Measuring Self-Compassion

27.2.1 Self-Compassion Scale (SCS)

The Self-Compassion Scale (SCS), developed by Neff (2003), is a self-report measure designed to assess an individual's level of self-compassion. It evaluates three key components: self-kindness versus self-judgment, common humanity versus isolation, and mindfulness versus over-identification. The original 26-item

E. S. Jaya, *Cognitive Behavioral Therapy for Psychosis as a Syndrome*,
https://doi.org/10.1007/978-981-95-9203-6_27

scale uses a 5-point Likert scale, ranging from "almost never" to "almost always," to gage how frequently respondents experience self-compassionate versus self-critical thoughts and behaviors. The SCS has been widely utilized in research to explore its relationship with mental health, emotional resilience, and overall well-being.

27.3 Compassionate Break

Compassionate breaks serve as powerful tools in fostering self-compassion, an essential component of emotional well-being. These breaks provide a dedicated space and time to pause, acknowledge difficult emotions or moments of suffering, and respond with kindness and understanding toward oneself. When engaging in a compassionate break, individuals deliberately shift their attention to embrace self-compassion, offering themselves the same care and support they would extend to a friend facing similar challenges. Through this practice, individuals develop a compassionate mindset, fostering resilience and emotional balance in the face of life's difficulties.

A compassionate break involves a deliberate shift in focus from self-criticism and judgment to self-compassion and understanding. It often starts with recognizing moments of distress or self-criticism, allowing oneself to pause and acknowledge these feelings without judgment. During this pause, individuals can employ various techniques, such as self-soothing activities, mindfulness, or guided imagery, to offer themselves comfort, care, and reassurance. Through these practices, individuals create a space for self-kindness and self-compassion, nurturing a supportive inner dialog and fostering emotional healing.

Regular practice of compassionate breaks can lead to profound shifts in self-perception and emotional resilience. By incorporating compassionate breaks into daily routines, individuals cultivate a greater sense of self-compassion, which can positively impact mental health and well-being. These moments of self-compassion enable individuals to approach life's challenges with greater understanding, self-acceptance, and resilience, ultimately fostering a more compassionate relationship with oneself and others.

References

Ferrari, M., Hunt, C., Harrysunker, A., Abbott, M. J., Beath, A. P., & Einstein, D. A. (2019). Self-compassion interventions and psychosocial outcomes: A meta-analysis of RCTs. *Mindfulness, 10*(8), 1455–1473. https://doi.org/10.1007/s12671-019-01134-6

Neff, K. D. (2003). The development and validation of a scale to measure self-compassion. *Self and Identity, 2*(3), 223–250. https://doi.org/10.1080/15298860309027

References

Abramowitz, J. S. (1996). Variants of exposure and response prevention in the treatment of obsessive-compulsive disorder: A meta-analysis. *Behavior Therapy, 27*(4), 583–600. https://doi.org/10.1016/S0005-7894(96)80045-1

Adelheid, T., Ramadhani, A. P., Novrianto, R., & Jaya, E. S. (2025). Case series of body dysmorphic disorder treatment using exposure and response prevention psychotherapy. *Asian Journal of Psychiatry, 108*, 104505. https://doi.org/10.1016/j.ajp.2025.104505

Addington, D., Addington, J., & Maticka-Tyndale, E. (1993). Assessing depression in schizophrenia: The Calgary depression scale. *British Journal of Psychiatry, 163*(S22), 39–44. https://doi.org/10.1192/S0007125000292581

Addington, J., & Tran, L. (2009). Using the brief core schema scales with individuals at clinical high risk of psychosis. *Behavioural and Cognitive Psychotherapy, 37*(2), 227–231.

Adelheid, T., Ramadhani, A. P., Novrianto, R., & Jaya, E. S. (2025). Case series of body dysmorphic disorder treatment using exposure and response prevention psychotherapy. *Asian Journal of Psychiatry, 108*, 104505. https://doi.org/10.1016/j.ajp.2025.104505.

Angelo, F. N., McDonell, M. G., Lewin, M. R., Srebnik, D., Lowe, J., Roll, J., & Ries, R. (2013). Predictors of stimulant abuse treatment outcomes in severely mentally ill outpatients. *Drug and Alcohol Dependence, 131*(1–2), 162–165. https://doi.org/10.1016/j.drugalcdep.2012.11.017

Antony, M. M., Bieling, P. J., Cox, B. J., Enns, M. W., & Swinson, R. P. (1998). Psychometric properties of the 42-item and 21-item versions of the depression anxiety stress scales in clinical groups and a community sample. *Psychological Assessment, 10*(2), 176.

Barlow, D. H. (2002). *Anxiety and its disorders: The nature and treatment of anxiety and panic* (2nd ed.). Guilford Press.

Barlow, D. H., & Craske, M. G. (2007). *Mastery of your anxiety and panic: Workbook* (4th ed.). Oxford University Press.

Barry, D., Sullivan, B., & Petry, N. M. (2009). Comparable efficacy of contingency management for cocaine dependence among African American, Hispanic, and white methadone maintenance clients. *Psychology of Addictive Behaviors, 23*(1), 168–174. https://doi.org/10.1037/a0014575

Beards, S., Gayer-Anderson, C., Borges, S., Dewey, M. E., Fisher, H. L., & Morgan, C. (2013). Life events and psychosis: A review and meta-analysis. *Schizophrenia Bulletin, 39*(4), 740–747. https://doi.org/10.1093/schbul/sbt065

Beck, A. T. (1976). *Cognitive therapy and the emotional disorders*. Penguin.

Beck, J. S. (2011). *Cognitive behavior therapy: Basics and beyond* (2nd ed.). Guilford Press.

E. S. Jaya, *Cognitive Behavioral Therapy for Psychosis as a Syndrome*, https://doi.org/10.1007/978-981-95-9203-6

Beck, A. T., Himelstein, R., & Grant, P. M. (2017). In and out of schizophrenia: Activation and deactivation of the negative and positive schemas. *Schizophrenia Research, 203*, 55. https://doi.org/10.1016/j.schres.2017.10.046

Ben-Zeev, D., Ellington, K., Swendsen, J., & Granholm, E. (2011). Examining a cognitive model of persecutory ideation in the daily life of people with schizophrenia: A computerized experience sampling study. *Schizophrenia Bulletin, 37*(6), 1248–1256. https://doi.org/10.1093/schbul/sbq041

Berg, K. C., Peterson, C. B., Frazier, P., & Crow, S. J. (2012). Psychometric evaluation of the eating disorder examination and eating disorder examination-questionnaire: A systematic review of the literature. *International Journal of Eating Disorders, 45*(3), 428–438.

Berking, M., & Znoj, H. (2011). *SEK-27. Fragebogen zur standardisierten Selbsteinschätzung emotionaler Kompetenzen*. Open Test Archive. Trier: ZPID. https://doi.org/10.23668/psycharchives.5261

Bleuler, E. (1950). *Dementia praecox or the group of schizophrenias*. International Universities Press.

Boersma, F. J., Den Hengst, S., Dekker, A. J., & Emmelkamp, P. M. (1976). Flooding in vivo versus imaginal systematic desensitization in the treatment of phobic patients. *Behaviour Research and Therapy, 14*(1), 63–70. https://doi.org/10.1016/0005-7967(76)90037-6

Borkovec, T. D., et al. (1988). Relaxation-induced anxiety: Paradoxical anxiety enhancement due to relaxation training. *Journal of Consulting and Clinical Psychology, 56*(6), 924–931.

Brohede, S., Wingren, G., Wijma, B., & Wijma, K. (2013). Validation of the body dysmorphic disorder questionnaire in a community sample of Swedish women. *Psychiatry Research, 210*(2), 647–652.

Buchanan, R. W., & Heinrichs, D. W. (1989). The neurological evaluation scale (NES): A structured instrument for the assessment of neurological signs in schizophrenia. *Psychiatry Research, 27*(3), 335–350.

Buckley, P. F., Miller, B. J., Lehrer, D. S., & Castle, D. J. (2009). Psychiatric comorbidities and schizophrenia. *Schizophrenia Bulletin, 35*(2), 383–402. https://doi.org/10.1093/schbul/sbn135

Budney, A. J., & Higgins, S. T. (1998). *A community reinforcement plus vouchers approach: Treating cocaine addiction*. National Institute on Drug Abuse Therapy Manuals for Drug Addiction.

Bush, G., Fink, M., Petrides, G., Dowling, F., & Francis, A. (1996). Catatonia. 1. Rating scale and standardized examination. *Acta Psychiatrica Scandinavica, 93*(2), 129–136. https://doi.org/10.1111/j.1600-0447.1996.tb09814.x

Carlyle, D., Green, R., Inder, M., Porter, R., Crowe, M., Mulder, R., & Frampton, C. (2020). A randomized-controlled trial of mentalization-based treatment compared with structured case management for borderline personality disorder in a mainstream public health service. *Frontiers in Psychiatry, 11*, 561916. https://doi.org/10.3389/fpsyt.2020.561916

Carmona i Farrés, C., Elices, M., Soler, J., Domínguez-Clavé, E., Pomarol-Clotet, E., Salvador, R., & Pascual, J. C. (2019). Effects of mindfulness training on borderline personality disorder: Impulsivity versus emotional dysregulation. *Mindfulness, 10*(7), 1243–1254. https://doi.org/10.1007/s12671-018-1071-4

Carpenter, W. T. (2016). Shifting paradigms and the term schizophrenia. *Schizophrenia Bulletin, 42*(4), 863–864. https://doi.org/10.1093/schbul/sbw050

Carpenter, W. T. (2022). Schizophrenia: A view of immediate future. *Schizophrenia Research, 242*, 15–16. https://doi.org/10.1016/j.schres.2021.12.004

Carroll, K. M., & Onken, L. S. (2005). Behavioral therapies for drug abuse. *The American Journal of Psychiatry, 162*(8), 1452–1460.

Chadwick, P. (2006). *Person-based cognitive therapy for distressing psychosis*. Wiley.

Chien, H. C., Ku, C. H., Lu, R. B., Chu, H., Tao, Y. H., & Chou, K. R. (2003). Effects of social skills training on improving social skills of patients with schizophrenia. *Archives of Psychiatric Nursing, 17*(5), 228–236. https://doi.org/10.1016/s0883-9417(03)00095-5

Clark, D. M., & Wells, A. (1995). A cognitive model of social phobia. In R. G. Heimberg, M. R. Liebowitz, D. A. Hope, & F. R. Schneier (Eds.), *Social phobia: Diagnosis, assessment, and treatment* (pp. 69–93). Guilford Press.

Clark, D. M., et al. (2003). Video feedback in the treatment of social phobia. *Behavior Research and Therapy, 41*(2), 179–187.

Connor, K. M., Davidson, J. R., Churchill, L. E., Sherwood, A., Foa, E., & Weisler, R. H. (2000). Psychometric properties of the social phobia inventory (SPIN): New self-rating scale. *The British Journal of Psychiatry, 176*(4), 379–386. https://doi.org/10.1192/bjp.176.4.379

Craske, M. G., Wittchen, U., Bogels, S., Stein, M. B., Andrews, G., & Lebeu, R. (2013). *Severity measure for specific phobia*. American Psychiatric Association.

Crush, E., Arseneault, L., Moffitt, T. E., Danese, A., Caspi, A., Jaffee, S. R., Matthews, T., & Fisher, H. L. (2018). Protective factors for psychotic experiences amongst adolescents exposed to multiple forms of victimization. *Journal of Psychiatric Research, 104*, 32–38. https://doi.org/10.1016/j.jpsychires.2018.06.011

Cuijpers, P., Quero, S., Noma, H., Ciharova, M., Miguel, C., Karyotaki, E., Cipriani, A., Cristea, I. A., & Furukawa, T. A. (2021). Psychotherapies for depression: a network meta-analysis covering efficacy, acceptability and longterm outcomes of all main treatment types. *World Psychiatry, 20*, 283–293. https://doi.org/10.1002/wps.20860.

Cuijpers, P., Miguel, C., Harrer, M., Plessen, C. Y., Ciharova, M., Ebert, D., & Karyotaki, E. (2023). Cognitive behavior therapy vs. control conditions, other psychotherapies, pharmacotherapies and combined treatment for depression: A comprehensive meta-analysis including 409 trials with 52,702 patients. *World Psychiatry, 22*(1), 105–115. https://doi.org/10.1002/wps.21069

Davis, J. P., Barr, N., Dworkin, E. R., Dumas, T. M., Berey, B., DiGuiseppi, G., & Rael Cahn, B. (2019). Effect of mindfulness-based relapse prevention on impulsivity trajectories among young adults in residential substance use disorder treatment. *Mindfulness, 10*(10), 1997–2009. https://doi.org/10.1007/s12671-019-01164-0

Dazzi, F., Shafer, A., & Lauriola, M. (2016). Meta-analysis of the brief psychiatric rating scale–expanded (BPRS-E) structure and arguments for a new version. *Journal of Psychiatric Research, 81*, 140–151. https://doi.org/10.1016/j.jpsychires.2016.07.001

DeAraujo, L. A., Ito, L. M., & Marks, I. M. (1995). Comparative efficacy of matching and mismatching imaginal and in vivo exposure for obsessive-compulsive disorder. *Journal of Consulting and Clinical Psychology, 63*(1), 331–341. https://doi.org/10.1037/0022-006X.63.2.331

Deckersbach, T., Rauch, S., Buhlmann, U., & Wilhelm, S. (2006). Habit reversal versus supportive psychotherapy in Tourette's disorder: A randomized controlled trial and predictors of treatment response. *Behaviour Research and Therapy, 44*(8), 1079–1090. https://doi.org/10.1016/j.brat.2005.08.007

Dimidjian, S., Barrera, M., Martell, C., Muñoz, R. F., & Lewinsohn, P. M. (2011). The Origins and Current Status of Behavioral Activation Treatments for Depression. Annual Review of Clinical Psychology, 7(1), 1–38. https://doi.org/10.1146/annurev-clinpsy-032210-104535.

Drake, R., Haddock, G., Tarrier, N., Bentall, R., & Lewis, S. (2007). The psychotic symptom rating scales (PSYRATS): Their usefulness and properties in first episode psychosis. *Schizophrenia Research, 89*(1–3), 119–122.

DuPont, R. L., Humphreys, K., Carr, C. J., & Shea, C. L. (2017). Random drug testing: A critical tool for preventing addiction and saving lives. *Journal of Global Drug Policy and Practice, 11*(1), 12–23.

Eisen, J. L., & Rasmussen, S. A. (1993). Obsessive compulsive disorder with psychotic features. *The Journal of Clinical Psychiatry, 54*(10), 373–379.

Eisen, J. L., Rasmussen, S. A., Phillips, K. A., Price, L. H., Davidson, J., Lydiard, R. B., Ninan, P., & Piggott, T. (2001). Insight and treatment outcome in obsessive-compulsive disorder. *Comprehensive Psychiatry, 42*(6), 494–497. https://doi.org/10.1053/comp.2001.27898

Emmelkamp, P. M., & de Lange, R. (1983). Agoraphobia: A comparative study of self-exposure in vivo and intensive exposure in vivo plus cognitive restructuring and exposure in sensu. *Behavior Modification, 7*(4), 489–501. https://doi.org/10.1177/01454455830074003

Emmelkamp, P. M., & Kuipers, A. C. (1980). Flooding vs. gradual desensitization in vivo: A case study. *Behaviour Research and Therapy, 18*(5), 429–435. https://doi.org/10.1016/0005-7967(80)90003-2

Emmelkamp, P. M., Kwee, M. G., & Muris, P. (1990). Symptom-specific effects of cognitive and behavioral interventions in the treatment of obsessive-compulsive disorder. *Behaviour Research and Therapy, 28*(2), 153–162. https://doi.org/10.1016/0005-7967(90)90023-M

Espelage, D. L., & Holt, M. K. (2001). Bullying and victimization during early adolescence: Peer influences and psychosocial correlates. *Journal of Emotional Abuse, 2*(2–3), 123–142. https://doi.org/10.1300/J135v02n02_08

Fairburn, C. G., & Beglin, S. J. (1994). Assessment of eating disorders: Interview or self-report questionnaire? *International Journal of Eating Disorders, 16*(4), 363–370.

Fairburn, C. G., & Harrison, P. J. (2003). Eating disorders. *The Lancet, 361*(9355), 407–416.

Felitti, V. J., Anda, R. F., Nordenberg, D., Williamson, D. F., Spitz, A. M., Edwards, V., Koss, M. P., & Marks, J. S. (1998). Relationship of childhood abuse and household dysfunction to many of the leading causes of death in adults: The adverse childhood experiences (ACE) study. *American Journal of Preventive Medicine, 14*(4), 245–258. https://doi.org/10.1016/S0749-3797(98)00017-8

Ferrari, M., Hunt, C., Harrysunker, A., Abbott, M. J., Beath, A. P., & Einstein, D. A. (2019). Self-compassion interventions and psychosocial outcomes: A meta-analysis of RCTs. *Mindfulness, 10*(8), 1455–1473. https://doi.org/10.1007/s12671-019-01134-6

Ferri, M., Amato, L., Davoli, M., & Bo, A. (2019). Respiratory health risks of smoking marijuana. *The. Cochrane Database of Systematic Reviews, 2*, CD003639. https://doi.org/10.1002/14651858.CD003639.pub2

Foa, E. B., & Kozak, M. J. (1980). Cognitive-behavioral versus exposure only treatment for social phobia: A meta-analysis. *Journal of Consulting and Clinical Psychology, 48*(6), 594–602. https://doi.org/10.1037/0022-006X.48.6.594

Foa, E. B., Abramowitz, J. S., Franklin, M. E., & Kozak, M. J. (1999). Feared consequences, fixity of belief, and treatment outcome in patients with obsessive-compulsive disorder. *Behavior Therapy, 30*(4), 717–724. https://doi.org/10.1016/S0005-7894(99)80035-5

Foa, E. B., Huppert, J. D., Leiberg, S., Langner, R., Kichic, R., Hajcak, G., & Salkovskis, P. M. (2002). The obsessive-compulsive inventory: Development and validation of a short version. *Psychological Assessment, 14*(4), 485–496. https://doi.org/10.1037/1040-3590.14.4.485

Foa, E. B., Kozak, M. J., Salkovskis, P. M., Coles, M. E., & Weiss, B. D. (1998). The validation of a new subscale for measuring obsessive-compulsive disorder. *Journal of Anxiety Disorders, 12*(1), 1–20. https://doi.org/10.1016/S0887-6185(97)00050-3

Foa, E. B., Liebowitz, M. R., Kozak, M. J., Davies, S., Campeas, R., Franklin, M. E., & Tu, X. (1984). Randomized, placebo-controlled trial of exposure and ritual prevention, clomipramine, and their combination in the treatment of obsessive-compulsive disorder. *The American Journal of Psychiatry, 141*(5), 581–585. https://doi.org/10.1176/ajp.141.5.581

Ford, A. C., Talley, N. J., Schoenfeld, P. S., Quigley, E. M. M., & Moayyedi, P. (2014). Efficacy of antidepressants and psychological therapies in irritable bowel syndrome: Systematic review and meta-analysis. *Gut, 63*(6), 997–1007.

Fowler, D., Freeman, D., Smith, B. E. N., Kuipers, E., Bebbington, P., Bashforth, H., Garety, P., et al. (2006). The brief Core schema scales (BCSS): Psychometric properties and associations with paranoia and grandiosity in non-clinical and psychosis samples. *Psychological Medicine, 36*(6), 749–759.

Fowler, D., Hodgekins, J., Howells, L., Millward, M., Ivins, A., Taylor, G., Freeman, D., et al. (2009). Can targeted early intervention improve recovery in psychosis? A historical control evaluation of the effectiveness of different models of early intervention service provision in Norfolk 1998–2007. *Health Services and Delivery Research, 14*(12), 1–174.

Franco, C., Amutio, A., López-González, L., Oriol, X., & Martínez-Taboada, C. (2016). Effect of a mindfulness training program on the impulsivity and aggression levels of adolescents with behavioral problems in the classroom. *Frontiers in Psychology, 7*, 1385. https://doi.org/10.3389/fpsyg.2016.01385

Freeman, D., Dunn, G., Startup, H., Pugh, K., Cordwell, J., Mander, H., Černis, E., Wingham, G., Shirvell, K., & Kingdon, D. (2015). Effects of cognitive behaviour therapy for worry on persecutory delusions in patients with psychosis (WIT): A parallel, single-blind, randomised controlled trial with a mediation analysis. *The Lancet Psychiatry, 2*(4), 305–313. https://doi.org/10.1016/S2215-0366(15)00039-5

Freeman, D., Pugh, K., Vorontsova, N., & Southgate, L. (2009). Insomnia and paranoia. *Schizophrenia Research, 108*(1–3), 280–284. https://doi.org/10.1016/j.schres.2008.12.001

Freeman, D., Sheaves, B., Goodwin, G. M., Yu, L. M., Nickless, A., Harrison, P. J., Waite, F., et al. (2017). The effects of improving sleep on mental health (OASIS): A randomized controlled trial with mediation analysis. *The Lancet Psychiatry, 4*(10), 749–758. https://doi.org/10.1016/S2215-0366(17)30328-0

Freeman, D., Taylor, K. M., Molodynski, A., & Waite, F. (2019). Treatable clinical intervention targets for patients with schizophrenia. *Schizophrenia Research, 211*, 44–50. https://doi.org/10.1016/j.schres.2019.07.016

Garety, P. A., & Freeman, D. (1999). Cognitive approaches to delusions: A critical review of theories and evidence. *British Journal of Clinical Psychology, 38*(2), 113–154. https://doi.org/10.1348/014466599162700

Garnefski, N., Kraaij, V., & Spinhoven, P. (2001). Negative life events, cognitive emotion regulation, and emotional problems. *Personality and Individual Differences, 30*(8), 1311–1327. https://doi.org/10.1016/S0191-8869(00)00113-6

Garner, D. M., Olmsted, M. P., Bohr, Y., & Garfinkel, P. E. (1982). The eating attitudes test: Psychometric features and clinical correlates. *Psychological Medicine, 12*(4), 871–878. https://doi.org/10.1017/S0033291700049163

Gilbert, P. (2010). Compassion focused therapy: The distinctiveness of a new mindfulness-based approach. In K. S. Dobson & D. J. A. Dozois (Eds.), *Handbook of cognitive-Behavioral therapies* (3rd ed., pp. 423–444). The Guilford Press.

Goldin, P. R., Jazaieri, H., Ziv, M., Kraemer, H., Heimberg, R. G., & Gross, J. J. (2013). Changes in positive self-views mediate the effect of cognitive-behavioral therapy for social anxiety disorder. *Clinical Psychological Science, 1*(3), 301–310. https://doi.org/10.1177/2167702613476867

Gollwitzer, A., Wilczynska, M., & Jaya, E. S. (2018). Targeting the link between loneliness and paranoia via an interventionist-causal model framework. *Psychiatry Research, 263*, 101–107. https://doi.org/10.1016/j.psychres.2018.02.050

Goodman, W. K., Price, L. H., Rasmussen, S. A., Mazure, C., Fleischmann, R. L., Hill, C. L., Heninger, G. R., & Charney, D. S. (1989). The Yale-Brown obsessive-compulsive scale: I. Development, use, and reliability. *Archives of General Psychiatry, 46*(11), 1006–1011. https://doi.org/10.1001/archpsyc.1989.01810110048007

Gratz, K. L., & Roemer, L. (2004). The difficulties in emotion regulation scale: Development and validation of an instrument to assess emotional dysregulation. *Journal of Psychopathology and Behavioral Assessment, 26*(1), 41–54. https://doi.org/10.1023/B:JOBA.0000007455.08539.94

Gross, J. J., & John, O. P. (2003). Individual differences in two emotion regulation processes: Implications for affect, relationships, and Well-being. *Journal of Personality and Social Psychology, 85*(2), 348–362. https://doi.org/10.1037/0022-3514.85.2.348

Gunderson, J. G., Stout, R. L., McGlashan, T. H., Shea, M. T., Morey, L. C., Grilo, C. M., Zanarini, M. C., Yen, S., Markowitz, J. C., Sanislow, C., Ansell, E., Pinto, A., & Skodol, A. E. (2011). Ten-year course of borderline personality disorder: Psychopathology and function from the collaborative longitudinal personality disorders study. *Archives of General Psychiatry, 68*(8), 827–837. https://doi.org/10.1001/archgenpsychiatry.2011.37

Haddock, G., McCarron, J., Tarrier, N., & Faragher, E. B. (1999). Scales to measure dimensions of hallucinations and delusions: The psychotic symptom rating scales (PSYRATS). *Psychological Medicine, 29*(4), 879–889.

Häfner, H., Maurer, K., Trendler, G., & an der Heiden, W., Schmidt, M., & Könnecke, R. (2005). Schizophrenia and depression: Challenging the paradigm of two separate diseases-a controlled study of schizophrenia, depression and healthy controls. *Schizophrenia Research, 77*(1), 11–24. https://doi.org/10.1016/j.schres.2005.01.004

Hartley, S., Barrowclough, C., & Haddock, G. (2013). Anxiety and depression in psychosis: A systematic review of associations with positive psychotic symptoms. *Acta Psychiatrica Scandinavica, 128*(5), 327–346. https://doi.org/10.1111/acps.12080

Hendrickson, K. L., & Rasmussen, E. B. (2017). Mindful eating reduces impulsive food choice in adolescents and adults. *Health Psychology, 36*(3), 226–235. https://doi.org/10.1037/hea0000440

Hennig, T., Jaya, E. S., & Lincoln, T. M. (2017). Bullying mediates between attention-deficit/hyperactivity disorder in childhood and psychotic experiences in early adolescence. *Schizophrenia Bulletin, 43*(5), 1036–1104. https://doi.org/10.1093/schbul/sbw139

Hermanto, E., Asih, S. R., & Jaya, E. S. (2020). The role of perceived discrimination in mediating the relationship between minority status and psychotic symptoms in a community sample. *Konselor, 8*(4), 104. https://doi.org/10.24036/0201983105924-0-00

Higgins, S. T., & Petry, N. M. (1999). Contingency management: Incentives for sobriety. *Alcohol Research & Health, 23*(2), 122–127.

Hilker, R., Helenius, D., Fagerlund, B., Skytthe, A., Christensen, K., Werge, T. M., & Nordentoft, M. (2018). Heritability of schizophrenia and schizophrenia spectrum based on the nationwide Danish twin register. *Biological Psychiatry, 83*(6), 492–498. https://doi.org/10.1016/j.biopsych.2017.08.017

Himle, M. B., Woods, D. W., Conelea, C. A., Bauer, C. C., Rice, K. A., & Investigative Team, T. I. C. S. (2007). Evaluating the contributions of ADHD, OCD, and tic severity in predicting functional competency and impairment in children with tic disorders. *Journal of Developmental and Behavioral Pediatrics, 28*(4), 274–281.

Hofmann, S. G., Bufka, L. F., Brady, S. M., Du Rand, C., & Goff, D. C. (2000). Cognitive-behavioral treatment of panic in patients with schizophrenia: Preliminary findings. *Journal of Cognitive Psychotherapy, 14*(4), 381–392.

Holman, R. R., Paul, S. K., Bethel, M. A., Matthews, D. R., & Neil, H. A. W. (2008a). 10-year follow-up of intensive glucose control in type 2 diabetes. *The New England Journal of Medicine, 359*(15), 1577–1589. https://doi.org/10.1056/NEJMoa0806470

Holman, R. R., Paul, S. K., Bethel, M. A., Neil, H. A., & Matthews, D. R. (2008b). Long-term follow-up after tight control of blood pressure in type 2 diabetes. *The New England Journal of Medicine, 359*(15), 1565–1576. https://doi.org/10.1056/NEJMoa0806359

Horton, L. E., Barrantes-Vidal, N., Silvia, P. J., & Kwapil, T. R. (2014). Worries about being judged versus being harmed: Disentangling the association of social anxiety and paranoia with schizotypy. *PLoS ONE, 9*(6), e96269. https://doi.org/10.1371/journal.pone.0096269

Hudiyana, J., Lincoln, T. M., Hartanto, T., & Witvliet, M. (2020). Measuring loneliness in Indonesia: Validating the UCLA loneliness scale version 3 and its six-item short form in Indonesian adolescents. *Assessment, 27*(8), 1540–1551. https://doi.org/10.1177/1073191119828410

Hunot, V., Churchill, R., Silva de Lima, M., & Teixeira, V. (2007). Psychological therapies for generalised anxiety disorder. *The. Cochrane Database of Systematic Reviews, 2007*(1), CD001848. https://doi.org/10.1002/14651858.CD001848.pub4

Insel, T. R., & Akiskal, H. S. (1986). Obsessive-compulsive disorder with psychotic features: A phenomenologic analysis. *The American Journal of Psychiatry, 143*(12), 1527–1533. https://doi.org/10.1176/ajp.143.12.1527

Jaya, E. S. (2017). Confirmatory factor analysis of the Indonesian version of community assessment of psychic experiences. *Makara Human Behavior Studies in Asia, 9*(1), 1–12. https://doi.org/10.7454/mssh.v21i1.3495

Jaya, E. S., & Lincoln, T. M. (2016). Social adversities and psychotic symptoms: A test of predictions derived from the social defeat hypothesis. *Psychiatry Research, 245*, 466–472. https://doi.org/10.1016/j.psychres.2016.09.002

Jaya, E. S., Ascone, L., & Lincoln, T. M. (2017). Social adversity and psychosis: The mediating role of cognitive vulnerability. *Schizophrenia Bulletin, 43*(3), 557–565. https://doi.org/10.1093/schbul/sbw104

Jaya, E. S., Ascone, L., & Lincoln, T. M. (2018). A longitudinal mediation analysis of the effect of negative-self-schemas on positive symptoms via negative affect. *Psychological Medicine, 48*(8), 1299–1307. https://doi.org/10.1017/S003329171700277X

Jaya, E. S., van Amelsvoort, T., Bartels-Velthuis, A. A., Bruggeman, R., Cahn, W., de Haan, L., Kahn, R. S., van Os, J., Schirmbeck, F., Simons, C. J. P., & Lincoln, T. M. (2021). The community assessment of psychic experiences: Optimal cut-off scores for detecting individuals with a psychotic disorder. *International Journal of Methods in Psychiatric Research, 30*, e1893. https://doi.org/10.1002/mpr.1893

Jaya, E. S., Pillny, M., Lincoln, T. M., & Riehle, M. (2022). Does social defeat cause negative symptoms? A prospective study in a multi-national community sample. *Comprehensive Psychiatry, 113*, 152289. https://doi.org/10.1016/j.comppsych.2021.152289

Jorovat, A., Twumasi, R., Mechelli, A., & Georgiades, A. (2025). Core beliefs in psychosis: A systematic review and meta-analysis. *Schizophrenia, 11*(1), 38. https://doi.org/10.1038/s41537-025-00577-2

Kuranova, A., Booij, S. H., de Jonge, P., Jeronimus, B., Lin, A., Wardenaar, K. J., Wichers, M., & Wigman, J. T. W. (2020). Don't worry, be happy: Protective factors to buffer against distress associated with psychotic experiences. *Schizophrenia Research, 223*, 79. https://doi.org/10.1016/j.schres.2020.05.019

Lim, M. H., Gleeson, J. F., Jackson, H. J., & Fernandez, K. C. (2014). Social relationships and quality of life moderate distress associated with delusional ideation. *Social Psychiatry and Psychiatric Epidemiology, 49*(1), 97–107. https://doi.org/10.1007/s00127-013-0738-3

Lincoln, T. M., Marin, N., & Jaya, E. S. (2017). Childhood trauma and psychotic experiences in a general population sample: A prospective study on the mediating role of emotion regulation. *European Psychiatry, 42*, 111–119. https://doi.org/10.1016/j.eurpsy.2016.12.010

Linscott, R. J., & van Os, J. (2010). Systematic reviews of categorical versus continuum models in psychosis: Evidence for discontinuous subpopulations underlying a psychometric continuum. Implications for DSM-V, DSM-VI, and DSM-VII. *Annual Review of Clinical Psychology, 6*(1), 391–419. https://doi.org/10.1146/annurev.clinpsy.032408.153506

Linscott, R. J., & van Os, J. (2013). An updated and conservative systematic review and meta-analysis of epidemiological evidence on psychotic experiences in children and adults: On the pathway from proneness to persistence to dimensional expression across mental disorders. *Psychological Medicine, 43*(6), 1133–1149. https://doi.org/10.1017/S0033291712001626

Octavia, S., Jaya, E. S., & Asih, S. R. (2019). Does negative-self-schema link the relationship between childhood trauma and psychotic symptoms in a community sample of Indonesians? *Konselor, 8*(3), 85. https://doi.org/10.24036/0201983105885-0-00

Strauss, J. S. (1969). Hallucinations and delusions as points on continua function: Rating scale evidence. *Archives of General Psychiatry, 21*(5), 581–586. https://doi.org/10.1001/archpsyc.1969.01740230069010

Kerbeshian, J., Peng, C. Z., & Burd, L. (2009). Tourette syndrome and comorbid early-onset schizophrenia. *Journal of Psychosomatic Research, 67*(6), 515–523. https://doi.org/10.1016/j.jpsychores.2009.08.002

Khemlani-Patel, S., Neziroglu, F., & Mancusi, L. M. (2011). Cognitive-behavioral therapy for body dysmorphic disorder: A comparative investigation. *International Journal of Cognitive Therapy, 4*(4), 363–380. https://doi.org/10.1521/ijct.2011.4.4.363

Kingdon, D. G., & Turkington, D. (1994). *Cognitive-behavioral therapy of schizophrenia*. Guilford Press.

Kraepelin, E. (1913). *Lectures on clinical psychiatry* (T. Johnstone, trans.). William Wood & Company. (Original work published 1905).

Kring, A. M., Gur, R. E., Blanchard, J. J., Horan, W. P., & Reise, S. P. (2013). The clinical assessment interview for negative symptoms (CAINS): Final development and validation. *American Journal of Psychiatry, 170*(2), 165–172. https://doi.org/10.1176/appi.ajp.2012.12010109

Kroenke, K., Spitzer, R. L., & Williams, J. B. (2001). The PHQ-9: Validity of a brief depression severity measure. *Journal of General Internal Medicine, 16*(9), 606–613. https://doi.org/10.1046/j.1525-1497.2001.016009606.x

Laskemoen, J. F., Simonsen, C., Büchmann, C., Barrett, E. A., Bjella, T., Lagerberg, T. V., Vedal, T. J., Andreassen, O. A., Melle, I., & Aas, M. (2019). Sleep disturbances in schizophrenia spectrum and bipolar disorders—A transdiagnostic perspective. *Comprehensive Psychiatry, 91*, 6–12. https://doi.org/10.1016/j.comppsych.2019.02.006

Leckman, J. F., Greene, D. J., & Pauls, D. L. (1997). Yale global tic severity scale (YGTSS): A multidimensional measure of tic severity. *Journal of the American Academy of Child and Adolescent Psychiatry, 36*(6), 1004–1013. https://doi.org/10.1097/00004583-199706000-00013

Lelliott, P. T., Noshirvani, H. F., Başoğlu, M., Marks, I. M., & Monteiro, W. O. (1988). Obsessive-compulsive beliefs and treatment outcome. *Psychological Medicine, 18*(3), 697–702. https://doi.org/10.1017/s0033291700008382

Lelliott, P., & Marks, I. (1987). Management of obsessive-compulsive rituals associated with delusions, hallucinations and depression: A case report. *Behavioural and Cognitive Psychotherapy, 15*(1), 77–87.

Levin, F. R., & Fishman, M. J. (2020). *Substance use disorders: A practical guide for clinicians* (6th ed.). Wolters Kluwer.

Levy, M. M., Evans, L. E., & Rhodes, A. (2018). The surviving sepsis campaign bundle: 2018 update. *Intensive Care Medicine, 44*(6), 925–928. https://doi.org/10.1007/s00134-018-5085-0

Liebowitz, M. R. (1987). Social phobia. *Modern Problems of Pharmacopsychiatry, 22*, 141–173. https://doi.org/10.1159/000414022

Linehan, M. M. (1993). *Cognitive-behavioral treatment of borderline personality disorder*. Guilford Press.

Linehan, M. M. (2014). *DBT skills training handouts and worksheets* (2nd ed.). The Guilford Press.

Linehan, M. M., Comtois, K. A., Murray, A. M., Brown, M. Z., Gallop, R. J., Heard, H. L., Korslund, K. E., Tutek, D. A., Reynolds, S. K., & Lindenboim, N. (2006). Two-year randomized controlled trial and follow-up of dialectical behavior therapy vs therapy by experts for suicidal behaviors and borderline personality disorder. *Archives of General Psychiatry, 63*(7), 757–766. https://doi.org/10.1001/archpsyc.63.7.757

Linehan, M. M., Goodstein, J. L., Nielsen, S. L., & Chiles, J. A. (1983). Reasons for staying alive when you are thinking of killing yourself: The reasons for living inventory. *Journal of Consulting and Clinical Psychology, 51*(2), 276–286. https://doi.org/10.1037/0022-006X.51.2.276

Lovibond, P. F., & Lovibond, S. H. (1995). The structure of negative emotional states: Comparison of the depression anxiety stress scales (DASS) with the Beck depression and anxiety inventories. *Behaviour Research and Therapy, 33*(3), 335–343. https://doi.org/10.1016/0005-7967(94)00075-U

Luck, A. J., Morgan Luck, J. F., Reid, F., O'Brien, A., Brunton, J., Price, C., Perry, L., & Lacey, J. H. (2002). The SCOFF questionnaire and clinical interview for eating disorders in general practice: Comparative study. *BMJ, 325*(7367), 755–756. https://doi.org/10.1136/bmj.325.7367.755

Ludwig, L., Mehl, S., Schlier, B., Krkovic, K., & Lincoln, T. M. (2020). Awareness and rumination moderate the affective pathway to paranoia in daily life. *Schizophrenia Research, 216*, 161–167. https://doi.org/10.1016/j.schres.2019.12.007

Lynam, D. R., Smith, G. T., Cyders, M. A., & Fischer, S. (2007). The UPPS-P impulsive behavior scale: Development and assessment of a new measure of impulsivity. *Psychological Assessment, 19*(1), 55–68. https://doi.org/10.1037/1040-3590.19.1.55

Maremmani, A. G. I., Rovai, L., Rugani, F., Pani, P. P., Pacini, M., Lamanna, F., & Maremmani, I. (2018). Skin complications in injecting drug use: Different prevalence by habit, drug, and gender. *Heroin Addiction and Related Clinical Problems, 20*(5), 79–88.

Mayhew, S. L., & Gilbert, P. (2008). Compassionate mind training with people who hear malevolent voices: A case series report. *Clinical Psychology & Psychotherapy, 15*(2), 113–138. https://doi.org/10.1002/cpp.566

McDonell, M. G., Leickly, E., McPherson, S., Skalisky, J., Srebnik, D., Angelo, F., Ries, R. K., et al. (2017). A randomized controlled trial of ethyl glucuronide-based contingency management for outpatients with co-occurring alcohol use disorders and serious mental illness. *American Journal of Psychiatry, 174*(4), 370–377. https://doi.org/10.1176/appi.ajp.2016.16050627

McGrath, J. J., Saha, S., Al-Hamzawi, A., Alonso, J., Bromet, E. J., Bruffaerts, R., Caldas-de-Almeida, J. M., Chiu, W. T., de Jonge, P., Fayyad, J., Florescu, S., Gureje, O., Haro, J. M., Hu, C., Kovess-Masfety, V., Lepine, J. P., Lim, C. C., Mora, M. E., Navarro-Mateu, F., Ochoa, S., Kessler, R. C., et al. (2015). Psychotic experiences in the general population: A cross-national analysis based on 31, 261 respondents from 18 countries. *JAMA Psychiatry, 72*(7), 697–705. https://doi.org/10.1001/jamapsychiatry.2015.0575

McMain, S. F., Chapman, A. L., Kuo, J. R., Dixon-Gordon, K. L., Guimond, T. H., Labrish, C., Isaranuwatchai, W., & Streiner, D. L. (2022). The effectiveness of 6 versus 12 months of dialectical behavior therapy for borderline personality disorder: A noninferiority randomized clinical trial. *Psychotherapy and Psychosomatics, 91*(6), 382–397. https://doi.org/10.1159/000525102

McNeely, J., Wu, L. T., Subramaniam, G., Sharma, G., Cathers, L. A., Svikis, D., Sleiter, L., Russell, L., Nordeck, C., Sharma, A., O'Grady, K. E., Bouk, L. B., Cushing, C., King, J., Wahle, A., & Schwartz, R. P. (2016). Performance of the tobacco, alcohol, prescription medication, and other substance use (TAPS) tool for substance use screening in primary care patients. *Annals of Internal Medicine, 165*(10), 690–699. https://doi.org/10.7326/M16-0317

Meuret, A. E., Rosenfield, D., Seidel, A., Bhaskara, L., & Hofmann, S. G. (2010). Respiratory and cognitive mediators of treatment change in panic disorder: Evidence for intervention specificity. *Journal of Consulting and Clinical Psychology, 78*(5), 691–704. https://doi.org/10.1037/a0019552

Morgan, J. F., Reid, F., & Lacey, J. H. (1999). The SCOFF questionnaire: Assessment of a new screening tool for eating disorders. *BMJ, 319*(7223), 1467–1468. https://doi.org/10.1136/bmj.319.7223.1467

Moritz, S., & Lysaker, P. H. (2014). Metacognitive training for schizophrenia spectrum patients: A review and synthesis of neurocognitive, social cognitive, and metacognitive perspectives. *Psychological Medicine, 44*(3), 647–658.

Morrison, A. P., & Barratt, S. (2010). What are the components of CBT for psychosis? A Delphi study. *Schizophrenia Bulletin, 36*(1), 136–142.

Morrison, A. P., Turkington, D., Pyle, M., Spencer, H., Brabban, A., Dunn, G., Christodoulides, T., Dudley, R., Chapman, N., Callcott, P., Grace, T., Lumley, V., Drage, L., Tully, S., Irving, K., Cummings, A., Byrne, R., Davies, L. M., & Hutton, P. (2014). Cognitive therapy for people with schizophrenia spectrum disorders not taking antipsychotic drugs: A single-blind randomised controlled trial. *The Lancet, 383*(9926), 1395–1403. https://doi.org/10.1016/S0140-6736(13)62246-1

Murray, R. M., Englund, A., Abi-Dargham, A., Lewis, D. A., Di Forti, M., Davies, C., Sherif, M., McGuire, P., & D'Souza, D. C. (2017). Cannabis-associated psychosis: Neural substrate and clinical impact. *Neuropharmacology, 124*, 89–104. https://doi.org/10.1016/j.neuropharm.2017.06.018

National Institute for Health and Care Excellence. (2005). *Obsessive-compulsive disorder and body dysmorphic disorder: Treatment* (clinical guideline CG31). https://www.nice.org.uk/guidance/cg31

National Institute for Health and Care Excellence. (2013). *Social anxiety disorder: Recognition, assessment and treatment* (clinical guideline CG159). https://www.nice.org.uk/guidance/cg159

National Institute for Health and Care Excellence. (2017). *Eating disorders: Recognition and treatment* (NICE guideline NG69). https://www.nice.org.uk/guidance/ng69

National Institute for Health and Care Excellence. (2020). *Generalised anxiety disorder and panic disorder in adults: Management* (clinical guideline CG113). https://www.nice.org.uk/guidance/cg113

National Institute for Health and Care Excellence. (2022). *Depression in adults: Treatment and management* (NICE guideline NG222). https://www.nice.org.uk/guidance/ng222

Neacsiu, A. D., Eberle, J. W., Kramer, R., Wiesmann, T., & Linehan, M. M. (2014). Dialectical behavior therapy skills for transdiagnostic emotion dysregulation: A pilot randomized controlled trial. *Behaviour Research and Therapy, 59*, 40–51. https://doi.org/10.1016/j.brat.2014.05.005

Neff, K. D. (2003). The development and validation of a scale to measure self-compassion. *Self and Identity, 2*(3), 223–250. https://doi.org/10.1080/15298860309027

O'Connor, S. S., Comtois, K. A., Wang, J., Russo, J., Peterson, R., Lapping-Carr, L., & Zatzick, D. (2015). The development and implementation of a brief intervention for medically admitted suicide attempt survivors. *General Hospital Psychiatry, 37*(5), 427–433. https://doi.org/10.1016/j.genhosppsych.2015.05.001

Oliver, J. E., O'Connor, J. A., Jose, P. E., McLachlan, K., & Peters, E. (2012). The impact of negative schemas, mood and psychological flexibility on delusional ideation—Mediating and moderating effects. *Psychosis: Psychological, Social and Integrative Approaches, 4*(1), 6–18. https://doi.org/10.1080/17522439.2011.637117

Orth, R. D., Hur, J., Jacome, A. M., Savage, C. L. G., Grogans, S. E., Kim, Y. H., Choe, E. K., Shackman, A. J., & Blanchard, J. J. (2022). Understanding the consequences of moment-by-moment fluctuations in mood and social experience for paranoid ideation in psychotic disorders. *Schizophrenia Bulletin Open, 3*(1), sgac 064. https://doi.org/10.1093/schizbullopen/sgac064

Öst, L.-G. (1987). Applied relaxation: Description of a coping technique and review of controlled studies. *Behaviour Research and Therapy, 25*(5), 397–409. https://doi.org/10.1016/0005-7967(87)90017-9

Öst, L. G. (1996). One-session group treatment of spider phobia. *Behaviour Research and Therapy, 34*(9), 707–715. https://doi.org/10.1016/0005-7967(96)00022-8

Overall, J. E. (1974). The brief psychiatric rating scale in psychopharmacology research. In P. Pichot & E. Olivier-Martin (Eds.), *Psychological measurements in psychopharmacology: Modern problems in psychopharmacology* (pp. 67–78). Karger.

Overall, J. E., & Gorham, D. R. (1962). The brief psychiatric rating scale. *Psychological Reports, 10*, 799–812. https://doi.org/10.2466/pr0.1962.10.3.799

Patton, J. H., Stanford, M. S., & Barratt, E. S. (1995). Factor structure of the Barratt impulsiveness scale. *Journal of Clinical Psychology, 51*(6), 768–774. https://doi.org/10.1002/1097-4679(199511)51:6<768::AID-JCLP2270510607>3.0.CO;2-1

Petry, N. M. (2000). A comprehensive guide to the application of contingency management procedures in clinical settings. *Drug and Alcohol Dependence, 58*(1–2), 9–25. https://doi.org/10.1016/s0376-8716(99)00071-x

Phillips, K. A. (1996). Body dysmorphic disorder: Diagnosis and treatment of imagined ugliness. *The Journal of Clinical Psychiatry, 57*(Suppl 8), 61–65.

Phillips, K. A. (1991). Body dysmorphic disorder: The distress of imagined ugliness. *The American Journal of Psychiatry, 148*(9), 1138–1149. https://doi.org/10.1176/ajp.148.9.1138

Phillips, K. A. (1995). Diagnostic instruments for body dysmorphic disorder. New research programs and abstracts. 57. In *American Psychiatric Association 148th annual meeting, 1995*. American Psychiatric Association.

Phillips, K. A. (2006). *Cognitive-behavioral therapy for body dysmorphic disorder: A treatment manual*. Guilford Press.

Phillips, K. A., & Hollander, E. (1996). Body dysmorphic disorder. In T. A. Widiger, A. J. Frances, H. A. Pincus, R. Ross, M. B. First, & W. W. Davis (Eds.), *DSM-IV sourcebook* (Vol. 2). American Psychiatric Association.

Phillips, K. A., Dufresne, R. G., Jr., Wilkel, C. S., & Vittorio, C. C. (2000). Rate of body dysmorphic disorder in dermatology patients. *Journal of the American Academy of Dermatology, 42*(3), 436–441.

Phillips, K. A., Hollander, E., Rasmussen, S. A., Aronowitz, B. R., DeCaria, C., & Goodman, W. K. (1997). A severity rating scale for body dysmorphic disorder: Development, reliability, and validity of a modified version of the Yale-Brown obsessive-compulsive scale. *Psychopharmacology Bulletin, 33*(1), 17–22.

Pokos, V., & Castle, D. J. (2006). Prevalence of comorbid anxiety disorders in schizophrenia spectrum disorders: A literature review. *Current Psychiatry Reviews, 2*(3), 285–307. https://doi.org/10.2174/157340006778018193

Pompoli, A., Furukawa, T. A., Imai, H., Tajika, A., Efthimiou, O., & Salanti, G. (2016). Psychological therapies for panic disorder with or without agoraphobia in adults: A network meta-analysis. *The. Cochrane Database of Systematic Reviews, 4*(4), CD011004. https://doi.org/10.1002/14651858.CD011004.pub2

Riemann, D., Baglioni, C., Bassetti, C., Bjorvatn, B., Dolenc Groselj, L., Ellis, J. G., Espie, C. A., Garcia-Borreguero, D., Gjerstad, M., Gonçalves, M., Hertenstein, E., Jansson-Fröjmark, M., Jennum, P. J., Leger, D., Nissen, C., Parrino, L., Paunio, T., Pevernagie, D., Verbraecken, J., Weeß, H. G., Spiegelhalder, K., et al. (2017). European guideline for the diagnosis and treatment of insomnia. *Journal of Sleep Research, 26*(6), 675–700. https://doi.org/10.1111/jsr.12594

Rosen, J. C., & Ramirez, E. (1998). A comparison of cognitive and behavior therapies for body dysmorphic disorder. *Behavior Therapy, 29*(3), 357–377.

Rosen, J. C., Reiter, J., & Orosan, P. (1995). Cognitive-behavioral body image therapy for body dysmorphic disorder. *Journal of Consulting and Clinical Psychology, 63*(2), 263–269. https://doi.org/10.1037/a0022-006x.63.2.263

Rosenheck, R., Stroup, S., Keefe, R. S., McEvoy, J., Swartz, M., Perkins, D., Hsiao, J., Shumway, M., & Lieberman, J. (2005). Measuring outcome priorities and preferences in people with schizophrenia. *British Journal of Psychiatry, 187*(6), 529–536. https://doi.org/10.1192/bjp.187.6.529

Rothe, U., Müller, G., Schwarz, P. E., Seifert, M., Kunath, H., Koch, R., Bergmann, S., Julius, U., Bornstein, S. R., Hanefeld, M., & Schulze, J. (2008). Evaluation of a diabetes management system based on practice guidelines, integrated care, and continuous quality management in a Federal State of Germany: A population-based approach to health care research. *Diabetes Care, 31*(5), 863–868. https://doi.org/10.2337/dc07-0858

Rus-Calafell, M., Gutiérrez-Maldonado, J., Ortega-Bravo, M., Ribas-Sabaté, J., & Caqueo-Urízar, A. (2013). A brief cognitive-behavioural social skills training for stabilised outpatients with schizophrenia: A preliminary study. *Schizophrenia Research, 143*(2–3), 327–336. https://doi.org/10.1016/j.schres.2012.11.014

Rush, A. J., Gullion, C. M., Basco, M. R., Jarrett, R. B., & Trivedi, M. H. (1996). The inventory of depressive symptomatology (IDS): Psychometric properties. *Psychological Medicine, 26*(3), 477–486. https://doi.org/10.1017/S0033291700035558

Saitz, R., Miller, S. C., Fiellin, D. A., & Rosenthal, R. N. (2014). *The ASAM principles of addiction medicine* (5th ed.). Lippincott Williams & Wilkins.

Salkovskis, P. M., & Warwick, H. M. (1985). Cognitive therapy of obsessive–compulsive disorder: Treating treatment failures. *Behavioural and Cognitive Psychotherapy, 13*(3), 243–255.

Scahill, L., & Riddle, M. A. (2000). The Yale global tic severity scale: A comprehensive measure of tic severity and impairment. *Journal of Child and Adolescent Psychopharmacology, 10*(1), 1–10. https://doi.org/10.1089/cap.2000.10.1

Schizophrenia Working Group of the Psychiatric Genomics Consortium. (2014). Biological insights from 108 schizophrenia-associated genetic loci. *Nature, 511*(7510), 421–427.

Schlier, B., Jaya, E. S., Moritz, S., & Lincoln, T. M. (2015). The community assessment of psychic experiences measures nine clusters of psychosis-like experiences: A validation of the German version of the CAPE. *Schizophrenia Research, 169*(1–3), 274–279. https://doi.org/10.1016/j.schres.2015.10.034

Schlier, B., Winkler, K., Jaya, E. S., & Lincoln, T. M. (2018). Fluctuations in hallucination spectrum experiences co-vary with social defeat but not with social deafferentation. A 3-week daily assessment study. *Cognitive Therapy and Research, 42*(1), 92–102. https://doi.org/10.1007/s10608-017-9871-8

Seeman, M. V. (2014). Eating disorders and psychosis: Seven hypotheses. *World Journal of Psychiatry, 4*(4), 112–119. https://doi.org/10.5498/wjp.v4.i4.112

Seeman, M. V. (2016). Eating disorders and psychosis. *Psychiatric Times, 33*(4), 1. https://www.psychiatrictimes.com/view/eating-disorders-and-psychosis

Shear, M. K., Brown, T. A., Barlow, D. H., Money, R., Sholomskas, D. E., Woods, S. W., Gorman, J. M., & Papp, L. A. (1997). Multicenter collaborative panic disorder severity scale. *The American Journal of Psychiatry, 154*(11), 1571–1575. https://doi.org/10.1176/ajp.154.11.1571

Singer, A. R., Addington, D. E., Dobson, K. S., & Wright, C. (2014). A pilot study of cognitive behavior therapy for depression in early psychosis. *Cognitive and Behavioral Practice, 21*(3), 323–334. https://doi.org/10.1016/j.cbpra.2013.08.004

Spitzer, R. L., Kroenke, K., Williams, J. B. W., & Löwe, B. (1999). Patient health questionnaire (PHQ). In *Pfizer* (pp. 1–9). https://doi.org/10.1007/s11606-006-0098-0

Spitzer, R. L., Kroenke, K., Williams, J. B., & Löwe, B. (2006). A brief measure for assessing generalized anxiety disorder: The GAD-7. *Archives of Internal Medicine, 166*(10), 1092–1097.

Soler, J., Pascual, J. C., Tiana, T., Cebrià, A., Barrachina, J., Campins, M. J., Gich, I., Alvarez, E., & Pérez, V. (2009). Dialectical behaviour therapy skills training compared to standard group therapy in borderline personality disorder: A 3-month randomised controlled clinical trial. *Behaviour Research and Therapy, 47*(5), 353–358. https://doi.org/10.1016/j.brat.2009.01.013

Stanford, M. S., Mathias, C. W., Dougherty, D. M., & Lake, A. M. (2009). Fifty years of the Barratt impulsiveness scale: An update and review. *Personality and Individual Differences, 47*(5), 385–395. https://doi.org/10.1016/j.paid.2009.01.061

Stefanis, N. C., Hanssen, M., Smirnis, N. K., Avramopoulos, D. A., Evdokimidis, I. K., Stefanis, C. N., Verdoux, H., & Van Os, J. (2002). Evidence that three dimensions of psychosis have a distribution in the general population. *Psychological Medicine, 32*(2), 347–358. https://doi.org/10.1017/s0033291701005141

Storch, E. A., Abramowitz, J. S., & Goodman, W. K. (2022). Understanding and improving treatment outcomes for obsessive-compulsive disorder. *Psychiatry Research, 317*, 114861. https://doi.org/10.1016/j.psychres.2022.114861

Storch, E. A., Bagner, D. M., Merlo, L. J., Shapira, N. A., Geffken, G. R., Murphy, T. K., & Goodman, W. K. (2007). Florida obsessive-compulsive inventory: Development, reliability, and validity. *Journal of Clinical Psychology, 63*(9), 851–859. https://doi.org/10.1002/jclp.20394

Substance Abuse and Mental Health Services Administration (SAMHSA). (2012). *Clinical drug testing in primary care: Technical assistance publication series (TAP 32).* U.S. Department of Health and Human Services.

Sucitra, E., Novrianto, R., Pasaribu, Y. T., Lincoln, T. M., & Jaya, E. S. (2024). An analysis of measurement invariance of the patient health Questionnaire-9 between Indonesia, Germany, and the USA.

Suinn, R. M. (1977a). Behavioral rehearsal with modeling and coaching. In A. Goldstein & P. H. C. Kendall (Eds.), *The evolution of behavior therapy: A conference* (pp. 317–323). Jossey-Bass.

Suinn, R. M. (1977b). Behavioral rehearsal with relaxation in treating test anxiety. *Journal of Counseling Psychology, 24*(5), 414–422.

Sutjiono, B., Ahmad, S. F., & Jaya, E. S. (2022). Feasibility and benefit of cognitive behavioural therapy for psychosis via teleconsultation in Indonesia: A case study of a 40-year-old schizoaffective disorder patient. *Behaviour Change, 40*, 1–14. https://doi.org/10.1017/bec.2022.11

Tandon, R., Keshavan, M., & Nasrallah, H. (2022). Reinventing schizophrenia: Updating the construct. *Schizophrenia Research, 242*, 1–3. https://doi.org/10.1016/j.schres.2022.02.024

Thompson, R. A. (1994). Emotion regulation: A theme in search of definition. *Monographs of the Society for Research in Child Development, 59*(2–3), 25–52.

Treasure, J., & Schmidt, U. (2013). The cognitive-interpersonal maintenance model of anorexia nervosa revisited: A summary of the evidence for cognitive, socio-emotional and interpersonal predisposing and perpetuating factors. *Journal of Eating Disorders, 1*(1), 13.

Tundo, A., & Necci, R. (2016). Cognitive-behavioural therapy for obsessive-compulsive disorder co-occurring with psychosis: Systematic review of evidence. *World Journal of Psychiatry, 6*(4), 449–455. https://doi.org/10.5498/wjp.v6.i4.449

van de Griendt, J. M., Verdellen, C. W., van Dijk, M. K., & Verbraak, M. J. (2013). Behavioural treatment of tics: Habit reversal and exposure with response prevention. *Neuroscience and Biobehavioral Reviews, 37*(6), 1172–1177. https://doi.org/10.1016/j.neubiorev.2012.10.007

Veale, D. (2004). Advances in a cognitive behavioural model of body dysmorphic disorder. *Body Image, 1*(1), 113–125.

Veale, D., Gournay, K., Dryden, W., Boocock, A., Shah, F., Willson, R., & Walburn, J. (1996). Body dysmorphic disorder: A cognitive behavioural model and pilot randomised controlled trial. *Behaviour Research and Therapy, 34*(9), 717–729. https://doi.org/10.1016/0005-7967(96)00025-3

Ventura, J., Lukoff, D., Nuechterlein, K. H., Liberman, R. P., Green, M. F., & Shaner, A. (1993). Brief psychiatric rating scale (BPRS) expanded version: Scales, anchor points, and administration manual. *International Journal of Methods in Psychiatric, 3*, 227–243.

Verdejo-Garcia, A., Lawrence, A. J., & Clark, L. (2008). Impulsivity as a vulnerability marker for substance-use disorders: Recent findings and clinical implications. *Current Drug Abuse Reviews, 1*(3), 207–221. https://doi.org/10.2174/1874473710801030207

Verdellen, C. W., Keijsers, G. P., Cath, D. C., & Hoogduin, C. A. (2004). Exposure with response prevention versus habit reversal in Tourettes's syndrome: A controlled study. *Behaviour Research and Therapy, 42*(5), 501–511. https://doi.org/10.1016/S0005-7967(03)00154-2

Vinokur, A. D., & van Ryn, M. (1993). Social support and undermining in close relationships: Their independent effects on the mental health of unemployed persons. *Journal of Personality and Social Psychology, 65*(2), 350–359.

Waugh, C. E., & Fredrickson, B. L. (2008). The emotional regulation scale: A brief measure of emotion regulation. *Journal of Personality Assessment, 90*(4), 319–327.

Wild, J., et al. (2008). Changing views of imagery rescripting: A qualitative study of patients' experience. *Behavioural and Cognitive Psychotherapy, 36*(2), 129–147.

Wilhelm, S., & Phillips, K. A. (2010). Cognitive-behavioral therapy for body dysmorphic disorder. *Psychiatric Clinics, 33*(3), 563–582.

Wilhelm, S., & Steketee, G. (2006). *Cognitive therapy for obsessive–compulsive disorder: A guide for professionals*. American Psychiatric Publishing.

Wilhelm, S., Berman, N. C., Keshaviah, A., Schwartz, R. A., & Steketee, G. (2016). Development and psychometric evaluation of the Lifetime History of Impulsive Behaviors Interview (LHIB). *Psychological Assessment, 28*(11), 1405–1417. https://doi.org/10.1037/pas0000266

Wilhelm, S., Greenberg, J. L., Fama, J. M., & Rosenfield, E. (2016a). Development and validation of the body dysmorphic disorder symptom scale. *Body Image, 17*, 82–87. https://doi.org/10.1016/j.bodyim.2016.02.002

Wilhelm, S., Greenberg, J., & McGlynn, S. (2016b). The lifetime history of impulsive Behaviors questionnaire: Development and validation. *Body Image, 17*, 89–98. https://doi.org/10.1016/j.bodyim.2016.03.007

Wilhelm, S., Peterson, A. L., Piacentini, J., Woods, D. W., Deckersbach, T., Sukhodolsky, D. G., Chang, S., Liu, H., Dziura, J., Walkup, J. T., & Scahill, L. (2012). Randomized trial of behavior therapy for adults with Tourette syndrome. *Archives of General Psychiatry, 69*(8), 795–803. https://doi.org/10.1001/archgenpsychiatry.2011.1528

Williams, D. R., Yu, Y., Jackson, J. S., & Anderson, N. B. (1997). Racial differences in physical and mental health: Socio-economic status, stress, and discrimination. *Journal of Health Psychology, 2*(3), 335–351.

Wolitzky-Taylor, K. B., Horowitz, J. D., Powers, M. B., & Telch, M. J. (2008). Psychological approaches in the treatment of specific phobias: A meta-analysis. *Clinical Psychology Review, 28*(6), 1021–1037. https://doi.org/10.1016/j.cpr.2008.02.007

Woods, D. W., Piacentini, J., Chang, S. W., Deckersbach, T., Ginsburg, G. S., Peterson, A. L., Scahill, L. D., Walkup, J. T., & Wilhelm, S. (2008). *Managing Tourette syndrome: A behavioral intervention for children and adults therapist guide*. Oxford University Press.

Xiang, Y. T., Weng, Y. Z., Li, W. Y., Gao, L., Chen, G. L., Xie, L., Chang, Y. L., Tang, W. K., & Ungvari, G. S. (2007). Efficacy of the community re-entry module for patients with schizophrenia in Beijing, China: Outcome at 2-year follow-up. *British Journal of Psychiatry, 190*(1), 49–56. https://doi.org/10.1192/bjp.bp.106.023697

Zaidens, S. H. (1950). Dermatologic hypochondriasis; A form of schizophrenia. *Psychosomatic Medicine, 12*(4), 250–253. https://doi.org/10.1097/00006842-195007000-00006

MIX
Papier aus verantwortungsvollen Quellen
Paper from responsible sources
FSC® C105338

If you have any concerns about our products,
you can contact us on
ProductSafety@springernature.com

In case Publisher is established outside the EU,
the EU authorized representative is:
Springer Nature Customer Service Center GmbH
Europaplatz 3, 69115 Heidelberg, Germany

Printed by Libri Plureos GmbH
in Hamburg, Germany